City
County
Forest

This book is dedicated to the memory of Tim Hughes, cyclist, photographer and writer, who was working on this second edition of *City County Forest* when he died unexpectedly in May 2002.

FORTY CYCLE RIDES TO SUIT ALL ABILITIES IN NOTTINGHAM'S

City County Forest

Second revised edition based on routes devised by members of Pedals and the Nottinghamshire District Association of the Cyclists' Touring Club

Cyclographic Publications

First published in 1997 by Cyclographic
Publications on behalf of Pedals and the
Nottinghamshire District Association of the
Cyclists' Touring Club

This edition published 2004 by Cyclographic
Publications, 51 Wood Lane, Hucknall,
Nottingham NG15 6LR on behalf of Pedals

Routes compilation by Jo Cleary and Tim
Hughes

Design and layout by Tim Hughes/Jo Cleary

Front cover: Clumber Park.

Back cover, top to bottom: on the Linby Trail; approaching Vimy
Ridge Farm; picnic at Creswell Crags

ISBN   0 907191 03 7

Printed and bound by Warwick Printing Co Ltd, Caswell Road,
Leamington Spa, Warwickshire CV31 1QD

Contents

Acknowledgments

The production of the first edition of *City County Forest* in 1997 was generously supported by (in alphabetical order) the Countryside Commission (now the Countryside Agency), the Cycle Touring and Countryside Trust, Gedling Borough Council, Nottingham City Leisure and Community Services Department, Nottingham Health Authority, Nottinghamshire County Council Green Grant, Nottingham Green Partnership, and RJB Mining PLC. The compilers wish to acknowledge the help of members of Pedals and the CTC upon whose suggestions many of the routes are based and who also supplied entries for the listings. They also gratefully acknowledge the considerable work of Gillian Moss, who drew the sketch maps, and Stephen Wallwork, who made the line drawings.

The production of this second revised 2004 edition has been supported by Going for Green East Midlands, Nottingham Green Partnership and the Nottingham Health Authority. Their generosity is acknowledged with thanks. More details of these sponsors' activities are given on pp221-222.

Welcome to cycling!

The twenty-first century began with bikes in fashion in a way they haven't been since the end of the nineteenth. A lot of it is because people are quite simply looking for a way to get out into the countryside that's healthy, inexpensive and fun. The mountain-bike boom has helped, too. Almost everybody can ride a bike. You may be much too young to hold a driving licence – but you can still ride a bike. If jogging makes your joints begin to feel a bit old, riding a bike is gentle by comparison. If you don't want to lash out a lot of money on a car, buying a reasonable bike is much cheaper. In any case, something like 14 million people in Britain have bikes already. These bikes may be leaning at the back of the garage, dusty, old and not very fashionable-looking; they may not have dozens of gears; they may look quite drab alongside the colours of this year's models. But even the oldest, simplest bike can take you along most of our routes.

A bike isn't just for weekend fun, though: it's a great form of everyday transport, too. Surveys show that almost a third of people's car journeys are less than a mile. You could cycle that in well under ten minutes – probably quicker than finding a parking space! Another third of all car journeys are less than three miles – less than twenty minutes' even quite gentle cycling. Not only is cycling much cheaper, but if you ride a bike for even a few of those trips you are helping to cut noise, pollution and save precious fossil fuel – and benefiting your own health as well as the planet's. Only swimming comes higher than cycling as a way of toning up heart, lungs, circulation and muscles – and you can't really swim to work or down to the shops! Twenty minutes of steady exercise – that 3 or 4-mile bike ride – three times a week, even better every day, will work wonders for your vitality.

The forty routes in this book, ranging from 4 to 45 miles, on-road, off-road and a mixture, have been specially selected, surveyed and described by experienced cyclists from Nottingham's cycle campaign group Pedals and Nottinghamshire CTC – all with beginners and the not-so-fit in mind. There's more on these two organisations – and a great deal more about bikes and how and where you can ride them – towards the back of the book, after the routes themselves.

Cycling in Nottinghamshire – as it is now. Riding along the magnificent avenue of poplars leading to Vimy Ridge Farm, near Hickling.

Welcome to Nottinghamshire

Nottinghamshire is one of England's finest counties to begin cycling in. For a start, there's a surprising range of scenery. The Robin Hood legend has made Sherwood Forest world-famous, but there are many other superb forests and woodlands. One of England's great rivers, the Trent, flows gently through the southern part of the county. The city of Nottingham dominates the south but throughout the county's 50-mile length and 25-mile breadth there are historic market towns, villages and secret, hidden hamlets, steeped in history and literary associations.

There are cycling associations, too: Beeston and Nottingham were important cycle manufacturing centres as early as the 1880s, while even today Raleigh is still the first cycle maker's name that springs to mind for most people, although no bicycles are actually made in Nottingham by Raleigh any more! The great Nottinghamshire coalfield, source of much of Britain's prosperity at the beginning of the century, has now dwindled to a handful of pits but enough is left to show that the county was at the centre of England's industrial heartland. With the passing of the coalfield the great spoil heaps that dominated the mining villages are being landscaped, planted with trees and opened to the public as country parks. Several feature on our routes.

Above all Nottinghamshire is gentle country at a human scale, rolling enough for you to find broad sweeping views from the tops of its modest climbs – yet even if you're new to cycling or making a long-delayed comeback, you won't have to walk up many hills!

The county has about 3000 miles of minor roads, most of them carrying very little traffic – ideal for cycling – and many miles of bridleway, on which you are legally entitled to cycle, canal towpaths where you can ride with a permit (free from British Waterways), firm-based forest roads and a growing number of special cycle routes, including *National Cycle Network Route 6*. This book shows you how to get the best out of them.

Cycling in Nottinghamshire – as it was then. A woodcut – 'The Humber Tandem' – from the 1891 edition of The Badminton Book of Cycling. *The Humber Tandem was made at Thomas Humber's then-renowned bicycle factory in Beeston. Parts of the original facade of the works are still there (see p16).*

THE ROUTES

How to follow our routes

All our routes start and finish in Nottinghamshire or the city of Nottingham. Except where it follows rivers – the Trent, Idle, Erewash and Soar – the county boundary is not a natural barrier, though, and we do cross the frontier a few times for a short distance, either to make a more pleasant or even possible route between two Nottinghamshire villages or to reach a tea-stop or place of interest just over the border.

The routes are listed in order of length, shortest first. The key map on page 13 shows roughly where in the city and county each one is situated. Each route description has a heading bar giving distance, whether it's on- or off-road, a rough idea of how hilly it is, and the name of the place where it starts. This is followed by a short introduction to the area, a sketch map, and a box giving the exact position of the starting point, more details on the surface quality, notes on possible refreshment stops, useful Ordnance Survey map sheets, public transport links and other possible linking routes, including links where appropriate to the 'National Cycle Network' Route 6 which runs north to south through the west of the county (see pp203-206). The main part of each route entry is a detailed route description that is meant for you to be able to follow without having to use a map if you don't want to.

We use one or two conventions in the route descriptions:

● We use *italic* type for information on signposts, while place names in **bold** type highlight the village or hamlet you have reached at that stage of the route – for example: 'In **Willaston**, turn left opposite the church into Main Street, signed *Nottingham*'.

● Distances (which are all approximate) are given in yards up to half a mile, and in miles for longer ones. If you have a cycle computer or old cyclometer in decimal miles, rough equivalents are: 0.1 miles = 200yds; 0.2 miles = 350yds; 0.3 miles = 500yds; 0.4 miles = 700yds. 0.5 miles is of course half a mile. If you have one calibrated in kilometres, or prefer to use metric measures any-way, you can take the yards figures as metres for all practical purposes, while practical equivalents for longer distances are: 1 mile = 1.5km; 2 miles = 3km; 3 miles = 5km; 4 miles = 6.5km; 5 miles = 8 km; 10 miles = 16km.

● We use the road number – A- or B-road – if there is one. Other roads we refer to as 'minor' or 'unclassified'. Anything we call a road is hard-surfaced. If you are emerging from an off-road sec-tion (or if you're going onto one), we refer to a hard-surfaced, metalled road as a 'tarred road' (unless it's clearly something dif-ferent, such as concrete). We use the word 'track' to mean a well-defined but unsurfaced road or track at least wide enough for a tractor or cart, and often give more details – such as 'firm stone-surfaced' or 'grassy'. We use the word 'path' to mean something narrower, usually too narrow for two cyclists to ride along side by side (what mountain-bikers call 'single-track'), again with more details if needed.

● Sometimes in the route description we give the instruction 'Turn left [or right]' followed by '(effectively straight on)'. In these cases, while the markings on the road indicate a left or right turn manoeuvre, you continue riding in roughly the same compass direction as before.

● There is no reason why you shouldn't follow only part of a route, and even return by the same route. For example, the bri-dleways on farm and estate roads and tracks north-east of Worksop to the hamlets of Scofton and Bilby (routes **12** and **21**) would make a good out-and-home traffic-free outing for a young family – with a possible side trip to the river and canal at Scofton. There are also obvious short cuts on some of the longer circuits.

● Although one or two routes are described as starting from a pub or inn, please note that this is only because they are promi-nent local landmarks. **We have not negotiated parking facili-ties for users of this book at these places.**

Our sketch maps

The route is shown as a bold black line: continuous where it follows roads and dashed for off-road sections. The starting point is marked with a little cycle symbol and an arrow to show the direction in which the route is described. There are repeat arrows at other points where there might be some doubt. Obviously you can go round a circular route in either direction, but we think our direction is the better one – and it isn't always too easy to follow route directions in reverse. It's also possible to link up some routes to make longer ones, and in several cases we give link routes between them. All the maps are the conventional way up – with north at the top. There's also a scale bar showing roughly how far a mile is on the map. And if you need to be told what the little steaming teacup symbol stands for, then you really have still got some way to go before you qualify as a *real* cyclist!

Routes index

(page number in italics)

(continued on p14)

Where the routes are

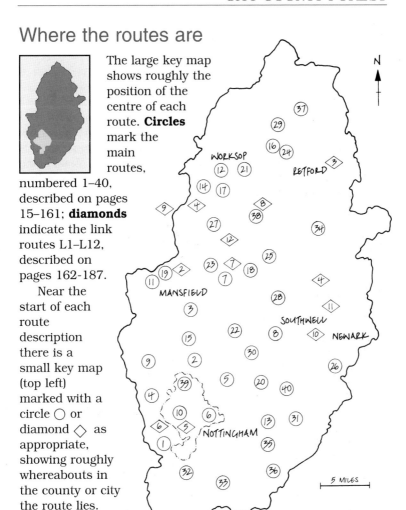

The large key map shows roughly the position of the centre of each route. **Circles** mark the main routes, numbered 1–40, described on pages 15–161; **diamonds** indicate the link routes L1–L12, described on pages 162-187.

Near the start of each route description there is a small key map (top left) marked with a circle ○ or diamond ◇ as appropriate, showing roughly whereabouts in the county or city the route lies.

Several routes lie within the area of the Greenwood Community Forest; these are marked with the Greenwood Community Forest symbol (right).

Helping to create the
GREENWOOD
COMMUNITY FOREST

13

Linear routes

38 Hardwick to Ollerton off-road 149

39 Leen Valley Path from Basford to Newstead *152*

40 Newark to Nottingham – south of the Trent *156*

Link routes

L1 Norwell village (links routes 28 and 34) *162*

L2 Mansfield Woodhouse to Pleasley Vale (links Robin Hood Line station and route 11) *163*

L3 North Leverton and Treswell (links routes 24 and 37) *164*

L4 Worksop Manor South Lodge and Creswell Crags (spur off route 14) *165*

L5 Beeston and Nottingham (links routes 1 and L6) *168*

L6 Beeston and Strelley village (links routes 4 and L4) *170*

L7 Sherwood Pines and Edwinstowe (links routes 18, 25 and 23) *174*

L8 Clumber Park and Walesby (links routes 27 and 28) *176*

L9 Whaley Common and Creswell Crags (links routes L4 and 27) *178*

L10 Newark and Fiskerton (links routes 30 and 40 to Newark) *180*

L11 Norwell and Newark (links routes 28 and 36 to Newark) *182*

L12 Langwith-Whaley Thorns station and Clumber Park (links Robin Hood Line station with routes 17, 27 and 38) *185*

Alphabetical index of starting points

(*route number in italics*)

CIRCULAR ROUTES
UP TO 10 MILES

Route

start

4 miles • on- and off-road • flat • Beeston

Attenborough Nature Reserve

This very short route from Beeston visits the wetlands of the Attenborough Nature Reserve. For centuries gravel has been dug from great pits along the flood-plain of the River Trent. Once extraction has finished in a particular spot, the gravel pits rapidly fill with water and become colonised by water-loving plants, with wildlife quickly following. The Reserve, which is managed by the Nottinghamshire Wildlife Trust, was opened some thirty years ago and covers over 350 acres of these former pits, which are now broad lakes fringed with reed beds and lush vegetation. The Reserve is noted particularly for its bird life – so it could be worth taking a bird book and binoculars – and otters have recently made a come-back to the area.

From **Beeston Square** go south-west through the pedestrianised area, leaving the HSBC bank and Post Office to the right. Just before the Post Office, join Chilwell Road. This comes to a T-junction with the B6464, which continues to the right still as Chilwell Road (although not signed at this point). Turn right on Chilwell Road which becomes High Road, **Chilwell**. Opposite Chilwell College House Junior School on the right after about ¾ mile, turn left into Meadow Lane. Cross Queens Road West, A6005, still on Meadow Lane (*'NCN' Route 6 briefly joins here*). Where Meadow Lane bears round to the right after the golf course, becoming Long Lane, turn left by the *Attenborough* sign into a short no-through road. Bear right on a gravel track and through a swing gate to cross the railway by the level crossing, then through a second swing gate. You next cross a little bridge over a stream to turn

15

1

continued

A plaque on the wall of Thomas Humber's original bicycle factory in Humber Road, Beeston

right on a bridleway through Attenborough Nature Reserve.

This well-surfaced track, signed as a bridleway to *Attenborough Village*, follows the railway line on its right for a short way, then veers away to the left alongside a stream. After about 400yds there is a 'crossroads' of paths, with the entrance to gravel workings to the right. Continue straight on over a humpbacked wooden-slatted bridge with metal sides, along a spit of land between two lakes. After leaving the water the path passes between a stone wall to the right and a fence on the left, to join a tarred road (The Strand, but not named at this point). At the far end of the playing fields on the left, where The Strand bears round to the right, there is a small anglers' car park on the left. Turn left into the car park. From this point the path is a footpath for a while.

For a short tour of the **Attenborough Nature Reserve**, go round the metal barrier at the end of the car park, then straight on to cross another wooden-slatted green humpbacked bridge and along the well-marked path with water both sides. Continue straight on to meet the bank of the River Trent. Turn right to follow the river for about ¾ mile until a stream joins it from the right. Don't cross the stream but turn right, inland, along a fairly wide track which by some stables becomes a bridleway. This wide but potholed track – although it is easy enough to avoid the holes – passes between two lakes with an attractive view across the water to Attenborough church on the right. Cross over a bridge which crosses a link between the two lakes; shortly after this there is a car park area. Just after this car park turn right on a marked bridleway towards **Attenborough** church. After about 300yds there is a fork in the paths; follow the right-hand path, signed *Attenborough Village*. This leads across a finger of land between waters, which takes you back to the anglers' car park where the Nature Reserve tour began.

Turn left to The Strand, then left on The Strand and follow this where it bears right and left to become Attenborough Lane to pass over a level crossing by Attenborough Station (*and to rejoin 'NCN' Route 6 again briefly*). Take the first right after the level crossing into Long Lane, and follow this until it becomes Meadow Lane and comes to a traffic-light-controlled junction with the A6005, Queen's Road West. Cross to the north side of the road and follow the shared-use cycle track on the north side of the road for about a mile to its junction with Dovecote Lane, just before a pelican crossing. Turn left (leaving *'NCN' Route 6*) into Dovecote Lane to its T-junction with Middle Street. Turn left and then second right into Chilwell Road to **Beeston Square** to complete the circuit. If you don't wish to use the shared-use cycle track, go straight on at the Meadow Lane/A6005 junction to follow the outgoing route back to Beeston Square.

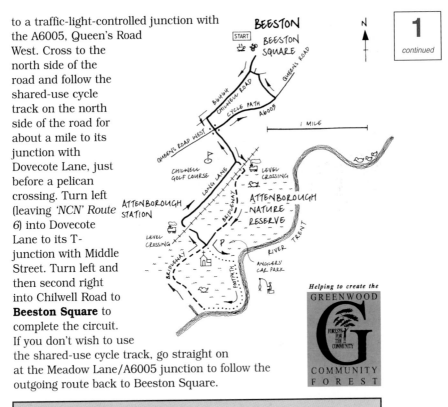

1 continued

Helping to create the
GREENWOOD
COMMUNITY
FOREST

Start: Beeston town centre (GR 528 369)

Distance: 4 cycling miles; optional 1 mile of footpath

Terrain: minor suburban roads and bridleway, with some footpath involved if you wish to explore the Nature Reserve

Refreshment opportunities: various cafés etc in Beeston town centre (GR 528 369).

Ordnance Survey maps: Landranger sheet 129 Nottingham and Loughborough, or Explorer sheet 260 Nottingham. The whole route is also on the *AZ Premier Street Map of Nottingham*

Public transport links: Central Trains services and some Midland Main Line Turbostar trains call at Beeston station, about ½ mile south-east of Beeston town centre; a few Central Trains services from Nottingham to Derby and vice versa call at Attenborough station (on the route).

Other routes: Route **L5** links the Beeston start of this route with Nottingham city centre and Midland Station, largely by the signed cycle route; this route also links with route **10**. Route **L6** links Beeston with Strelley village, where route **4** starts. The route briefly joins '**NCN**' **Route 6** in Attenborough village.

6 miles • off-road • hilly • Bestwood Lodge

Bestwood Country Park and Mill Lakes

Bestwood Country Park, like many of the country parks that have emerged to the north of Nottingham, owes its existence largely to the demise of coalmining. The old spoil heaps had become naturally colonised by vegetation, and careful landscaping has made for a seamless graft between the open and airy artificial hill and the extensive established woodland which is a remnant of an old deer park to the east. Bestwood's mining past is commemorated by the old pit-head gear and engine house, now a listed building and preserved as a feature at the entrance to the park. Once in the park, cyclists and walkers share most of the paths that are not marked as 'horse trails'. Many of them are broad tracks or untarred roads, but some are narrower paths, so take care. This route also goes round the Mill Lakes, a nature reserve adjacent to Bestwood Country Park, to the west. Information leaflets on the wildlife to be seen around the lakes and woodland are obtainable from the Country Park Administration Office at Bestwood Country Park, tel (0115) 967 0042. The park is easily accessible by bike from the northern areas of Nottingham, or by the Robin Hood Line to Bulwell or Hucknall.

At the entrance of the **Bestwood Lodge Drive car park** turn right up the hill; the road bears quite sharply round to the left, then right, past **Bestwood Lodge Hotel**. You are on Main Drive, following signs to *Alexandra Lodges*, and a short distance after the hotel the tarred surface of this road gives way to crushed stone. About ½ mile from the hotel Main Drive continues through a five-barred gate. Here, turn right along a fenced track (not signed). At the end of the wood, after about 600yds, turn left at the track crossroads into Colliers' Path and

18

follow this down to **Alexandra Lodges**. Turn right onto the tarred minor road, past the field studies centre, and immediately left along Woodman's Path, signed to the *Adventure Playground*.

Go up the hill, past toilets and the Adventure Playground. At the top the path bears round to the left and shortly after turn right downhill, towards the 'Winding House'. This descent is fairly steep, with a loose surface. Just before the Winding House – the preserved pithead gear of the old Bestwood Colliery – take the path which heads off to the left up a gentle incline. Follow this path as it contours round the landscaped spoil heaps, and avoid straying on to any horse trails, which tend to cross and recross the firm-surfaced path on this stretch. After about ½ mile turn right on to the first path not signed as a horse trail, which heads downhill, across a small bridge and then bears round to the right. Continue on this path, ignoring any turnings, through a metal kissing gate, and when it joins a disused rail line path turn very sharp right – almost doubling back ('NCN' Route 6 joins here, marked by a prominent signpost). After about 400yds this track crosses over the B683 by a bridge. (The Leen Valley Path, route 39, from or to Bulwell Station joins/leaves here.) Follow the broad firm-surfaced path over a wooden bridge which crosses the River Leen at a small weir and then in a clockwise direction around the Mill Lakes – keeping the water on your right. At the far end of the lakes pass through one kissing gate onto a tarred path. (The Leen Valley route from or to Hucknall Station and 'NCN' Route 6 join/leave here.) Turn right across a wooden bridge over the River Leen and immediately right through another kissing gate, to rejoin the waterside path, here narrower but still firm crushed-stone-surfaced.

Having completed a tour of the lakes, you will need to retrace your

2

continued

Mill Lakes, Bestwood Country Park

route back into Bestwood Park, via the disused rail line. From the kissing gate leading into Bestwood Park, go straight on, ignoring any side turnings. This path soon passes through two wooden farm gates and climbs a fairly steep hill. At the summit follow the path as it bears round to the right and then curves to the left until you reach an entrance to Bestwood Park from a housing estate. Take the second left path, which runs along the perimeter of the park. Stick to the main path through the woods, and when this veers away from the housing estate, bear right at a Y-junction, and right at the next T-junction, signed to *Lodge Gardens and Bestwood Lodge Drive*. At the next fork, just after a sign for Woodman's Path, keep right. Through a wooden kissing gate you emerge onto Main Drive; turn right and follow this ½ mile or so down to **Bestwood Lodge Drive car park**.

Start: Bestwood Lodge Drive car park, Bestwood Park (GR 572 464)

Distance: 6 miles

Terrain: An entirely off-road route, undulating

Refreshment opportunities: Bestwood Lodge Hotel (en route) offers morning coffee, afternoon tea, lunches etc; as the route is situated on the urban fringe there are also some shops and pubs near to this route. If you're picnicking, there are several sets of wooden benches and tables dotted around the park.

Ordnance Survey maps: Landranger sheet 129 Nottingham and Loughborough, or Explorer sheet 260 Nottingham.

Public transport links: Robin Hood Line to Bulwell or Hucknall stations, then follow the Leen Valley Path, route **39**; in either case you join the circuit part-way round.

Other routes: The Leen Valley Path, route **39**, follows part of this route, and also forms a link to route **15**, Hucknall and Newstead Abbey. A short section of the route runs along 'NCN' Route **6**.

6 miles • off-road • undulating • Mansfield

Harlow Wood

THIS is a short, off-road route route, going round Harlow Wood and Thieves Wood, two woodlands divided by the A60, south of Mansfield. The forest tracks are not signed, but the route sticks to the main thoroughfares used by forestry vehicles, which are clearly differentiated from the numerous minor footpaths which criss-cross the area. The woodland is a characteristic Nottinghamshire mix of conifers and broad-leaved trees, with attractive clearings, and some open views where the route skirts the edge of the wood.

Close to the edge of Harlow Wood and just off the route itself, on the east side of the A60, is a memorial stone marking the spot where a 17-year-old Papplewick girl, Elizabeth Sheppard, was murdered in 1817. The motive was apparently theft, since a man was later apprehended, tried and hanged after trying to sell her shoes and umbrella. The stone is marked on the Ordnance Survey maps as 'Sheppard's Stone' (GR 551 563). It is rather hidden, a little down a bank from the road verge and about 50 yds on the Nottingham side of the point where the route crosses the A60. The site is said to be haunted.

With **Bellamy Road**, **Mansfield**, behind you, start by travelling a short distance eastwards along Old Newark Road. Just after Shelton Road, but before Syerston Road on the left, turn right along a signed bridleway. Follow this for about ¾ mile up a slight hill, and on reaching some farm buildings turn right on a bridleway indicated by a *blue arrow* – ignore the narrower bridleway that goes straight ahead (*this leads, after about 1¼ miles to 'NCN' Route 6*). This is a sandy track in places and progress many be fairly slow in very dry weather when the sand is loose. After about ½ mile, soon after entering Harlow Wood, you come to a significant crossroads of woodland tracks; turn left passing a low wooden barrier and follow this track for a further mile. Soon after passing another low wooden barrier you emerge onto the A60, Nottingham Road; there is a coffee shop just off to the right.

21

3
continued

Cross straight over the main road, onto a track leading into Thieves Wood. Continue straight on for about ½ mile, ignoring any smaller paths leading off to left or right. This track eventually comes to a 'T-junction' of forest tracks, where you turn right. Carry straight on when this track is crossed by another major one after about ½ mile and, at the bottom of the hill – just beyond a further low wooden barrier – turn right to return to the A60 via a wide, unsurfaced track.

Cross back over the main road, bearing slightly right to re-enter **Harlow Wood**, again passing a low wooden barrier. This wide, undulating track winds through the trees for nearly a mile before you reach a distinctive crossroads of forest tracks just after another low wooden barrier – you should recognise this spot from earlier on the route. Turn left, then left again after a short way – just before leaving the woods – down an unsigned bridleway. Descend with care as the sandy surface can be quite unpredictable. When this bridleway ends at a T-junction with an unsurfaced minor road on the outskirts of **Mansfield** – Old Newark Road, in fact – turn right and after a further ½ mile the route comes back to the junction where it started.

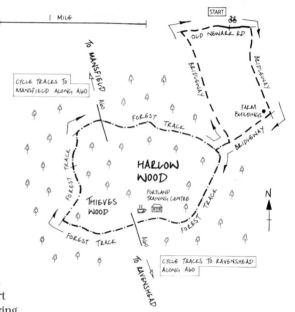

Helping to create the

GREENWOOD

COMMUNITY
F O R E S T

3
continued

Start: Junction of Old Newark Road and Bellamy Road – these are fairly minor residential roads in south-east Mansfield – (GR 562 588)

Distance: 6 miles

Terrain: An almost entirely off-road route on forest tracks and bridleways, which are loose-surfaced in places so sturdy tyres and low gears are advisable.

Refreshment opportunities:There is a coffee shop at Portland Training Centre – on the Nottingham Road (A60) – about half way round.

Ordnance Survey maps: Landranger sheet 120 Mansfield and Worksop; Explorer sheet 28 (270) Sherwood Forest

Public transport links: Robin Hood Line to Mansfield or Mansfield Woodhouse (no Sunday service)

Other routes: About 1½ miles of the A60, southwards, links this route to route **15**, Hucknall and Newstead, at The Hutt, Ravenshead. There is a narrow shared-use cycle-and-pedestrian path on the west side of the A60 for part of the way. '**NCN**' **Route 6** is about ½ mile south of the southernmost point of the route.

Route

4

start

5 miles • mostly off-road • undulating • Strelley village

Strelley, Cossall and the Nottingham Canal

THIS short route follows bridleways, towpath cycle tracks and a small proportion of minor road through rural agricultural land right on the fringes of the city.

The little village of Cossall, about halfway round, has several features of interest, including some attractive almshouses dating from 1685. Church Cottage in the village is notable as the home of Louise Burrow, at one time D H Lawrence's fiancée. The disused Nottingham Canal which the route follows for a while is now a small nature reserve and the naturalised home of many water birds. The wrought-iron Bennerley Viaduct which you can see down in the valley on the left just after you leave the canal towpath is now a listed 'building'. It was built in the 1870s for a branch of the Great Northern Railway using a

23

4

continued

patented lattice design to overcome possible unstable foundations as a result of mining activity. It was in use right up to 1968 when the line closed and there is now a proposal to incorporate it in a cycle route.

From **Strelley** church head south-east (towards Nottingham) for about 300yds, then at the sharp left bend in the road, turn onto a bridleway on the right (where the grass verge has a line of posts with red and white markers). Go through the gap at the side of the metal gate. The bridleway, between hedges, bears round to the left. Ignore the first wide track on the right after about 150yds. About 300yds farther on turn right by the *bridleway sign* with step-over bars at the gateway. Continue straight on for about ½ mile through four more gates and past a small wood on the right to a junction with a wide hard-surfaced track. (*This junction is where the Beeston to Strelley link route* **L6** *joins or leaves.*)

Turn right on this track as it winds under the M1 motorway. Continue for about a mile through two large five-barred gates and two bridleway gateways. (The path becomes narrow for a short section so take care to avoid the ditch on the right.) The path emerges onto a tarred road at a bend, by a bridge where it crosses a short arm of disused canal. Turn right towards Cossall village for about 300yds. At a T-junction on the outskirts of the village, where the right-hand arm is signed *No through road,* turn left and, at the right-hand bend about 150yds later, go straight on onto a track, Mill Lane, signed *Bridleroad to Ilkeston.*

(If you want to explore **Cossall** village itself, go right at this last bend and then retrace your route to this corner, where it will of course now be a right turn. Take care turning right: visibility is poor at this corner.)

Follow the track (which has a surface that can be loose and dusty in dry weather) downhill for about 300yds until it crosses the disused **Nottingham Canal**. On

Start: Strelley church (GR 506 421)

Distance: just under 5 miles

Terrain: quite undulating but with no really sharp hills. Over two-thirds of the route is off-road, on easily ridable firm-surfaced bridleway and canal towpath

Refreshment opportunities: the route doesn't appear to pass any pubs, though there are some in Awsworth, while the Broad Oak, Strelley, just under 1/2 mile on the Nottingham side of the starting point, also serves food.

Ordnance Survey maps: Landranger sheet 129 Nottingham and Loughborough; Explorer sheet 260 Nottingham

Public transport links: none, really

Other routes: Route **L6** links this route with Beeston town centre via Bramcote

24

the far side of the canal, turn right on the old towpath which is a firm-surfaced bridleway (*unsigned* when we last checked) for just under a mile. At one point the path dips from the canal, goes over a road bridge and then climbs up again: continue on

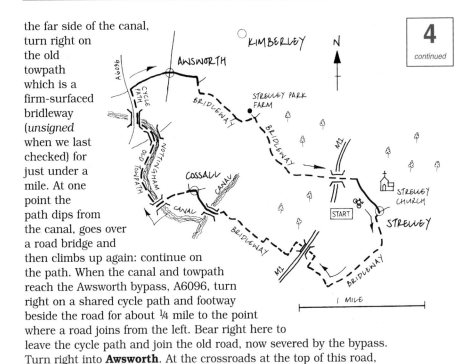

the path. When the canal and towpath reach the Awsworth bypass, A6096, turn right on a shared cycle path and footway beside the road for about ¼ mile to the point where a road joins from the left. Bear right here to leave the cycle path and join the old road, now severed by the bypass. Turn right into **Awsworth**. At the crossroads at the top of this road, Newton Lane, go straight across on Westby Lane, a 'no through road' and signed *Babbington 1¼*. Continue downhill for about 300yds to a sharp right-hand bend, followed by an even sharper left one.

At this left-hand corner, go straight ahead on a track signed *Bridleway Strelley, footpath Cossall*: keep to the bridleway. This reasonably-surfaced track climbs steadily for about ½ mile and bears round to the left to a junction of tracks, with the left leading to Strelley Park Farm. Turn right onto a wide firm-surfaced track, signed *Bridleway*. Ignore two tracks on the right and the one on the left (to Turkey Fields Farm) which appears to be the main track. Instead go straight ahead on a narrower path – the official public bridleway – between a hedge on the left and a wire fence on the right. After about 350yds this path rejoins a wide stone-surfaced track from the left (the other entrance to Turkey Fields Farm). Go straight ahead on this track for about 500yds to cross over the M1 motorway and join the tarred road opposite the gateway to Strelley Hall. Turn right; **Strelley** church is 200yds or so farther along this road.

Helping to create the
GREENWOOD

COMMUNITY
F O R E S T

25

Route 5 start

8 miles • on- and off-road • hilly • Woodborough

Woodborough Rounds

These two short circuits – one an all-weather version, the other with some fine-weather off-road sections – have one main attraction: the views across the tumbling hills just to the north-east of the city. The intricate interlocking of the spurs of the hill and the changing light and colour make this a pleasant diversion well worth a visit at any season. This is by no means the highest part of the county but four of Nottinghamshire's very few steeper-than-1-in-7 hills, marked on the OS map by a black arrow, are on these roads. The on-road version of the route touches the large former mining village of Calverton, whose pit closed in 1999. However, another industry was here even earlier: at the foot of Bonner Hill is a run of restored cottages, with the characteristic long windows to let in the light that frame-knitters needed in those pre-electricity days.

The rough – or fair-weather – version: Leave **Woodborough** westwards towards Calverton on Foxwood Lane, signed *Calverton*. This climbs away from the village and at the crest of the hill, just after Foxwood Lodge and just before the road drops steeply into Calverton, turn left onto a public bridleway. Follow this rather variably-surfaced bridleway for about 1½ miles until you reach a tarred road at a bend in the road. Turn left on the road from the bridleway to climb gently to a crossroads junction with B684 at **Dorket Head**; turn left on B684, signed *Mapperley 3*. Continue for about 1½ miles, ignoring the first turning on the left to Woodborough but taking the second, Catfoot Lane, just after the Traveller's Rest, signed *Lambley*. (About 200yds further along the B684 is a teashop at Brookfields Garden Centre, Mapperley Plains.) Follow Catfoot Lane for about 2 miles gently downhill through a pleasant valley, becoming steeper at the end into Lambley. At the T-junction by the Nags Head in **Lambley** turn

left, signed *Lowdham.*
After about 500yds, just after going by Lambley Post Office on the right, take the first turning left, Church Street, signed *Woodborough.*
About 300yds farther on the road bears round to the right and begins to go steeply uphill, becoming Green Lane. After about ¾ mile, the road becomes Lingwood Lane and bears round to the right to go steeply downhill into Woodborough. **Do not go down the hill** but continue straight ahead

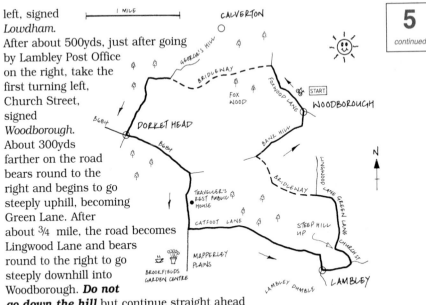

on a wide unsurfaced track, with a bridleway sign. After about 50yds go round a metal gate, then after about ¾ mile, just before a green metal barrier, there is a sign on the left reading 'Private road ahead: turn right for bridleway'. The bridleway runs between hedges and is signed with a blue bridleway arrow. After about 450yds it emerges onto a tarred road. This is Bank Hill (not signed at this point); turn right downhill into **Woodborough**.

The smooth all-road version: Leave **Woodborough** westwards towards Calverton on Foxwood Lane, signed *Calverton*. This climbs away from the village and then drops steeply down Bonner Hill to its T-junction with Bonner Lane, **Calverton**. Turn left along Bonner Lane, which becomes Main Street and after about ½ mile, beyond a children's playground on the left, turn left into George's Lane, signed *Arnold 3*, to go up George's Hill. This is quite a tough climb for the first part but with the reward of fine views to the left. The upper part of the climb is more gentle and brings you to a crossroads junction with B684 at Dorket Head; turn left on B684, signed *Woodborough, Mapperley* and *Nottingham*. Continue for about 1½ miles, ignoring the first turning on the left to Woodborough but taking the second, Catfoot Lane, just after the Traveller's Rest, signed *Lambley*. (About

Helping to create the
GREENWOOD
G
FOREST FOR THE COMMUNITY
COMMUNITY
FOREST

27

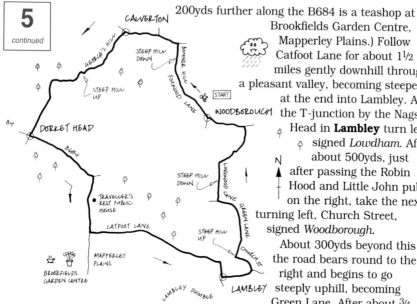

5 continued

200yds further along the B684 is a teashop at Brookfields Garden Centre, Mapperley Plains.) Follow Catfoot Lane for about 1½ miles gently downhill through a pleasant valley, becoming steeper at the end into Lambley. At the T-junction by the Nags Head in **Lambley** turn left, signed *Lowdham*. After about 500yds, just after passing the Robin Hood and Little John pub on the right, take the next turning left, Church Street, signed *Woodborough*.

About 300yds beyond this the road bears round to the right and begins to go steeply uphill, becoming Green Lane. After about ¾ mile, the road becomes Lingwood Lane and bears round to the right to go steeply downhill into **Woodborough**. Turn left by the church on Main Street to complete the circuit.

Start: At the western end of Woodborough (GR 624 478). You could also start from Lambley or Dorket Head. Note, however, there is no car parking at Dorket Head.

Distance: 8 miles for the *bridleway* version; about a mile longer for the *all-road alternative*

Terrain: decidedly hilly – but rewarded by fine views. The mix on the *bridleway* version is about 1½ miles of B-road, which can be quite busy at times on weekdays, 4 miles of minor road and 2½ miles of bridleway. The bridleway surfaces are reasonable for most of the time but with a definite tendency to muddiness in wet weather. They would be best tackled on a mountain-bike or by experienced riders on touring bikes – definitely not for smooth, narrow racing tyres. Despite the short distance, we wouldn't recommend the bridleway route for absolute beginners. However, we first checked it when it was frozen hard and it was fine!

Refreshment opportunities: Brookfields Garden Centre, Mapperley Plains.

Ordnance Survey maps: Landranger sheet 129 Nottingham and Loughborough; Explorer sheet 260 Nottingham.

Public transport links: none.

Other routes: Route **30**, Daybrook to Southwell uses some of the same roads near Dorket Head and between Woodborough and Arnold. The westernmost point of route **20**, Lambley and Lowdham, lies only about 200yds east of this route in Lambley village.

9 miles • on- and off-road • almost flat • Nottingham Station

Route

6

start

Colwick Country Park

This short route lies entirely within the boundaries of the City of Nottingham and uses sections of marked cycle route to reach out to one of the city's fine green spaces: Colwick Country Park, an area of lakes between the heights of Sneinton and the River Trent.

From **Nottingham Midland Station** turn left, signed as *cycle route to Trent Bridge and West Bridgford,* and keep in left-hand traffic lane. At traffic lights, go straight ahead on Arkwright Street, signed as *no through road except buses and cycles.* After about 100yds at a crossroads with traffic lights, go straight ahead and bear almost immediately right on a pedestrian and cycle route underpass below a road and straight on up the other side. In about a further 100yds you reach the Bridgeway Shopping Centre, passing between houses. Turn left following cycle route sign to Trent Bridge and West Bridgford passing Bridgeway Hall Methodist Mission on the left. Turn right, still following *cycle route sign to Trent Bridge and West Bridgford;* there is also a red and blue metal fingerpost signed *Trent Bridge* and *St Xavier's Church.* This is Arkwright Walk (not named at this point), a heavily traffic-calmed area. Continue to the end of Arkwright Walk to its junction with Meadows Way. Turn right across four traffic lanes to the bus and cycle lane at the traffic lights. Keep in the left hand lane at this complex junction for 35yds, to a second set of traffic lights, where you use the cycle cut-through in the central reservation to join Meadow Lane, following blue *cycle route sign to Colwick.* Pass Notts County football ground to the left and at a T-junction go right, effectively straight on, still on Meadow Lane, following brown *tourist route signs for Colwick Park and Nottingham Racecourse.* After about 400yds, just before a light-controlled junction (part of a large roundabout), some more *cycle route signs* appear: follow them using a shared-use path. After about 20yds, blue *cycle route signs marked All routes* direct you to the central island of the roundabout so that you can cross to the far side of busy Manvers Street.

29

6

continued

Turn left on the shared-use pedestrian and cycle path on the far, east, side to go over a railway bridge. Just before the light-controlled junction, bear right (unsigned), almost a U-turn, through a wooden entrance gateway to join

a gravel path, the start of the **Gedling Greenway**. Follow this path which bears round to the left to follow the railway line. After about ½ mile, the path goes down a gentle slope, and at the foot go right through a pair of swing gates to cross the railway line at a pedestrian-and-cyclist level crossing (again no signs). Immediately after crossing the railway, turn left on another path, this time keeping the railway on your left. After about ½ mile this path emerges onto Racecourse Road, by a roundabout junction with Daleside Road. On the right is the entrance to Colwick Park. Follow *cycle path markings* to cross Daleside Road **(with care!)** into Colwick Park.

Pass the entrance to the racecourse and the park-and-ride site; do not turn into these but continue straight ahead. Follow this access road as it bears round to the left, following the curve of the racecourse; the River Trent appears to the right. Just as the road you are on begins to bear round to the left and as it approaches a church tower and the maple avenue comes to an end, a broad and distinct track bears off to the right. It is fenced on the right-hand side and follows the line of the river but is unsigned at this point. Follow this track and, after a short distance at a T-junction of paths just before a children's playground, bear right to continue to follow the river. Go through two wooden five-barred gates towards a large lake; the path splits to go either side of the lake. Take the right-hand branch, with lake to the left and the river to the right. The Holme Pierrepont water sports centre is on the opposite side of the river at this point.

At the far side of the lake the path splits again, and once again take the right-hand option to follow the river. This path shortly also bears round to the left, leaving the river and passing a marina on the

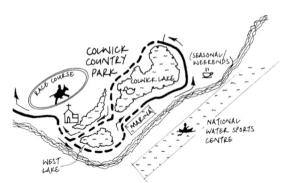

6
continued

right. About 50yds after the bend, the path joins a tarred road. Turn right on the road, still with the marina to the right. Another lake, Colwick Lake, appears to the left. Continue on this traffic-calmed road round the lake. Shortly after an information hut on the right, the tarred road bears sharp right to leave the park. Continue straight on past a five-barred gate along a cinder path round the lake, with the lake still on the left.

When you reach the head of the lake, the path you are on bears left and two cinder tracks go off to the right. Take the middle path and follow this to rejoin your outward route, this time with the River Trent on your left. At the children's playground, turn left to retrace your incoming route out of Colwick Park. At the roundabout junction on Daleside Road, go straight across into Racecourse Road.

From here it is possible **either** to **retrace your outgoing route** via the Greenway path, or to take an **alternative road route**. To follow this **alternative**, continue on Racecourse Road, which soon bears round to the left to become Colwick Road, and go over a level crossing. At a light-controlled junction go straight on into Sneinton Hermitage and on to another light-controlled

Start: Nottingham Midland Station (GR 574 393)

Distance: about 9 miles

Terrain: a mix of minor roads, shared-use cycle-and-pedestrian path, some tarred, some crushed stone and park roads and tracks – but all suitable for any type of bike. The route is virtually flat.

Refreshment opportunities: Cosy Teapot Café, Carrington Street (about 150yds north of Midland Station)

Ordnance Survey maps: Landranger sheet 129 Nottingham and Loughborough; Explorer sheet 260 Nottingham. The whole route is also on the *AZ Premier Street Map of Nottingham*.

Public transport links: Midland Main Line, Robin Hood Line and Central Trains services go to Nottingham Midland Station

Other routes: Routes 10, City Canals and Castles; 32, Sutton Bonington; 33, Villages beginning with W; 36, Grantham Canal; and 40, Newark to Nottingham, all start or finish at Nottingham Midland Station. Link route L5 joins this route to routes 4, Attenborough Nature Reserve, and L6, Beeston to Strelley.

6

continued

junction with Manvers Street. This junction has an advance stop-line for cyclists.

Go straight across (bearing slightly right), to join a shared-use path on the far side of Manvers Street (there are pedestrian crossing lights on the left if you don't want to ride across); turn right on this path. After a short distance the path goes round to the left at a signalled junction; follow it round past a *blue-and-white cycle route sign London Road* pointing straight ahead, on a road named City Link (ignore the cycle route sign to City centre on the right, and its accompanying 'Cyclists dismount' notice). Follow the path as it crosses a number of minor access roads (ignore the 'Private road' sign – this is a designated cycle route) until you reach NHS Direct Drop-In Centre (on the left) and BBC East Midlands (on the right). Just after this the path turns right past an access barrier onto an access road which joins London Road by the Premier Lodge motel. Turn left on the dual carriageway London Road for about 100yds to a signalled junction to turn right into Station Street. (You can walk along the pavement if you feel the road is too busy and cross into Station Street by the press-button 'toucan' crossing.) Follow Station Street to its T-junction with Carrington Street, then turn left to **Nottingham Midland Station.**

Route

7

start

6–9 miles • off-road • gently rolling • Sherwood Pines

Sherwood Pines Forest Park

Sherwood Pines Forest Park – Clipstone Forest – is the largest single tract of woodland open to the public in the East Midlands and is very popular with visitors, particularly at weekends. There is a wide variety of trees, which support a range of wildlife, although much of the area is planted with conifers. The attraction for cycling, particularly for beginners, is that there are about 12 to 15 miles of firm-surfaced but untarred traffic-free tracks with mostly gentle gradients. Cycling in a forest gives a exhilarating feel of adventure, an

7

continued

impression that you're in far wilder country that you actually are, even though you are only a few miles from the centres of both Nottingham and Mansfield.

You may cycle on any of the firm tracks in the Forest but *not* on way-marked walking or horse paths (marked with a horseshoe). There is also a general mountain-bike play area at the south-west corner of the Forest, and two waymarked cycle

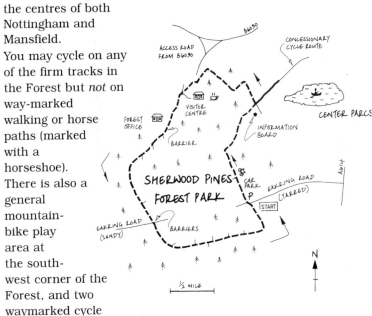

routes: a 5km 'family' route, waymarked in green, and a 10km route, waymarked in blue. In any working forest, tracks may be closed temporarily for timber operations: see the noticeboards on the official cycle route and also the Sherwood Pines Forest Park 'Cycling in the Forest' leaflet available from Forest Enterprise, Edwinstowe, Mansfield, Notts NG21 9JL; tel (01623) 822447 and Tourist Information Centres.

The route suggested here incorporates part of the waymarked cycle route and there is no difficulty in following its route markers. Even so, forest roads do look very similar and it is possible to get lost if you go off the waymarked route. However, remember that the main waymarked cycle route is a big irregular-shaped loop quite near to the edge of the forest, so that if you carry straight on in any direction you will eventually see the reassuring blue or green waymarker posts of one of the official cycle routes once more.

7

continued

Turn left out of **Eakring Road car park** to the road and follow the *blue cycle waymarkers* left and then right past a green and yellow barrier onto a forest track; follow this over a slight hill for about 1 mile to a cross-tracks. Turn right to follow the waymarked route for about 1 mile to another green metal barrier by a cross-tracks with an information board marked 'Sherwood Pines' and signposted *Visitor Centre and Cycle Trail.* Turn left on the forest road and follow the blue and green cycle route signs as far as the **Sherwood Pines Forest Park visitor centre** area. Here, ignore cycle waymarking to go through the car park and follow car park *Exit* signs until you reach a tarred road, where *Exit* is signed to right. Turn left on the tarred road to go past the Forest Office. At the end of the tarred road continue straight on past the barrier on a firm-surfaced sandy track, following the line of electric power line poles on the right. (*The route briefly joins 'NCN' Route 6 here: don't let the Route 6 signs lead you off to the right.*) Ignore the first left-hand turn and continue straight on to rejoin the waymarked cycle route. Follow the *route posts,* ignoring all left-hand turns until you reach two yellow and green barriers, either side of a sandy road about 1½ miles after the Forest Office. Go straight across, following the *cycle markers,* for about 2 miles on a wide track which curves round to the left through an open area and then climbs gently into mixed woodland, then pine forest. At the end of the pine woodland, bear left for about 800yds and slightly downhill to a green metal barrier by **Eakring Road car park**.

If you are staying at **Center Parcs' Sherwood Holiday Village** it is possible to join the route part way round. Turn left out of the village down the slope and at the foot bear left on a firm-surfaced but untarred track – a concessionary cycle way, marked with a red *'No entry' sign (for vehicles) and two-way blue cycle route signs* – keeping Center Parcs perimeter fence on left. After 1¼ miles, there is a cross-tracks with an information board marked 'Sherwood Pines'. Turn right, signed *Visitor Centre,* and follow the route as described round as far as the Eakring Road car park and continue as far as the cross-tracks with the information board. Then go straight on on the firm-surfaced concessionary cycle route back to **Center Parcs**.

7

continued

Start: As described, the route starts from the Eakring Road car park (GR 620 616). (At the time of writing, 2004, the Eakring Road car park was closed because of a deep and persistent puddle in the middle, but it is easy to park nearby.) If you are on holiday there, it would also be possible to start from Center Parcs' Sherwood Holiday Village (GR 637 640) as described, or from the Visitor Centre (GR 612 642).

Distance: about 6½ miles (or 9 including the link to and from Center Parcs' Sherwood Holiday Village)

Terrain: almost entirely off-road on forest tracks, with generally only slight gradients.

Refreshment opportunities: Sherwood Pines Forest Park visitor centre.

Ordnance Survey maps: Landranger sheet 120 Mansfield and Worksop; Explorer sheet 28 (270) Sherwood Forest

Public transport links: by rail to Mansfield Woodhouse (Robin Hood Line), then follow route **23** (either outward or return legs as described) as far as Old Clipstone, then follow B6030 east for ½ or ¾ mile to the Sherwood Pines Forest Park Visitor Centre to join this circuit.

Other routes: Routes **18** and **25** give alternative 13- and 26-miles road routes east of Sherwood Pines. Route **L7** links the northern end of this route to Edwinstowe and Sherwood Forest, and so to route **23**. The route very briefly joins '**NCN' Route 6**.

---

9 miles • on-road • some hills • Southwell

Route

8

start

Halam and Southwell

The pleasing little town of Southwell which figures on several of our routes is dominated by the Minster's twin grey square spires, technically known as 'Rhenish caps'. The great Minster stands four-square right in the centre of the town and is the cathedral for the Diocese of Southwell, which covers most of Nottinghamshire and parts of the surrounding counties. Southwell's other claim to fame is as the home of the Bramley cooking apple. Grown from pips by two ladies of the town, it was commercialised by Henry Merryweather whose descendants still run a nursery and garden centre to the west of the town. The centre also houses a display giving the history of this cook's favourite. In the town itself, down Church Street beyond the Minster, the Bramley Apple pub stands close to the spot

8

continued

where the original tree grew. There are many other delightful corners to Southwell, with one of the most refreshing being the wide open green of the Burgage. A 'burgage' was an area of freehold properties in an otherwise leased estate, and one of the Burgage's more celebrated residents was Lord Byron's mother. Southwell was, like many small East Midlands towns, once almost self-sufficient with its range of trades, crafts and products but now most are commemorated only in street and house names.

This route follows a short circuit round the town, visiting the attractive little village of Halam. This village's name comes from the Old English word '*halh*' meaning a hidden-away corner and, sure enough, it is hidden away at the foot of its small valley. At one time it was famed for its orchards and described as a sea of blossom in spring. Enough remnants are left to give a hint of what it must have been. The second part of the route swings south of Southwell giving some of the best views of Southwell's Minster.

From **Southwell Minster car park**, turn right on A612 opposite the Minster to the mini-roundabout by the Saracen's Head. Turn right into *King Street*, then almost immediately left following the one-way system into *Queen Street*. At the next junction, where Queen Street bears right, turn left – effectively straight on – on *Halam Road*. Before long you pass Merryweather's garden centre then a relatively new housing development, both on the right, beyond which you turn right into *Hopkiln Lane* (not signed at this junction). After about 300yds, at a T-junction, turn left into *Kirklington Road*, and at the next T-junction after about ¼ mile, again left, signed *Kirklington*. Follow this road for about 1½ miles, still following signs to Kirklington. Just after a brick bridge (*over the Southwell Trail, see route 28*) the road bears

Start: Southwell Minster (car park opposite, off A612, Church Street) (GR 702 538)

8
continued

Distance: 9 miles

Terrain: entirely on-road, undulating, quite hilly from Halam to Westhorpe

Refreshment opportunities: several teashops in Southwell, including the Minster Refectory and Gossips Coffee House; picnic area where the route crosses the Southwell Trail for the second time.

Ordnance Survey maps: Landranger sheet **120** Mansfield and Worksop; Explorer sheet 28 (270) Sherwood Forest

Public transport links: The nearest rail station to Southwell is Fiskerton on the Nottingham to Newark Castle line, about 2½ miles south-east of Southwell. Fiskerton is a request stop: trains stop there if you tell the conductor when you get on, or give a hand signal as the train approaches. Not all trains on this route will stop at Fiskerton.

Other routes: Route **22**, Blidworth and Halam, joins this one at Halam. Route **28**, Southwell Trail and the Dumbles, starts and finishes at Southwell. Route **30**, Daybrook and Southwell, gives a link to Nottingham and, at Fiskerton, by way of link route **L10** to Newark-on-Trent.

sharply round to the left. About 200yds after this bend, take the first left gently uphill, signed *Edingley* (and also to *picnic area*).

After recrossing the Southwell Trail continue for about 500yds to a staggered crossroads. Turn left, then very shortly right on Holme Lane (not named at this junction), signed *Halam*. After about 1 mile at a T-junction on the outskirts of Halam, turn left. At the next crossroads, in **Halam**, continue straight up Halam Hill, signed *Southwell*, Just over the crest of Halam Hill turn right into *Saversick Lane*, otherwise unsignposted. At the next crossroads (give way sign), cross B6386 and continue straight on downhill on an unsigned road, bearing left at the bottom of the hill into **Westhorpe**. After about 200yds, turn right into *The Holme* to leave the village and climb up Cundy Hill.

8
continued

The road makes a right-angle bend to the left and about 200yds beyond this go straight on at a T-junction where the slightly larger of these two very minor roads goes right.

At the T-junction with the main road, A612, turn right, slightly uphill, then after about 200yds, take the first turn left, signed *Brackenhurst College*. After passing a playing-field on the left go straight on (right then left) at the staggered crossroads. The road bends sharp left and about 150yds later at a T-junction, turn right (no signpost). The road winds round with some fine views across to Southwell Minster on the left, eventually coming to a T-junction with Fiskerton Road, where you learn that the road you have been on is Crink Lane. On the right at the junction is a wooden bench seat with the intriguing inscription 'This seat was donated by a cyclist' – we don't know any more about it. Turn left; the road sweeps downhill to a T-junction with the A612, opposite the Old Coach House Inn, turn left on A612, Easthorpe, past the Minster School and then **Southwell Minster** itself to complete the route.

Route
9
start

10 miles • on- and off-road • undulating • Ram Inn, Eastwood

Beauvale to Bogend!

This figure-of-eight route makes use of tracks and country lanes north-east of the town of Eastwood – taking in woods, water (Moorgreen Reservoir) and Robin Hood's Well! The area is one of historical interest, with the remains of Beauvale Priory and the site of Edward III's castle, not to mention Eastwood's claim to fame as the birthplace of D H Lawrence.

Turn right out of the car park of the ***Ram Inn***, along a road known as Beauvale. After approximately 300yds, just beyond Greasley Beauvale Infant School (where D H Lawrence was a pupil), turn right into Mill Road, which you follow down a hill to its T-junction with Lower Beauvale. Turn right, then almost immediately left along a bridleway signed *Willey Lane*. Continue for about 1½ miles on this track,

Moorgreen Reservoir

ignoring any minor paths which branch off, but following the *blue arrows* which indicate bridleway status. The track winds around one farm, and soon after passing a second, emerges onto a tarred road at a T-junction. Turn left and follow this – the B600, which becomes the A608 – for ¾ mile to the outskirts of **Underwood**.

Shortly past the sign, turn right at an unsigned crossroads into the minor road, Felly (or Felley) Mill Lane. At the bottom of this lane, turn right onto an unclassified road which becomes a public bridlepath at a metal barrier. Shortly after the end of the tarred surface, bear off to the right to follow a track with a stream running along its right-hand side. Soon you will see *bridleway signs* for *Moorgreen*; follow the *blue arrows* through the woods, keeping **Moorgreen Reservoir** at some distance to your right. After about ¾ mile the bridleway emerges onto a tarred minor road; bear right and continue as far as the gatehouse. Turn left onto the B600 – itself known as Moorgreen – up the hill, and soon after the Horse and Groom, turn left signed *New Road leading to Narrow Road*. This virtually traffic-free lane goes past the remains of Beauvale Priory and Robin Hood's Well – hidden in the woods after about 1½ miles. It's worth stopping to look back from the top of this road to look at the view over typical D H Lawrence country, backed by the foothills of the Peak District.

Eventually the lane emerges at a T-junction with the B6009; turn right and right again after about 50yds into *Church Road* – which runs parallel to the

9

continued

main road and takes you through the picturesquely named **Bogend**! At the T-junction, the knoll on the opposite side of the main road is the site of Edward III's castle: go right and up the hill – with Minton's Tearooms on the left offering a welcome break. Opposite the same Horse and Groom, turn left down Moorgreen, B6010, signed *Newthorpe*, which leads back to the **Ram Inn**.

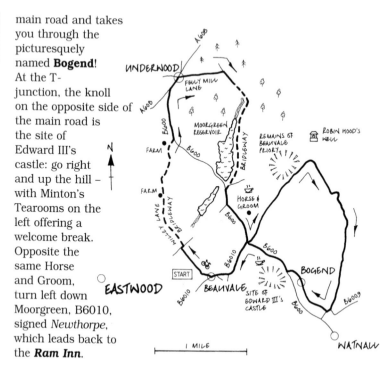

Start: The Ram Inn, Beauvale (road), Eastwood (GR 481 471)

Distance: 10 miles

Terrain: About a third of this route is **off-road** – but on bridleways ridable all year round; the on-road sections are primarily on B-roads. It is fairly undulating so, with the looser surfaced off-road elements, both sturdy tyres and low gears are recommended.

Refreshment opportunities: The Horse and Groom at Moorgreen does food lunchtimes and evenings; and the route passes Minton's Tearooms.

Ordnance Survey maps: Landranger sheets **120** Mansfield and Worksop and 129 Nottingham and Loughborough; Explorer sheets **260** Nottingham and **28** (being renumbered as **270**) Sherwood Forest

Public transport links: Bogend is about 3½ miles west of Hucknall station on the Robin Hood Line. To reach the route, leave the station by the one-way system, turning left to the traffic lights by the Byron Entertainment Centre. Turn right into the High Street, then at the next traffic lights turn left on Watnall Road, B6009. Continue on this road, crossing the Hucknall bypass, A611, and the M1 to the junction with B600 at Bogend.

Other routes: The nearest of the other routes are **15** and **39** which pass through Hucknall (see 'Public transport links' above).

City Canals and Castles

Although this route is essentially an urban one – starting and finishing in Nottingham city centre, and not straying beyond the city boundary – it takes riders on an intricate tour through the more leafy south-west section of the built-up area. It follows part of the Nottingham and Beeston Canal, which was opened up to cyclists by British Waterways in 1994, together with beautifully-kept Wollaton Park, which together give the route a deceptively rural feel. The route makes extensive use of the relatively comprehensive network of cycle routes in this part of the city, and finally heads back to the city centre by way of the Castle – where the Buttery cakes and view are worth a detour into the grounds. *Note: The majority of the 'signs' referred to in the directions that follow are the official white-on-blue cycle route signs.*

With **Nottingham Midland Station** behind you, turn right down Carrington Street. After a short way, before you cross the canal, take the ramp off to the left – opposite the Cosy Tea Pot Café. Go straight on at the bottom along the towpath of the Nottingham and Beeston Canal, which you follow for nearly 2 miles. The path crosses a number of small bridges, some with quite steep inclines, and passes under a number of road bridges. Eventually, the towpath goes under a very tall main road bridge which carries the A52 Nottingham ring road, and it is at the smaller arched bridge after this that the route leaves the towpath via a ramp off to the left. Bear right part way up the ramp to cross the canal via the arched bridge and, on reaching a minor road, turn left, signed *University (south)*. Take the first right, Cavendish Street, and go straight on at the end under the low railway bridge, negotiating the barriers barriers, following signs for *University (south entrance)*. Approximately 500yds beyond the railway bridge, opposite the Dunkirk Inn, turn left down a cycle path which runs between fenced gardens and past Highfields Science Park. On

41

10

continued

emerging, go right and straight over at the traffic lights, crossing the dual carriageway. The University Arts Centre café, which is open to the public, is just off the route to the right. Without entering the University grounds, turn left onto the cycle track (*'NCN' Route 6 joins here*), and follow it for its entire length along the northern side of University Boulevard.

At the end of University Boulevard, *leave 'NCN' Route 6* but keep on the cycle track which bears round to the right into Woodside Road, past the west entrance to the University and straight on following signs for *Wollaton*. The cycle track crosses numerous side-road turnings, but keep to the track, with the dual carriageway on your left. On reaching Priory roundabout – named after a nearby pub which has sinced changed it's name – cross Derby Road using the pedestrian crossing, then straight on into Wollaton Vale, continuing along the cycle track. Leave the track after a short distance, at the first right turn up Parkside. Soon after the top of the gentle climb, opposite Wollaton Rise, turn right through a small gate next to a pair of large brown gates into **Wollaton Park**. (*Note that the Wollaton Park gates close at dusk.*) Go through two more sets of gates, down a gently sloping well-defined path, then through a further wooden swing gate to emerge by a lake; turn left over a small bridge and straight on towards Wollaton Hall. Just beyond the Heritage Shop (and courtyard café if you explore through the archway), follow the path which bears round to the left – skirting below **Wollaton Hall** while keeping the courtyard

---

Start: Nottingham Midland railway station (GR 574 393)

Distance: 10 miles

Terrain: A generally flat route, using some of the more scenic sections of the Nottingham cycle route network.

Refreshment opportunities: As the route doesn't leave the City of Nottingham, you are never very far from corner grocery shops and pubs. On the route itself there are four tea shops: Café Lautrec – at the University Arts Centre, the courtyard cafe in Wollaton Park, and The Buttery in the grounds of Nottingham Castle, while the Cosy Teapot in Carrington Street is only about 150yds north of Nottingham Station.

Ordnance Survey maps: Landranger sheet **129** Nottingham and Loughborough and Explorer sheet **260** Nottingham. The whole route is also on the *AZ Premier Street Map of Nottingham*, which might be more useful.

Public transport links: Midland Main Line, Robin Hood Line and Central Trains services go to Nottingham Midland Station

Other routes: Routes 9, Colwick Country Park; 32, Sutton Bonington; 33, Villages beginning with W; 36, Grantham Canal; and 40, Newark to Nottingham, all start or finish at Nottingham Midland Station. Link route **L5** joins this route to routes 4, Attenborough Nature Reserve, and L6, Beeston to Strelley. The route briefly joins **'NCN'** Route 6 near the Queen's Medical Centre.

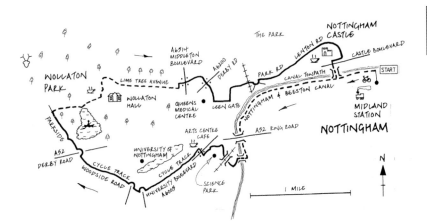

buildings on the left. At a 'crossroads' in the paths, marked by a telephone box, go right but ignore any further right-hand forks up to the Hall. This park road leads down a gentle slope and along the aptly named 'Lime Tree Avenue' to where the route leaves the park beside the impressive main wrought-iron gates.

On reaching the A6514 dual carriageway, go left for a short distance along the shared cycle/pedestrian path, then cross the main road just before Sutton Passeys Crescent via the signalled crossings, and into Charnock Avenue. (*'NCN' Route 6 joins shortly after this point.*) At the give-way markings bear right – although this is still Charnock Avenue – and right again at the end, between the bollards, to follow the *cycle route signs* for *Lenton*. Go straight over the signalled cycle crossing at the end of the shared-use path, into Hill Side, which continues as a cycle/pedestrian path behind the Queen's Medical Centre. Go left where the shared-use path meets a minor road, Leen Gate, signed *City centre* (*leaving 'NCN' Route 6*), and left again at the T-junction opposite the White Hart. Take the second right into Church Street, bearing immediately right into Sherwin Road, passing under the railway bridge towards the far end of this street.

Go right onto the cycle track just before Sherwin Road meets Lenton Boulevard, but use the signalled cycle crossing to cross the latter after a short distance – just before Broadholme Street. Bear right to continue along the cycle track until it ends on the opposite side of the roundabout to the Grove pub. Turn left, *signed for cyclists to the city centre* and straight on at the 'dead end', passing through an iron gate into The Park estate. Continue along Lenton Road, straight over at the small roundabout, to emerge from The Park residential area beside **Nottingham Castle** – there are public conveniences and

10
continued

The Buttery tea shop in the grounds. (*Note that there's an entry charge to the Castle grounds at weekends and bank holidays and you can't take bikes in at any time.*)

Go right just beyond the Castle, down the cobbled street known as Castle Road, straight on at the 'no-entry' signs, where there is provision for cyclists to cut through, and continue down the hill. Just before the T-junction, turn right onto the cycle track, which meanders between trees for a short way before taking you across Castle Boulevard, via a signalled cycle crossing, signed *Lenton*. Turn right to continue along the cycle track at the far side and, just before an HSS Hire Shop, turn left up a path to cross the **Nottingham and Beeston Canal** via a wooden bridge. On reaching the towpath, turn right – now keeping the canal to your left – to retrace the first part of the route back to **Nottingham Midland Station**.

Route

11

start

> **10 miles • on- and off-road • gentle • Skegby**

Pleasley and Teversal Trails

This route uses the track beds of disused rail lines that once served the long-since-closed local collieries and have now been turned into paths for cyclists and walkers. The tracks are generally well surfaced, but do tend to be dusty in dry weather and loose on the few short inclines. Much of the network of trails has been designated a Local Nature Reserve, containing a rich variety of plants and wild life. More information on what to look out for is available from the visitor centre – signed from various points along the route, tel (01623) 442021.

Teversal, towards the end of the route, is a surprisingly pretty village, with warm stone cottages surrounding a green open space. It is said to be the basis for the fictional 'Wragby Hall', home of D H Lawrence's Sir Clifford and Lady Chatterley, while the woodlands between the village and Hardwick Hall are the inspiration for the setting of the book's most, er, notable happenings.

Start: Teversal Trail – Skegby car park, Buttery Lane, off B6014 (GR 495 614)

Distance: 10 miles

Terrain: Half **off-road**, easy going with one or two steep pitches; remainder on quite hilly minor roads.

Refreshment opportunities: The Visitor Centre – well worth a visit – offers drinks and light snacks (open daily 10.30am–3.45pm); several pubs near the start/finish and in Pleasley – about half way along the route.

Ordnance Survey maps: Landranger sheet **120** Mansfield and Worksop; Explorer sheet **28** (270) Sherwood Forest

Public transport links: Mansfield Woodhouse station on the Robin Hood Line (no Sunday service): see link route **L2**, Mansfield Woodhouse to Pleasley Vale,

Other routes: Route **19**, Ault Hucknall and Hardwick Hall, overlaps at Pleasley Vale and crosses again at Moorhaigh.

11 continued

Head northward from **Skegby** trail car park along the Teversal Trail, and where it forks after about 400yds keep to the right-hand path. Stay on this path for a further 2 miles, following blue bridleway arrows signed *Teversal Trail to Pleasley*. This trail crosses a couple of minor roads which involve short steep climbs and descents as the original railway bridge and tunnel have been removed. At the end of the **Teversal Trail** pass through a wooden kissing gate and turn right onto a minor road. At the T-junction, opposite Pleasley Surgery, turn right again. After about 600yds, just before Pleasley Post Office, take the *signed footpath* off to the left which follows a small river – the Meden – under the A617.

On the other side of the main road, turn left to join the **Meden Trail** keeping the river on your left. After

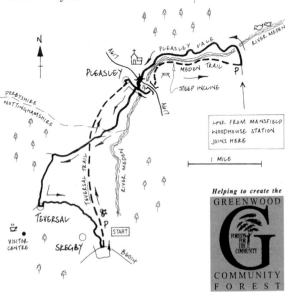

45

11
continued

about 400yds, opposite an informal stepping-stone river crossing, bear right up a fairly steep incline to join a disused railway line. Follow this track for some 1½ miles, until it emerges in a small, car park – the gates of which seem to be permanently locked! At the vehicle entrance to the abandoned car park, turn left into Common Lane, unsigned at this point (*the link* **L2** *from Mansfield Woodhouse station joins here*). Follow this minor road, which becomes Outgang Lane, some 2 miles back through **Pleasley Vale**, past some imposing mill buildings and an attractive mill pond, derelict until recently but now brought back into use as a business park and outward-bound centre.

Beyond Outgang Lane car park, turn left at the sign for *Pleasley Parish Church*. At the end of this 'no-through road', use the footbridge over the dual carriageway – the A617 again. Go straight on at the other side, along Church Lane, and at the staggered crossroads 'jog-right-jog-left' into Newboundmill Lane – signed for *Teversal and Skegby*. Continue along this lane – becoming Newbound Lane – for about ¾ mile: where the road bears sharp left, turn right, signed for *Terversal*. In **Teversal**, turn left into Buttery Lane and back to **Skegby** car park.

Route

12

start

> **10 miles • mostly off-road • rolling • Worksop**

Worksop and Thievesdale

This circuit makes extensive use of the mass of bridleways north of Worksop. These are mainly farm, park and estate roads with firm surfaces, easily ridable with any type of bike at most seasons. There are, though, one or two short stretches that are inclined to be loose and dusty or sandy in very dry weather, when they would be easier on a mountain bike – or you could walk these bits. The countryside is an incredibly quiet mixture of parkland, grazing and arable fields, with some surprisingly open views over the valley of the River Ryton with its French-style willow coppices to the east of Worksop.

From **Worksop Town Hall** in the corner of the Market Place, bear right at pedestrian lights into Potter Street, then at mini-roundabout turn left into Watson Road, signed *Tickhill 10 (A60).* Continue straight on at the next two sets of traffic lights, then at the next set opposite Mothercare, turn right over the bridge, signed *A60, Tickhill.* At the traffic lights immediately after the bridge, get into the right-hand waiting lane then turn right into Eastgate, just in front of the King's Head. ('NCN' Route 6 crosses here.)

12
continued

From **Worksop Station**: the street-level exits from the platforms are at the level-crossing (eastern) end. Once on the road, turn right downhill towards the town, to the first set of traffic lights, by the King's Head, and turn left into Eastgate.

After about 600yds, at the Kilton Inn, Eastgate becomes Kilton Road. Continue straight on to a mini-roundabout, and go straight on, still on Kilton Road. After about 500yds this bears round to the left under a railway bridge; immediately after the bridge, turn right onto a completely *unnamed, unsigned minor road* which starts by running close to the railway. After about ½ mile the tarred surface stops (go round the motor-vehicle barrier) and the road continues as a firm-surfaced gravel track. In about a further 1½ miles the track crosses the grounds of **Osberton Hall**, which is a prominent white building to the right, visible across a small lake. The track emerges onto a tarred road, which still only has bridleway status, with a wooden three-way signpost marking the junction of bridleways.

This is the hamlet of **Scofton**. Turn left on the tarred road, up a gentle slope. After about ½ mile the route crosses straight over a former airfield runway. Immediately after the runway, turn left between a metal gate and a concrete plinth, to follow an

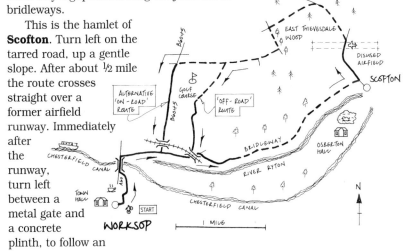

47

Between Worksop and Scofton

unsigned firm-surfaced track which runs to the left of a fir plantation. After about 700yds the bridleway divides, take the left hand track which runs along the bottom of a field. Some ½ mile later you reach a T-junction of tracks (which is actually a 'crossroads' of bridleways – the one straight on just crosses a grassy meadow). Turn left up hill to a line of trees (this is one of the sections which gets sandy in dry weather), and follow the track when it bears round to the right between wooden fences to a small water-treatment station almost hidden on the right, where the track jogs right and left.

About 700yds beyond this point there is a crossing of tracks. The right-hand leg aligns with a radio mast, and to the left there is a misleading green, grassy track – which you *don't* take. A bridleway (*unsigned*) strikes off to the left at this point, roughly midway in the angle between the green track and the track you are already on. If you look towards the three squat blocks of flats on the horizon, you'll be facing in the right direction. In the late spring we first prospected this route, the field it crosses was newly ploughed and harrowed and only a couple of lines of footprints and a mountain-bike tyre track revealed its line. In summer it is clearly visible through the crops.

(*If you don't want to risk this cross-country bridleway*, the alternative is to continue straight on to the junction with the B6045 at the exit to the Kilton Forest Golf Club, then left down hill on B6045 into Worksop, following *signs* for the town centre.)

The **bridleway** carries on across open country downhill to a gap in the hedge at the bottom of the field. Go through the gap in the hedge, then turn left on a stone-based track beside the golf course for about 200yds to a pair of *pink posts with blue bands* on the right. Turn right and head across the fairways for other pairs of *pink posts*. When you reach the back fences of some houses, turn left for about 150yds, and then right on a path bordered by green metal railings between two blocks of five-storey flats.

This path emerges on to Osberton View, a short dead-end road. At the head of Osberton View, turn left onto Browning Close (*not signed* at this point) to the T-junction with Coleridge Road (*not signed* at this point), where you turn right. At the next T-junction, turn left down Plantation Hill (also *not signed* at this point) past a pub called the Lord Byron. At the second road after the Lord Byron, turn left on Rayton Spur, signed *Bracebridge and Town Centre* and follow the road round under the railway bridge into Kilton Road. At the T-junction with High Hoe Road turn right, then immediately left at the mini-roundabout, still on Kilton Road. This becomes Eastgate. At the traffic lights by the King's Head, turn left over the bridge, and left again at the next set of lights into Watson Road. Continue straight on at all traffic lights to the mini-roundabout junction with Potter Street, turn right, signed *Ollerton and Edwinstowe* to return to **Worksop Town Hall**.

To return to the **station**, turn right at the lights by the King's Head up Carlton Road to the level crossing.

Start: Worksop Station (GR 585 798) or Worksop Town Hall (GR 584 786)

Distance: 10 miles

Terrain: a large proportion is **off-road on untarred farm and estate roads** which have the status of bridleways; they are for the most part firm-surfaced and easily ridable. The terrain rolls a little but there is only one appreciable short hill, towards the end of the bridleway section.

Refreshment opportunities: Worksop has a number of cafés and pubs, though most of the cafés seem to be closed on Sundays.

Ordnance Survey maps: Landranger sheet **120**, Mansfield and Worksop; Explorer sheet **28** (being renumbered as **270**) Sherwood Forest.

Public transport links: Arriva Trains Northern services run from Sheffield, Retford and Gains-borough to Worksop, while Central Trains' Robin Hood Line services run from Nottingham, Mansfield and intermediate stations to Worksop.

Other routes: Routes **14**, **17** and **21** also start from Worksop, while '**NCN**' **Route 6** passes through the town.

12
continued

CIRCULAR ROUTES
FROM 11 TO 20 MILES

Route

13

start

11 miles • on-road • rolling • Bingham

A tour round Bingham

This short on-road circuit based on Bingham has some surprising delights. The little hamlet of Tythby (or Tithby*) is charming – and so remote that you wonder why the AA thought it worth their while in the 1920s to put up one of their round yellow signs giving the distance to London! The next village, Cropwell Butler, is larger and perhaps a little more self-consciously picturesque with its old water pump preserved by the shaded green in the village centre. About three miles later you come out onto a tiny open hedgeless road that crosses a gentle rolling hill – in high summer, nothing to be seen but the corn and the sky – and then as it rolls over the brow reveals one of the most attractive views in south Nottinghamshire, across the village of Shelford, nestled in a bend of the Trent.

*The hamlet appears as 'Tithby' on the OS map but generally as 'Tythby' on the ground. As far as we can we use the version you'll see on the actual sign.

From **Bingham** station go south on Station Street, then right along the edge of Market Place to Market Street, where you turn left. At the T-junction opposite the Wheatsheaf Inn, turn right into Long Acre, unsigned at this junction. After a short distance, turn left at the signalled cross-roads into Tithby Road, signed *Tithby* and *Langar*. There is now quite a steep climb up to the A52. Cross the main road

50

at a staggered crossroads, right and left, still on Tithby
Road.

13

continued

Head southwards and after about 1½ miles
take the first right, signed *Tithby*. The road
bears round to the left into the hamlet of Tythby.

At a minor crossroads by the church, turn
right, signed Cropwell Butler. After 1 mile, turn
right at T-junction. The road bears left then
right through the centre of Cropwell Butler:
follow signs for Bingham. At the staggered
crossroads over the A46 go right then left –
effectively straight on – into Henson Lane. After about 1 mile at a
new housing development, Upper Saxondale, on the site of a former
hospital, go straight on at the staggered cross-roads – still on Henson
Lane. Pass to the right of a wooden gate which bars access to motor
vehicles. Then, about 100yds before the junction with the A52 the
road is again blocked to cars but a cycle gap has been left. At the A52
go left, then almost immediately right, signposted *Shelford*. Follow this
open unfenced road with its fine views over the Trent valley for about
1 mile to a crossroads. Turn right, signposted *Newton*, and continue
through Newton to the junction with the
A46. Turn right (care), or cross over to the
footway on the
south-east side of
the road, riding or
walking as
appropriate for
about 250yds,
then turn left at
a footpath
fingerboard
just before a
white house
to join a
blocked-off
track. Follow
this track which
becomes tarred, to
a T-junction with a
minor road. Turn
right (no signs) to go
over the level
crossing up a slight
hill into Bingham,

13
continued

then left into Newgate Street, signed Library and health centre. Just after the road bears round to the right, turn left along the edge of Market Square, then first left by two telephone boxes into Station Street; the station is at the end of this road.

Start: Bingham station (GR 705 401)

Distance: 11 miles

Terrain: entirely on-road, gently rolling

Refreshment opportunities: Dickie's on theSquare café at the Market Place in Bingham

Ordnance Survey maps: Landranger sheet 129 Nottingham and Loughborough; Explorer sheet 260 Nottingham

Public transport links: Central Trains services to Bingham on the Nottingham–Grantham line (not all services on this line stop at Bingham)

Other routes: Route **31** is a longer (31-mile) version of this one; route **40**, Newark to Nottingham, meets this one at the crossroads above Shelford.

Route
14
start

11 miles • on- and off-road • moderate • Worksop

Rhodesia and the Manor Hills

Note: do not confuse Worksop Manor South Lodge (this route and link L4) with Clumber Park South Lodge (route 27)

This route can be used either as a short circular trip south and west of Worksop, or as an alternative route (to route 17) from Worksop to Clumber Park. Used with link route L4 it can also be used to reach the Creswell Crags archaeological site. The forested section of the route includes some fine trackways through the western remnant of the once-continuous Sherwood Forest.

From **Worksop Town Hall** in the corner of the Market Place, bear right at pedestrian lights into Potter Street, then at mini-roundabout turn left into Watson Road, signed *Tickhill 10 (A60)*. Continue straight on at the next two sets of traffic lights, then at the next set opposite Mothercare,

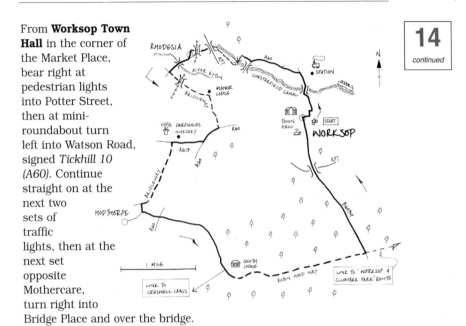

14 continued

turn right into Bridge Place and over the bridge. Keep in the left-hand lane, signed *The North, Sheffield*. After about 400yds, turn left at a mini-roundabout into Sandy Lane.

From **Worksop Station**: the street-level exits from the platforms are at the level-crossing (eastern) end. Immediately after the lower station exit turn right into Clarence Road (rather than cross the B-road twice in rapid succession, you may find it easier to walk round this corner on the right-hand side). Take the first left, Welbeck Street, and at the end of this road turn right on Overend Road (although no road sign visible here). At the end of this road go left and almost immediately right at a mini-roundabout, into Sandy Lane.

At the next T-junction turn left, still on Sandy Lane, and at the next mini-roundabout turn right, once more still on Sandy Lane, this time marked as *leading to Shireoaks Road*, with the Chesterfield Canal to the left. After a short distance, bear left across a canal bridge by the Lockkeeper Inn, then turn right along the canal towpath which is part of 'NCN' Route 6. (The canal bridge does involve negotiating a few shallow steps.) Leave the towpath – and Route 6 – at the next exit, just after you pass under a brock road bridge. Bear left, then right, to pass almost immediately under the A57.

After **Rhodesia** village centre the road bears round to the right and

14
continued

Start: Worksop Station (GR 585 798) or Worksop Town Hall (GR 584 786)

Distance: 11½ miles if used as a circuit starting and finishing in Worksop; about 9½ miles if ridden from Worksop to its junction with route **17**.

Terrain: the first section is relatively flat but there is quite a stiff climb for a short distance from South Lodge on the Robin Hood Way into the forest. The off-road sections are firm-based and reasonably surfaced, except for the central portion of the Darfoulds–Hodthorpe bridleway which can be muddy in or after wet weather.

Refreshment opportunities: Worksop

Ordnance Survey maps: Landranger sheet 120, Mansfield and Worksop; Explorer sheet 28 (270) Sherwood Forest.

Public transport links: Arriva Trains Northern services run from Sheffield, Retford and Gainsborough to Worksop, while Central Trains' Robin Hood Line services run from Nottingham, Mansfield and intermediate stations to Worksop. There is a Robin Hood Line station at Whitwell, near to the route at Hodthorpe. From Whitwell station, turn left downhill for 700yds, then take the first road on the left.

Other routes: This route joins route **17**, Worksop and Clumber Park near Truman's Lodge. Routes **13** and **21** also start from Worksop. Link route **L4** joins Worksop Manor South Lodge to the Creswell Crags archaeological site, by way of Welbeck Park. **'NCN' Route 6** passes through Worksop and crosses the route twice.

under a railway bridge, then bends immediately round to the left. In about 600yds there is a bridge over a stream, the infant River Ryton, and immediately after that, turn left on an untarred track signed *Public Bridleway Lodge Farm*, opposite a road signed to Shireoaks. Pass some farm buildings near the entrance to the bridleway, then go through a gap beside a large metal swing gate and under a high railway arch. Continue on this firm-surfaced track until you pass round another white metal gate, about ½ further on, onto a minor tarred road opposite the imposing Manor Lodge. Turn right (the surface improves) as far as the T-junction with the A60.

Turn right on the A60 for about 400yds, then turn right on A619, signed *Chesterfield*. *If you do not wish to ride on the A60 and A619, there is a footpath on the north side of the road which avoids the main roads and right turn. This will involve walking with your bike for about half a mile.* About 500yds further on, just after Darfoulds Nursery on the right, turn left on a signed bridleway, opposite a red pillar box. After about a mile the track bears right and passes between a farm and a cottage and then bends sharply round to the left as far as a minor tarred road. Turn left for about 300yds to a crossroads with the A60. Go straight across into Broad Lane, a minor road which winds gently for about 1½ miles up to the forest, eventually reaching Worksop Manor **South Lodge**. (*Link route L4 to Creswell Crags joins/leaves here.*) At the Lodge, go straight ahead following a bridleway fingerpost beside a metal fence. The path bears round to the left and climbs quite steeply through a small sandstone gorge, then becomes flat. The path through the wood is well-defined and occasionally marked with *bridleway posts, blue arrows and Robin Hood Way bow-and-arrow* signs – ignore any turnings to either side. After about 2 miles the track reaches the B6034.

14
continued

To return direct to Worksop, turn left on B6034 for about 1 mile, then turn left on an unclassified road where the B6034 swings right, signed *Worksop Town Centre*. Go down the hill, Sparken Hill; the road becomes Park Street, leading to **Worksop** Town Hall.

To continue to Clumber Park go straight across the B6034, signed as a *bridleway*. This emerges after some 500yds on a minor tarred road to join route **17**, Worksop and Clumber Park. Turn right for Clumber Park.

12 miles • on-road and cycle track • gentle • Hucknall station

Route
15
start

Hucknall, Newstead and Papplewick

This gentle circular route inevitably has strong Byron connections. Newstead Abbey became the home of the Byron family in 1539, although there had been an Augustinian priory on the site since the 12th century. The Byrons always seemed to be plagued by financial problems, and when the poet inherited the place and the title as the 6th Lord Byron only one room, the scullery, was habitable. Byron was fond of the place and brought more of it into use – living there, on and off, from 1809 to 1814. However, his lifestyle once more brought on money problems and he was forced to sell it in 1817. He died in 1824 in exile in Greece, a country that still reveres him for his support for Greek independence. He is buried in the Byron family vault in Hucknall church.

Another landmark on the route is Papplewick Pumping Station, a prominent Victorian building whose tall chimney is visible for miles. Built around 1880 as one of several to supply water to

15
continued

On the Linby Trail

the city of Nottingham, it contains a superb restored steam beam-engine which worked the pumps, housed in an ornate temple to industry. It can be seen working at specified times, mainly on summer Sundays and Bank Holidays. It is actually about 2½ miles from Papplewick, the nearest identifiable village at the time it was built.

The little village of Papplewick sits around what is at times a rather busy crossroads, with some attractive runs of light stone-built cottages leading towards the imposing Papplewick Hall. Just west of the village centre lies Castle Mill Farm. In the 17th century Castle Mill was a large employer of child labour, with children being brought from as far as London to toil over the machines. Many died and are buried in Papplewick churchyard. What is now a pleasant small patch of wetland north of the road was the site of the dam impounding the waters of the River Leen to power the mill.

From **Hucknall** station car park vehicle entrance, turn right opposite the Tesco store. Then right and left at the two mini-roundabouts on Station Road by the Station Hotel into Linby Road. (*'NCN' Route 6 joins here.*) After about ½ mile the road passes over a level crossing, then after another 700yds, just after a turn (unsigned) for Linby

Helping to create the GREENWOOD

COMMUNITY FOREST

village on right, join the *signed cycle/pedestrian path* on the right which brings you to the B6011, just east of a roundabout. Cross the B6011, onto the cycle path following blue *'NCN' Route 6* cycle route signs to *Newstead Abbey*, passing through a wooden barrier. Just beyond a second wooden access control barrier after about a mile continue straight ahead and in ½

56

mile or so the path bears round to the right between two wooden fences to join a tarred road.

15
continued

Turn right on this road past the gatehouse into Newstead Abbey grounds (note: there is a charge to enter the Abbey grounds which is reduced – to 50p at the time of writing, 2004 – for cyclists following the cycle route). Go straight ahead along a tree-lined avenue for ½ mile or so, then between the stone pillars of another gateway. Continue straight on, up a slope and then down to some lakes, with a waterfall on the left; **Newstead Abbey** (and the far-from-ruined tea shop) are on the right. The road sweeps round to the left, then right, with traffic-calming humps, then climbs between rhododendrons to the east gateway where the route leaves the Abbey grounds (*and also leaves 'NCN' Route 6*). Keep left at the small grassed triangle after the park gates to the main road, A60.

Go straight over the A60 into Longdale Lane, which bears round to the right (you may find it worth using the pedestrian crossing lights to your left if traffic is heavy). After about 2½ miles turn right at a minor crossroads, signed *Papplewick Pumping Station*. Pass this Victorian pumping station on your right and follow the road for about 1 mile to a T-junction. Turn right (unsigned) to traffic lights at the A60 junction opposite Seven Mile Cottages. Turn right on A60, signed *Mansfield*, over the railway bridge, then first left into Forest Lane, B6011, signed *Hucknall*. Continue for about 1½ miles to **Papplewick**, then left at the Griffin's Head on B683, signed *Hucknall*.

After about 500yds, turn right into Papplewick Lane, signed *Hucknall*. After about 1 mile turn right at a mini-roundabout just before the railway bridge into Station Road. Continue over the railway bridge, bearing left at the two mini-roundabouts to complete the circuit at **Hucknall** station car park.

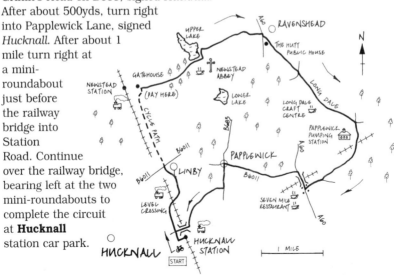

57

15
continued

Start: Hucknall Station (GR 540 493). Alternatively you could start at Newstead station (GR 522 528), following the cycle route signs for Newstead Abbey to join the circuit, or start at Newstead and finish at Hucknall, to give a total of about 9 miles.

Distance: 12 miles

Terrain: mostly on-road but making use of the cycle track from Linby to Newstead (tricky barriers for anything other than solo bicycles). Nearly all gradients are gentle, with the exception of the climb from Newstead Abbey to the east gatehouse opposite The Hutt.

Refreshment opportunities: there is a tea shop at Newstead Abbey and another at the Longdale Craft Centre, the Seven Mile Beefeater at the Seven Mile traffic lights on the A60. and the Griffin's Head restaurant in Papplewick.There are also cafés in Hucknall.

Ordnance Survey maps: Landranger sheets **120** Mansfield and Worksop, **129** Nottingham and Loughborough; Explorer sheets **260** Nottingham and 28 (**270**) Sherwood Forest.

Public transport links: Robin Hood Line from Nottingham, Mansfield, Worksop and intermediate stations to Hucknall or Newstead stations (no Sunday service)

Other routes: Route 39, Leen Valley Path, follows the same line as this one from Hucknall station to near Newstead station. Route **39** also gives a link (just over 1 mile) to route **2**, Bestwood Country Park. The route follows pretty well the line of '**NCN**' **Route 6** from Hucknall station to the exit gate of Newstead Abbey at Ravenshead.

Route
16
start

12 miles • on- and off-road • flat • Retford

Retford wetlands

Just as in the south of the county – at Attenborough beside the River Trent on route 1 – gravel extraction beside the River Idle, north of Retford has left an array of lakes in the flat landscape. This route goes round them on a mixture of mostly minor roads and gravel tracks – though the first couple of miles follow in the hoofmarks of characters such as Dick Turpin: along the Great North Road, the old coaching route between London, York and Edinburgh. Now the broad road is relatively quiet, with today's traffic hurtling along a mile or two to the west on the tarmac wastelands of the near-motorway A1.

Just under halfway round, on the first section of gravel track, the route passes the Wetlands Waterfowl Reserve, which now offers a habitat for many varieties of waterfowl in a series of lagoons created from the old gravel workings. There are nature trails and hides from which the birds can be seen. There is a charge for admission – and also a teashop (which you *don't* have to pay to get to). The River Idle, beside which an optional section of the route runs, begins only four or five miles

16
continued

The River Idle

south of Retford, where the Rivers Maun and Meden that feature on several of the other routes come together and lose their names. As in all really flat landscapes, the sky dominates the scene and this area is a great place to be on a breezy showery day with tall cumulus clouds sweeping across the sky.

Leave **Retford** Market Square at the northern end, turning left at the mini-roundabout by the White Hart into Bridgegate to cross the *River Idle*. At the next roundabout take the second exit, signed *Bawtry A638*; this is the old Great North Road, the original coaching route from London to York and Edinburgh. After about 1½ miles, just before the main road begins to climb to a railway bridge, fork right at an oblique crossroads onto a minor road, Sutton Lane, signed *Sutton and Wetlands Wildfowl Reserve*. Follow the road round through **Sutton**, then turn right about 150 yds past the Gate Inn, opposite the turn to the church, on Church Way, a very narrow road only about 200yds long. At the far end, turn left (unsigned). Where the tarred road bends left about ¾ mile farther on, turn right onto a gravel track, signed *Wetlands Waterfowl Reserve*.

This track passes the reserve, then after about a mile, just past Sutton Grange Farm, there is a junction of tracks. Turn right (this is

16
continued

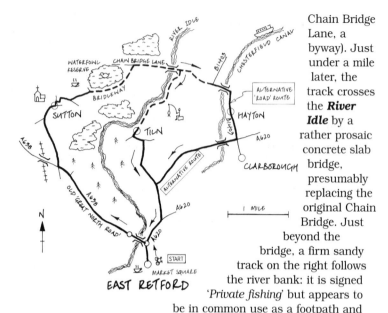

Chain Bridge Lane, a byway). Just under a mile later, the track crosses the **River Idle** by a rather prosaic concrete slab bridge, presumably replacing the original Chain Bridge. Just beyond the bridge, a firm sandy track on the right follows the river bank: it is signed 'Private fishing' but appears to be in common use as a footpath and bridleway, although we have to emphasise that its status is not clear. After about ½ mile there is a gateway marking the limit of the private fishing and vehicle access, and after about a further ¾ mile the track reaches a gate (locked but with a stile when we checked), marking the limit of vehicle access, onto a tarred road at **Tiln** Farm. From here, follow this road for about 1 mile until it joins a larger road on a bend.

Alternative road route from Chain Bridge to this point: continue straight on along Chain Bridge Lane, which now becomes a firm earthy track passing between wide, open fields. After about ¾ mile, this reaches the B1403 at a very sharp bend in the B-road. Continue straight on on B1403 to cross the Chesterfield Canal by the Boat Inn. Follow the B1403 round to the right through the long village of **Hayton**. Just before the give way sign at the approach to the A620 crossroads, opposite Corner Farm, turn right on Smeath Lane (not otherwise signed at this point).

At the junction with the lane from Tiln, turn left, signed *Retford Market Place*. This soon enters the built-up outskirts of Retford and after about ¾ mile joins the A620, Moorgate. Turn right downhill, turn left at the traffic lights at the foot of the hill onto Arlington Way, then right at the next set of lights into Chapelgate to return via the short pedestrianised section to **Retford** Market Place.

Start: Market Square, Retford (GR 704 811)

Distance: 12 miles following the road version through Hayton; 10 miles following the River Idle bank to Tiln.

Terrain: virtually flat; minor roads with the off-road sections firm-surfaced tracks.

Refreshment opportunities: there is a tearoom at the Wetlands Waterfowl Reserve.

Ordnance Survey maps: Landranger sheet 120, Mansfield and Worksop; Explorer sheets 271 Newark-on-Trent (part of route only)

Public transport links: East Coast Main Line trains (well, some of them) stop at Retford, and the Arriva Trains Northern service from Sheffield to Lincoln via Worksop and Gainsborough calls at the lower station at Retford.

Other routes: Routes **24** and **29**, and the longest one in the book, **37**, also start from Retford and use some of the same roads.

16
continued

12 miles • mostly on-road • gentle • Worksop

Route
17
start

Worksop and Clumber Park

Worksop lies at the heart of what has come to be known as the Dukeries. Two centuries and more ago, wealthy titled families created their parklands out of the rapidly-shrinking Sherwood Forest: Clumber Park was the domain of the Dukes of Newcastle, Welbeck Abbey the family home of the Dukes of Portland, Thoresby of the Dukes of Kingston, while Worksop Manor was owned by the Dukes of Norfolk. (And when you consider that Chatsworth in nearby Derbyshire is the seat of the Dukes of *Devonshire* you begin to have serious doubts about ducal map-reading!) The result is that the natural landscape is enhanced by great houses, fine parks and enlarged or artificial lakes. The 3800 acres of the largest of the parks, Clumber, is now without its great house but safe in the hands of the National Trust, and open to the public. There is a fine network of tarred and untarred roads and paths in the park – and, best of all, cyclists can go anywhere free, while car-drivers have to pay to get into the central part of the Park. We suggest a pleasant route to, from and round the park, but there is

17
continued

plenty of scope for other rides in this mixture of heath, open space and fine woodland, including some spectacular avenues.

Worksop station to Worksop Town Hall. The street-level exits from Worksop station are at the level-crossing (eastern) end of the platforms. Once on the road, turn right downhill towards the town, straight on to the second set of traffic lights. Here there are two choices: **1** continue straight ahead into Bridge Place and then walk up the pedestrianised section, which becomes Bridge Street, to reach the Market Place beside the Town Hall; **2** turn left to begin the road route, going straight on at the next two sets of traffic lights to a mini-roundabout junction with Potter Street. Turn right, signed *Edwinstowe and Ollerton*: the Town Hall is on the left after about 200yds. A third possibility is to follow the 'NCN' Route 6 signs to rejoin our route later near Truman's Lodge

From **Worksop** Town Hall, go south on Park Street. This becomes Sparken Hill, which crosses the A57 by an overbridge and climbs quite steeply through woodland to a T-junction with the B6034. Turn right on B6034 for just over ½ mile, then fork left onto an unclassified road signed *Clumber Park* with a brown National Trust sign. After ¾ mile this reaches Truman's Lodge, the entrance to the Park. (*The short bridleway link from route 14 Rhodesia and Manor Hills, joins here.*) Just after a road forks to the left, go straight ahead on a tarred road through a stone arch

17

continued

into the Park. Continue gently downhill for about 1 mile to a crossroads, marked with a 'Give way' sign. Go straight across, continuing downhill. At the foot of

The ford in Clumber Park

the hill, the road bears round to the left, signed *car park, cycle hire and chapel.* To visit the **Clumber Park** shop, restaurant and toilets, go straight ahead on a firm-surfaced track.

Otherwise, bear left to pass between low yellow posts and past the cycle hire centre and church on the right, then bear round to the left again after the car park to climb and descend a short hill. At the foot of the descent go round a low wooden barrier, then straight on on a tarred road, past the conservation office on the right to a T-junction. Turn right, and continue straight on past a notice reading *'No unauthorised vehicles beyond this point'*; this refers specifically to motor vehicles. Shortly afterwards the tarred surface changes to a firm-surfaced but untarred track. Continue straight on, ignoring crossing tracks and passing occasional wooden barriers, downhill to cross the lake by a causeway to a tarred road. Turn right uphill to a T-junction, with **Hardwick Village** to the right. Turn left (unsigned) for just over ¾ mile to a crossroads. Go straight across, signed *Clumber Park Caravan Site,* ignore the turning to the caravan site and continue to a barrier and through the white wooden gates by Manton Lodge, the northernmost entrance to Clumber Park.

Immediately after passing through the gates, turn left on a minor road, then after about 150yds fork right (unsigned) on a minor road for about 2½ miles to a T-junction with the B6034, just south of a roundabout junction with the A57. Go straight over the B6034 (well, slightly left-and-right) under a high black metal barrier next to the speed limit and derestriction sign onto a bridleway (unsigned). Continue straight ahead for about 300yds to a tarred road. This is the foot of Sparken Hill; turn right to cross the A57 by the overbridge to Park Street and **Worksop** Town Hall in the Market Place.

17 *continued*

Start: Worksop Station (GR 585 798) or Worksop Town Hall (GR 584 786)

Distance: 12 miles

Terrain: mostly on-road, with some stone-surfaced track in Clumber Park; mostly gently rolling, although there's quite a determined hill to be conquered right at the start as you leave the centre of Worksop.

Refreshment opportunities: Worksop and Clumber

Ordnance Survey maps: Landranger sheet 120, Mansfield and Worksop; Explorer sheet 28 (270) Sherwood Forest

Public transport links: Arriva Trains Northern services run from Sheffield, Retford and Gainsborough to Worksop, while Central Trains' Robin Hood Line services run from Nottingham, Mansfield and intermediate stations to Worksop.

Other routes: This route is joined by route **14**, Rhodesia and Manor Hills near Truman's Lodge, and joins route **27**, Clumber Park and Meden Vale in Clumber Park, route **38**, Hardwick and Ollerton in Hardwick village, and link routes **L8**, Clumber and Walesby, and **L12**, Whaley Thorns to Clumber, in Clumber Park. Routes **12** and **21** also start and finish in Worksop. The route coincides with a short stretch of '**NCN' Route 6** in Clumber Park.

Route

18 *start*

13 miles • forest track and on-road • rolling • Sherwood Pines

Wellow and Rufford from Sherwood Pines Forest Park

This route – and the longer version, route 25 – reaches out into the pleasant and remarkably quiet rolling farmlands to the east of Clipstone Forest. The first village on the route, Eakring, was at one time, particularly during the 1939–1945 war years, the unlikely centre of the British oil industry; even up to the 1960s the 'nodding donkey' pumps, scattered around the fields and nodding into action when the oil level was high enough, were a feature of the surrounding countryside. Several are preserved as a combined memorial and nature trail in Duke's Wood above Eakring, while you can see two still working near Bothamsall (on route 38 and link route L8).

Eakring is also the village to which the Reverend William Mompesson moved from Eyam in Derbyshire in 1670. Five years earlier Mompesson had been the hero of the Plague-

64

stricken village of Eyam, closing it off from the outside world and preventing the spread of the disease. Because of Eakring villagers' fear of the Plague – still a recent memory – he had to preach in the open air for the first few years of his ministry here, at a spot now marked by a monument which is signed from the village. The next village on the

18

continued

A 'nodding donkey' near Eakring

route, Wellow, is one of only three in England to have a permanent traditional maypole on the village green – though the current 55ft tubular steel mast is hardly the traditional material! Nevertheless, the May Queen is still crowned and children dance their intricate interweaving steps round the pole at the Spring Bank Holiday at the end of May.

The route returns through Rufford Country Park, based on the grounds of the ruined Rufford Abbey, part wild with lakes and woodland, part lawn and formal garden. The coach-house in the grounds near the Abbey ruins now houses a craft centre, a café and restaurant. Although Rufford lies in heart of the 'Dukeries', it was really a notch down the social league table, the home not of a Duke but a mere Marquess.

Turn left and right out of **Eakring Road car park** eastwards along Eakring Road for about 1½ miles to the A614. Cross the A614, and continue straight on, signed *Eakring 2¼* After climbing a longish hill, this road becomes Bilsthorpe Road, **Eakring**, where you turn left at the Savile Arms, into Wellow Road, signed *Wellow*, for about 2½ miles. In **Wellow**, at the T-junction at the far end of the green, turn left on the A616, signed *Sheffield*. Follow the main road as it swings round right and left, then after about 500yds turn first left on a minor road, Rufford Lane, signed *Rufford*. Follow this road for about 1½ miles, then down the hill to **Rufford** and through the ford (there is a footbridge). After about 200yds turn left, signed *Rufford Mill and Country Park*, into the car park area.

18
continued

An exhibit in Rufford Sculpture Park

Keep round to the left of the car park to join a path by the Lakeside Garden Shop. Cycling isn't permitted in the Park, so you'll have to walk the next 800yds or so as far as the Old Coach House. Bear right on the lakeside path, with the lake on the left, and at a junction of paths, bear right, signed *Rufford Abbey* and *Craft Centre*. Keep following signs to these destinations until you reach the ruin. The second – and more modern – building beyond the Abbey is the Old Coach House craft centre and tearooms.

To leave Rufford Park turn right into the car park: you can now start riding again. At the T-junction with the rather busy A614 there are two choices, neither ideal.

The first is to turn left on the A614 for about 400yds to where a track crosses it (signed *Manor Farm* to the left).There is a pavement beside the A614 which you can walk down if you don't feel comfortable riding on the main road. Turn right **with extreme care** on to the old road, now a bridleway, for about 300yds as

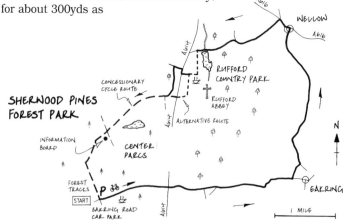

far as the tarred road which leads to Center Parcs Sherwood Holiday Village. Go straight on on a firm-surfaced but untarred track which is a concessionary cycle way, marked with a 'No entry sign' (for vehicles) plus *two-way blue cycle route* signs – keeping Center Parcs' perimeter fence on the left.

The second possibility is to turn right at the Rufford Park exit, either crossing the main road and riding up it for about 200yds or walking along the pavement on the right-hand side of the road (there isn't one the other side). In either case, turn left by the Rose Cottage pub on to the B6034, signposted *Edwinstowe, Sherwood Holiday Village and Sherwood Pines*. After about 200yds take the first left, signed Center Parcs, for about ½ mile to a double bend at the foot of a slight slope. Turn right on the concessionary cycle way.

From here all options follow the concessionary cycle route. After about 1¼ miles, at a cross tracks with information board marked '*Sherwood Pines*', go straight on, past the green metal barrier, for about 1 mile, then left, at a cross tracks up a slight hill. (You are following a waymarked cycle route in reverse: you can check that you're on the right track by the blue cycle route signs, mounted on short wooden posts.) Follow this track to a green metal barrier at the T-junction of tracks. Turn left into **Eakring Road** car park.

18

continued

Start: As described, the route starts from the Eakring Road car park (GR 620 616). (At the time of writing, 2004, the Eakring Road car park was closed because of a deep and persistent puddle in the middle, but it is easy to park nearby.) It would also be possible to start from either of the Rufford Abbey car parks (GR 643 647 or 646 656) or, if you are staying there, from Center Parcs' Sherwood Holiday Village (GR 637 640).

Distance: 13 miles

Terrain: Except for the finish section through Clipstone Forest on forest tracks and a short section which has to be walked through Rufford Country Park, entirely on-road through rolling country-side.

Refreshment opportunities: There are pubs serving food in several of the villages and a teashop in Rufford Park.

Ordnance Survey maps: Landranger sheet 120 Mansfield and Worksop; Explorer sheet 28 (270) Sherwood Forest.

Public transport links: by rail to Mansfield Woodhouse (Robin Hood Line), then follow route **23** (either outward or return legs as described) as far as Old Clipstone, follow B6030 east for ½ or ¾ mile to the Sherwood Pines Visitor Centre, then follow link **L7** to the cross-tracks west of Center Parcs' holiday village to join this route.

Other routes: Route **7** is a circuit in Sherwood Pines Forest Park. Route **25** is a longer (26-mile) version of this one; link **L7** leads from Sherwood Pines to Edwinstowe and Sherwood Forest, giving another link to route **23**. Route **28**, Southwell Trail and the Dumbles, shares a short stretch of road with this one, west of Eakring. '**NCN**' Route **6** crosses Eakring Road (which is pretty rough here with quite a bit of loose sand in dry weather) about 1¼ miles west of the Eakring Road car park.

Route
19
start

17 miles • mostly on-road • undulating • Mansfield Woodhouse

Ault Hucknall and Hardwick Hall

This route is one of several which makes use of the Robin Hood Line to get out to a different part of the county – and it's also one of the routes that venture a mile or two over the border into a neighbouring county, in this case Derbyshire. Although it is never more than five or six miles from the large town of Mansfield the route ventures into some remarkably quiet – and quite hilly – country.

There are several attractive warm stone-built hamlets on the route – such as Ault Hucknall and Rowthorne – but the obvious star of the show is Hardwick Hall and its park. There are in fact two halls at Hardwick: the partially ruined Old Hall, which is in the care of English Heritage, and the better-known 16th-century Hardwick Hall, which belongs to the National Trust. It is the latter with its six towers that is such a landmark in its commanding position overlooking the valley of the River Doe Lea (and nowadays the M1, too).

The great west-facing windows are taller on the upper storeys than the lower – giving rise to the local jingle when it was built: 'Hardwick Hall – more glass than wall'. The rooms are still furnished much as they were in the days of Elizabeth Shrewsbury ('Bess of Hardwick' – said to have been the richest woman in England apart from Queen Elizabeth I) for whom it was built. There is also a fine formal garden and recreated herb garden. The National Trust charges non-members for entry to the house and garden; the Old Hall can also be visited, and a combined ticket is available. Both are open Wednesday to Sunday (plus Bank Holidays) from the end of March to the end of October. The park, formerly a deer park but now used for cattle and sheep grazing, is open free throughout the year from dawn to dusk.

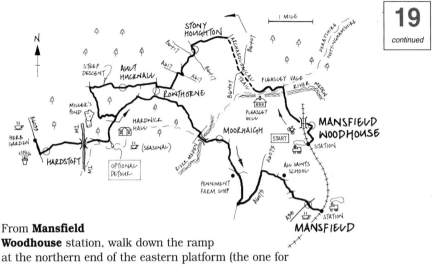

19
continued

From **Mansfield Woodhouse** station, walk down the ramp at the northern end of the eastern platform (the one for Nottingham-bound trains) and turn left, following blue *cycle route to town centre* sign, to exit beside steel gate at the north end of the station car park into Oxclose Lane (unsurfaced and unnamed at this point). Turn right on Oxclose Lane then, after a short distance, at a diagonal crossroads where the road bears round to the right, sharp left and left again into Thoresby Road. (When we surveyed this route late 2003 Thoresby Road was being redeveloped and there were no signposts in evidence.) Towards the end of this road, just before the railway embankment, turn right into Manor Road. At a T-junction, turn left into Vale Road (not signed). Where the road bears round to the right and continues as Brown Avenue, turn left – effecively straight on – on Vale Road under a low railway bridge becoming Common Lane (not signed). Follow this road for about 1 ½ miles to the foot of Pleasley Vale, then up the valley of the River Meden to **Pleasley Mills**.

Use the cycle gap to the right of the road barrier and continue up Pleasley Vale past the imposing mill buildings, derelict until recently but now brought back into use as a business park. Just after the exit barrier turn right through a small gate to the left of a steel gate marked *J Thompson Engineering (Mansfield) Ltd*, where there are also metallic *gold-coloured arrows* marking the *Archaeological Way Trail*. Continue past the buildings to a second steel gate, pass to the left of it, and go straight on. The path continues as a full-width tarred road, then becomes a tarred path, which reaches a road (B6407 but unmarked at this point) at a wooden gate. Cross the B-road on to an

69

19
continued

Part of the restored Pleasley Mills

unsurfaced bridleway, still following the metallic *gold-coloured arrows* of the Archaeological Way Trail. The surface of this ¾ miles of track is grassy, with a possible slightly muddy patch after wet weather halfway along it. After this the surface improves. Continue to a T-junction with a tarred road. Turn left for about 1 mile up a steady climb, then about 200yds after the electricity pylons, where the major road goes right and is signed *Bolsover 3 Clowne 6*, turn left on the *unsigned* road into **Stony Houghton**. The road drops and curves round to the right through the hamlet, meeting the B6417 at a 'Give way' sign. Turn right on B6417, then straight on on Green Lane where the B6417 bears right. Continue on Green Lane to a T-junction with the A617. Turn right for about 300yds, then first left left on an unsigned minor road. (*If you don't want to ride on the A617, which can be quite busy, you can wheel your bike along the pavement on the north (right-hand) side of the road briefly until you are opposite the turn.*)

Continue for about ¾ mile, following the road round to the right to a T-junction on the outskirts of **Rowthorne**. Turn right under pylons and then first left after about 300yds, signed *Ault Hucknall and Stainsby*. From this road there are views to the right across to the Peak District hills, with Hardwick Hall's towers clearly visible to the left. Follow *Hardwick Hall signs* for about 1½ miles through **Ault Hucknall**, then down a quite steep winding descent, with a double bend at the bottom. Immediately after the bend and stone bridge, bear left through some blue-grey gates towards Hardwick Hall. Cross cattle grids and climb steadily but not too steeply for about 1 mile through the park to a T-junction about 300yds before **Hardwick Hall**. (To visit

19
continued

the Hall turn right: note that a one-way traffic system operates here – if you visit the Hall, you must take extreme care when retracing against the traffic flow to this junction to rejoin the route.)

The route itself turns sharp left at this junction, along a broad avenue signed *No Entry or Exit* (this refers explicitly to car traffic). Continue on this broad straight avenue for about ¾ mile to the lodge and another set of blue-grey gates. Go through the swing wicket gate to the left of the main gates and continue for about 300yds to a T-junction at a small triangular green; turn right, signed *Rowthorne*. In **Rowthorne**, by a large house and stone wall on the left, turn right (unsigned) and follow this road for nearly 2 miles. Eventually it drops in a winding descent between high banks. At the T-junction at the foot of the hill, turn right and immediately left, signed *Skegby*, over a small river bridge and then first left into Moorhaigh Lane (just after a *sign warning of horses* for 2½ miles) along the flank of the stream valley. This road eventually climbs away from the stream and valley; keep round to the right where a road joins from the left, along the road signed *Penniment Lane* and up to a T-junction with Top Lane opposite a farm shop. Turn left on Top Lane and continue to its junction with the A6075. Turn left at the T-junction, following the cycle route signs to *Mansfield Woodhouse*. After ¾ mile turn right into Westfield Lane.

This is the beginning of the **Mansfield** built-up area (for alternative route from All Saints RC School through Mansfield town centre, see below). After about ½ mile, by the entrance to All Saints RC School on the left, turn right into Harrop White Road. At the end of the road, after about 400yds, turn left into Ladybrook Lane and almost immediately first right into Oakdale Road. At the T-junction at the end of Oakdale Road, turn left on Bancroft Lane (not signed at this point). Follow Bancroft Lane to its junction with Stockwell Gate, A38. Cross the A38 with care into Dallas Street and at a T-junction turn left into Peacock Lane and immediately right into Rooth Street to its T-junction with Victoria Street (unsigned at this point but marked as *no through road*). At the end of this road follow the

Directional signs at Mansfield Woodhouse station

19
continued

ramp down to the left to a light-controlled pedestrian crossing of the A6009 dual carriageway. Cross on foot to the opposite side, then still on foot left to the junction with Station Road (unsigned). Take the first turn on the right behind the Midland Hotel and Rumours Wine Bar to the restored station buildings, brought back into railway use in 2000. Follow *signs* under the subway to the far platform of Mansfield Station for Nottingham trains, or remain on the nearside to return to Mansfield Woodhouse.

If you want to visit Mansfield town centre, there is an alternative route but it involves quite a distance to be walked through a pedestrianised area: From All Saints RC school entrance, continue straight over the inner ring road at traffic lights, still on Westfield Lane. At the next T-junction, with *compulsory right turn sign*, dismount and walk to the street opposite, Westgate, and continue on foot through the pedestrianised area to Market Square. Opposite Leeming Street turn right across Market Square, following *pedestrian signs to Mansfield Station*. Go up Market Street which becomes Queens Walk. Cross the road, still on foot, into a subway marked *Crown Walk to buses*. At the far end of the subway, turn sharp left, then to the right into the car park. Follow *car park exit arrows* up a steep pitch and under a yellow barrier to the T-junction with Station Road (unsigned). Turn right and then almost immediately first left into a road signed to *Station Road South car park*, and marked as no through road. This leads to the station buildings. Follow signs under the subway to the far platform of Mansfield Station for Nottingham trains, or remain on the nearside to return to Mansfield Woodhouse.

Start: As described, the route starts at Mansfield Woodhouse station (GR 534 633).

Distance: 17 miles

Terrain: Except for the 3/4-mile stretch of bridleway between Pleasley Mills and Stony Houghton, entirely on-road through rolling countryside.

Refreshment opportunities: There are few pubs on the route, but there is a restaurant (seasonal opening) at Hardwick Hall and a number of refreshment places of different kinds in Mansfield. The teashop at the Herb Garden, Hardstoft, is about 2 miles west of the official car exit from Hardwick Hall and is marked on the Landranger map.

Ordnance Survey maps: Landranger sheet 120 Mansfield and Worksop; 28 (270) Sherwood Forest, 269 Chesterfield and Alfreton

Public transport links: by rail to Mansfield Woodhouse, returning from Mansfield (both Robin Hood Line)

Other routes: Route 23, Mansfield Woodhouse to Sherwood, also starts from Mansfield Woodhouse station.

12 miles • on- and off-road • some hills • Gunthorpe

Route

20

start

Lambley and Lowdham

This circular route east of Nottingham gives a chance to follow the north bank of a rural section of the River Trent for some distance on easily ridable and mainly grassy bridleways. Gunthorpe, where the route starts, has been a crossing of the River Trent for millennia. Long before the first bridge (not built until 1875), and before the rapids were tamed with a weir and lock, the river was fordable here. In Roman times it lay on a route between the town of MARGIDVNVM (on the Fosse Way between what are now East Bridgford and Bingham) and the Derbyshire lead mines. Later it was here that Queen Boudicca (or Boadicea) of the Iceni saw off the Romans' Tenth Legion. The first stretch of bridleway leads to Burton Joyce, then by way of quite a stiff climb over the ridge to Lambley, rewarded by a particularly fine view of Lambley and the hills and valleys behind it. Considering how near it is to Nottingham, Lambley remains a secluded village nestling in the narrow valley alongside the tumbling waters of the Cocker Beck. Its sheltered position must have given it its name – the 'lea' or field where lambs were raised. Like many other Nottinghamshire villages it grew in the early 19th century with the coming of the cottage frame-knitting machine: local records list 381 in 1844!

The road beside the Cocker Beck leads gently down to Lowdham, a village separated from its parish church by the main A6097, which the route crosses safely at traffic lights. Lowdham Mill, to the north of the village, is one of the dozen which once surrounded Lowdham but is now a private house. The bridle path which the route follows passes close to the mill and its millpond, and you can see the mill race where the wheel once turned. From Lowdham Mill the route follows very quiet byroads until it reaches the Trent once more, to follow a fine stretch of riverside path through wide grassy meadows.

20

continued

Start in **Gunthorpe** from the car park in front of The Unicorn pub. Take the unsigned narrow path (actually a public bridleway) which psses underneath Gunthorpe Bridge, and the A6097, to join a vehicle track on the west side of the bridge. Follow this anglers' access track for 200y, then fork left onto a narrow riverside bridleway. After about ½ mile the track forks at the edge of a wood: keep to the right hand path which is the bridleway (the riverside path continues as a footpath). Follow the bridleway for ¾ mile, between thick

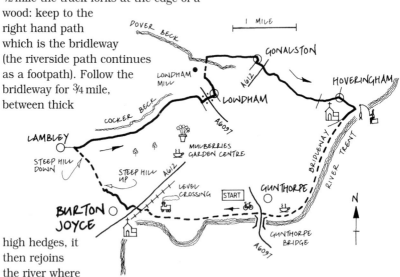

high hedges, it then rejoins the river where the path opens out. It continues along the river bank for 200yds, then turns inland to pass some allotments. Cross a narrow tarmac road to the level crossing, passing through the small swing gate, and then continue along the road to cross the main A612 into Meadow Lane, **Burton Joyce**. At the T-junction by Burton Joyce Methodist Church, turn left, then take the fifth minor road on the right, Lambley Lane. Go up this lane for about 500yds to where a public bridleway forks off to the right. Take this path, signed as a *Bridle Road*, that drops sharply for a few yards then gradually climbs between high fences on a hard-packed earth surface, which becomes tarmac where Glen and

Helping to create the
GREENWOOD

COMMUNITY
FOREST

Foxhill Roads cross. Continue on the bridleway, climbing steeply on a deteriorating tarmac surface. At the brow of the hill fork left, effectively straight on, on a track signed for *Stockhill Farm*. The surfaced road becomes an open grassy track which descends steeply across an open field into **Lambley**.

When the track eventually emerges on to a tarred

road, turn right and continue along the valley of the Cocker Beck for a couple of miles into Lowdham. Cross straight over the dual carriageway (A6097) at the traffic lights into Ton Lane, which leads into **Lowdham**. At the T-junction, almost opposite the old school building with its prominent clock, turn left onto Main Street (not signed at this point). At the top end of main street, now signed Epperstone Road, just before the road rejoins the dual-carriageway Lowdham bypass, A6097, and immediately before the '50' speed limit sign, turn right on what is obviously a short section of the old road by a small silver birch tree. After about 40yds, turn right into the entrance to Lowdham Mill (signed *public bridleway* on a wooden finger post), then about 150yds down this track, go through the small wicket gate to the right of the track, marked with a blue bridleway arrow (the larger white gates to the left mark the private entrance to Lowdham Mill). This attractive little firm-surfaced path looks almost as though it's going through somebody's garden as it goes over a little wooden bridge and then passes between the lower mill pool on the left and a tennis court on the right, to emerge by the upper millpond. After crossing a small stone bridge over a weir go through a second gate and 150yds later reach the tarred road.

Start: Gunthorpe Bridge, north side of the River Trent (GR 681 437). You could also start in Burton Joyce, Lambley or Lowdham.

Distance: 12 miles

Terrain: Fairly flat with one steep hill, about two-fifths is off-road on bridleways – most of the off-road section is along the banks on the River Trent; otherwise on minor roads.

Refreshment opportunities: Although fairly short, this route passes through a number of villages offering pubs and shops. There is a tea room (Mulberries Coffee House, if that isn't a contradiction) at the Tall Trees Garden Centre, about 1 mile east of Burton Joyce on the A612, and another at Gunthorpe Lock.

Ordnance Survey maps: Landranger sheet 129 Nottingham and Loughborough; Explorer sheet 260 Nottingham

Public transport links: Burton Joyce and Lowdham stations are on the Nottingham to Newark line, served by Central Trains. Not all services on this line stop at all the stations.

Other routes: The westernmost point of this route, where the bridleway comes down to the road in Lambley village, is only about 200yds from the nearest point of route 5, the Woodborough rounds. Route 30, Daybrook to Southwell, uses the same roads as this one between Gonalston and Hoveringham, while route 40, Newark to Nottingham, passes on the south side of Gunthorpe Bridge.

20
continued

Turn right on the road through **Gonalston** to a crossroads with the A612. Go straight across on a minor road signed *Hoveringham light traffic only*. Go into **Hoveringham** and at a T-junction with the church on the right, turn right (effectively straight on) on Boat Lane, signed *Caythorpe and Lowdham*. After about 500yds the road meets the River Trent and turns sharp right to leave the river on the left; about 400yds later there is a car parking area on the left as the road bears to the right away from the Trent again. Go left through a white swing gate to join a signed *bridleway* which runs along the northern bank of the river. This bridleway is not so much a well-defined track as an open grassy area popular with walkers and anglers. Pass through a number of distinctive swing gates, keeping the river on your left, to reach a tarred path at Gunthorpe Lock. Continue straight on to return to **Gunthorpe Bridge** where the route started.

Route
21
start

16 miles • on- and off-road • gentle • Worksop

Worksop, Scofton and Bilby

Like route 17, this route makes extensive use of the network of farm and estate roads north and east of Worksop. These have the status of bridleways and range from tarred roads to firm-based stone-surfaced tracks. Although this countryside is no more than a couple of miles from the busy A1, some of the little settlements, such as the hamlets of Scofton and Bilby, set in their wide open fields and copses, seem incredibly remote. This is not the pretty parkland of the Dukeries but a working landscape which even so has its picturesque corners.

From **Worksop Town Hall** in the corner of the Market Place, bear right at pedestrian lights into Potter Street, then at mini-roundabout turn left into Watson Road, signed *Tickhill 10 (A60)*. Continue straight on at the next two sets of traffic lights, then at the next set opposite Mothercare, turn right over the bridge, signed *A60, Tickhill*. At the traffic lights immediately after the bridge, get into the right-hand waiting lane then turn right into Eastgate, just in front of the King's Head.

From **Worksop Station**: the street-level exits from the platforms are at the level-crossing (eastern) end. Once on the road, turn right downhill towards the town, to the first set of traffic lights, by the King's Head, and turn left into Eastgate.

After about 600yds, at the Kilton Inn, Eastgate becomes Kilton Road. Continue straight on to a mini-roundabout, and go straight on, still on Kilton Road. After about 500yds this bears round to the left under a railway bridge; immediately after the bridge, turn right onto a completely unnamed, unsigned minor road which starts by running close to the railway. After about ½ mile the tarred surface stops (go round the motor vehicle barrier if it's shut) and the road continues as a firm-surfaced gravel track which crosses the grounds of Osberton Hall after about 1½ miles. The Hall is a prominent white building to the right, visible across a small lake.

21
continued

The track emerges onto a tarred road, which still only has bridleway status, with a wooden three-way signpost marking the junction of bridleways. Turn right on the tarred-surfaced bridleway through the hamlet of **Scofton**, leaving the church to the right. Don't try to ride through the ford through the River Ryton to the left of the much more obvious bridge: the road surface has crumbled away and you'll come to a stop in the middle! The road crosses the **Chesterfield Canal** at a lock on a double bend and then climbs through an avenue of trees to the B6079.

Turn left on the B6079 to pass under the A1 dual carriageway. About 300yds past the A1 bridge, turn left into **Ranby**,

signed *Ranby village*. Follow the road round to the right into the village, then continue to follow it as it sweeps round to the right in front of the Chequers Inn, to rejoin the main road, which has now become the A620. Turn left on the A620 (no sign) past Ranby House school and Ranby Prison. About 300yds past the prison entrance, turn left on a minor road,

21

continued

signed *Barnby Moor*. After just over a mile, and just past Green Mile Farm, by a very striking tall beech hedge, fork left (no sign) onto a very minor road by some farm cottages. (You can check that you're in the right place because this small road continues as a grassy track on the opposite side of the road behind you – possibly the 'green mile' that gives the farm its name.) After about 200yds the road becomes a firm earth-based track that leads to a picturesque willow-fringed bridge over the **Chesterfield Canal**. The track continues for about 1½ miles, with the surface improving for a while near a junction of tracks by Ranby Hall, then getting earthy again, eventually emerging onto a tarred minor road with the noisy A1 about 100yds to the left.

Go straight across onto a tarred path, where it's better to walk. This bears round to the left to cross the southbound carriageway of the A1 to the central reservation: **take great care, since this road carries heavy, fast traffic**. (As a guide if you can see that the road is clear to the next bend – to the right on this carriageway, to the left on the other – you have time to walk briskly but steadily across. Do *not* try to ride across: you probably won't accelerate fast enough.) Follow the path along the central reservation for about 50yds, then cross over the northbound carriageway to a path on the other side.

After a few yards this path joins a minor tarred road, signed *Bilby Farms only* and firmly marked with discouraging notices stating that it is a private road. However, a small sign to the left of the gateway concedes that it is also a bridleway. After about ½ mile the tarred road turns sharp left and over a bridge crossing the River Ryton into the hamlet of **Bilby**, little more than a farm and two cottages.

Shortly after the farm, the tarred road gives way to a firm gravel

---

Start: Worksop Station (GR 585 798) or Worksop Town Hall (GR 584 786)

Distance: 16 miles

Terrain: a mixture of minor road and farm and estate roads with the status of bridleways, some untarred but firm and easily ridable. The route rolls gently but the biggest hill is climbing up from the underpass below the A1.

Refreshment opportunities: Worksop has a number of cafés and pubs, though most of the cafés seem to be closed on Sundays. in Ranby there's the Chequers Inn.

Ordnance Survey maps: Landranger sheet 120, Mansfield and Worksop

Public transport links: Arriva Trains Northern services run from Sheffield, Retford and Gainsborough to Worksop, while Central Trains' Robin Hood Line services run from Nottingham, Mansfield and intermediate stations to Worksop.

Other routes: Routes **12**, **14** and **17** also start from Worksop. '**NCN**' **Route 6** goes through Worksop, just touching this route near the King's Head, at the foot of the hill from the station.

track which first climbs a short slope and then passes between open fields. After about 500yds, there is a T-junction of tracks, with a discreet blue bridleway on a post to the left of the junction. Turn left (the track to the right is firmly marked *'Private road, keep out'*) for about ½ mile to join a tarred road at a set of metal gates. Go straight on on the tarred road, still a bridleway, across an old airfield runway, then down to the three-way junction of bridleways in **Scofton**.

21
continued

Turn right and retrace the outgoing route to the outskirts of Worksop, turning left under the railway bridge into Kilton Road. At the T-junction with High Hoe Road turn right, then immediately left at the mini-roundabout, still on Kilton Road, which becomes Eastgate. At the traffic lights by the King's Head turn left over the bridge, and left again at the next lights into Watson Road. Carry straight on at all traffic lights to the mini-roundabout junction with Potter Street, signed Ollerton and Edwinstowe; turn right to return to **Worksop Town Hall**.

To return to **Worksop Station**, turn right at the lights by the King's Head up Carlton Road to the level crossing.

Route
22
start

18 miles • on-road • mostly gentle • Blidworth

Blidworth and Halam

This compact circular route follows some intricate country lanes – most of which carry no more than very light traffic – in a pocket of countryside to the north-east of Nottingham, known as the Dumbles. ('Dumble' is a local word for a usually narrow stream valley.) The going is not entirely flat, but any climbs are rewarded by fine views over rolling farmland. The route leads through the large village of Farnsfield past the

22

continued

trim fields of a stud farm, and then on through Edingley to Halam. The name of this little village, the easternmost point of the route, comes from the Old English word 'halh' meaning a hidden-away corner and Halam is certainly hidden away at the foot of its small valley. At one time it was famed for its orchards and was said to have been a sea of blossom in spring. Enough is left to give a hint of what it must have been. The little valley road that leads up to the B6386 above Oxton is a delight at any season and well worth the stiff little pitch you have to climb at the end. And of course there's the reward of swooping down Oxton Bank on the other side: mind the S-bend halfway down! Oxton, at the foot of the hill, is a pleasant light stone-built village, now quietly bypassed.

From the car park of the **Jolly Friar,** turn left along Dale Road up the hill leaving Blidworth behind. After 1½ miles there is a cross-roads with the A614; go straight over (care – it can be a very busy road!) on to the minor road opposite, and follow this for a further 1½ miles into **Farnsfield**. At the T-junction, opposite the Red Lion, turn right along Main Street. Leave Farnsfield and continue on this road for about 2 miles – through Edingley, then to Halam. Just after the Waggon and Horses in **Halam**, turn right into Radley Road. Follow this as it winds out of the village and up a quiet valley, climbing to the

---

Start: Jolly Friar pub, Dale Road, Blidworth (GR 603562)

Distance: 18 miles

Terrain: Entirely on-road, making use of quiet country lanes; quite undulating with one or two stiffish but not too long climbs.

Refreshment opportunities: The villages the route passes through offer a good selection of pubs, most of which offer food; there are shops in Blidworth and Farnsfield. Slightly off the route there are numerous tea shops in Southwell. Just after you cross the A614 on the way back, there is a cycle-friendly refreshment van at the Blidworth Woods car park off Longdale Lane.

Ordnance Survey maps: Landranger sheet 120 Mansfield and Worksop; Explorer sheets 28 (270) Sherwood Forest

Public transport links: none, really

Other routes: Route **8**, Halam and Southwell, also visits Halam, and route **15**, Hucknall and Newstead, just touches this one at the crossroads between Blidworth Bottoms and Papplewick Pumping Station. Route **30**, Daybrook to Southwell, shares a short stretch of the B6386 near Oxton. 'NCN' Route **6** passes through Blidworth about ¾ mile west of the Jolly Friar.

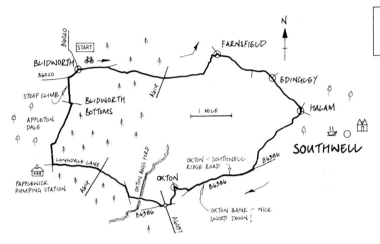

22 continued

Southwell–Oxton ridge road, B6386. At the T-junction, turn right.

Having swooped down Oxton Bank, take the first turn on the right – Blind Lane – into **Oxton** village. Go past the Green Dragon pub, then left at the T-junction, signed *Nottingham*. Turn right onto Nottingham Road at the T-junction just after Ye Olde Bridge Inn, and straight over at the roundabout – crossing the A6097 – onto the B6386, then, after a very short distance, first right onto Beanford Lane. After about ½ mile the road goes through a ford, part of 'Oxton Bogs'. This can be quite deep, especially after wet weather, so you may wish to use the footbridge. Turn right at the T-junction onto Whinbush Lane, which meets the A614 after about 1½ miles.

Cross straight over the main road at the roundabout to Longdale Lane – which is long and straight and slightly uphill! After approximately 1¼ miles there is a minor cross roads: **Papplewick Pumping Station** is signed off to the left, but turn right onto Rigg Lane. This climbs to Rigg Lane car park, used by visitors to Blidworth Woods, and then swoops down Appleton Dale to **Blidworth Bottoms**. At the junction opposite the Fox and Hounds, go left then first right after a short distance to climb the hill back into **Blidworth**. At the top, turn right at the T-junction on the B6020, signed for *Mansfield and Rainworth*. Just after the petrol station at the bottom of the hill, right into Dale Lane – signed for *Sherwood Forest*, and back to the **Jolly Friar**.

Helping to create the
GREENWOOD
G
FORESTS FOR THE COMMUNITY
COMMUNITY
FOREST

Route

23

start

15 miles • on- and off-road • gentle • Mansfield Woodhouse

Mansfield to Sherwood Forest

This route skirts the eastern fringes of Mansfield, using a bridleway as a traffic-free exit to the countryside. For the first few miles the route picks its way round the remnants of Clipstone colliery, now closed along with the majority of pits in the Nottinghamshire coalfield, but you hardly realise it until you glimpse the great towers of the pithead gear to your left. The little path follows a series of water features – ponds, streams – now Vicar Water Country Park. A minor road section leads to Edwinstowe, then on into Sherwood Forest, tracing a semi-circular route on delightful woodland tracks. Another section of minor road leads to Old Clipstone, from where there are two bridleway possibilities before you reach the last couple of road miles back to Mansfield Woodhouse station. Edwinstowe gets its name from King Edwin of Northumbria, who was killed in battle nearby in 632. It became quite a popular Victorian resort on the edge of Sherwood Forest, and in early cycling papers is frequently noted as the destination for cycle rides from Nottingham. In the 1890s, local members of the Cyclists' Touring Club (CTC) would ride out from Nottingham and the other towns on a Saturday afternoon, enjoy a tea and evening sing-song followed by a ride home by lamplight. In those days there was no Sunday riding – and in any case the founder of the local association was the Vicar of Annesley! Edwinstowe did not become a mining village until 1925, but nearby Thoresby Colliery is another of the last remnants of the once-great Nottinghamshire coalfield.

From **Mansfield Woodhouse** station go down the ramp at the end of the eastern platform (the one for Nottingham-bound trains) and left through the pedestrian exit beside a steel gate into Oxclose Lane (unsurfaced and unnamed at this point). Turn right on Oxclose Lane and continue to follow it round to the right as Grove Way and Grove Street, eventually becoming Station Hill. On reaching the T-junction

82

at the end, turn left into Station Street (no sign post), which becomes High Street, and follow this road through the centre of **Mansfield Woodhouse** and round to the right where it becomes Portland Street, signed *Warsop and Worksop*. After a short distance you reach a crossroads with traffic lights; go straight over into New Mill Lane. At a second set of traffic lights, at the crossroads with the A60, go straight on again, still on New Mill Lane. The road leaves the built-up area and climbs with open country to the left. After about ¾ mile at the top of the steepest

23
continued

On 'NCN' Route 6

part of the slope, turn left, still on New Mill Lane and signed *Clipstone*, to an oblique T-junction with B6030, Clipstone Road East.

Go right and left across the B6030 into Lime Grove. At the bottom of this narrow residential road, turn left (not signed) along a firmly surfaced track which is also a bridleway. After about 250yds pass round a metal gate, and go across a road and straight on, following the *cycle route sign to Vicar Water*. Keep to the right of the more prominent track to Newlands Farm, going through a small gate and over a step barrier to continue along the valley – passing various ponds and an attractive poplar-lined stream on your right. This track is a bit loose and sandy in places, with the odd cycle-unfriendly gate. You soon enter Vicar Water Country Park and get to a good tarred surface leading to Vicar Pond – a popular fishing spot. At the far end of this small lake, bear round to the right – through the car park – then turn left at the far side of the head of the water at a wooden three-armed bridleway signpost to continue along the bridleway, signed by a *blue arrow*. ('NCN' Route 6 joins here.) Go under a couple of bridges, passing fairly close to the

Helping to create the
GREENWOOD
COMMUNITY
FOREST

23

continued

pithead gear of Clipstone Colliery, visible to the left. Follow the *blue bridleway* or '*NCN*' *Route 6 arrows* – essentially straight on – for a further mile until you reach the B6030 beside the car park of the Dog and Duck. (*'NCN' Route 6 leaves here.*) Turn right on the B6030, under a railway bridge, then first left, signed *Edwinstowe*.

At the T-junction, after about 1½ miles, turn left into **Edwinstowe**. The village has a one-way system through its narrow streets, and northbound traffic (the direction you are travelling) is diverted to the left on West Lane. You may find it easier when you reach the 'no-entry' signs into the High Street to get off and wheel your bike up this main shopping street – not only is it shorter, but here's where you'll find several of the tea and cake shops. If you follow the one-way system, turn right at the junction with Mansfield Road, A6075, then left at the traffic lights at the top of High Street into Church Street. (If you've walked up the High Street, go straight on at these traffic lights into Church Street.) After about 300yds, turn left signed *Art and Craft Centre, Youth Hostel.* When the tarred road finishes, continue along a path, bordered by a wooden fence, which keeps the small amusement park on the right. When the fence ends, before you reach the cemetery, bear right between low wooden posts onto a path which bears left and up a gentle incline – signed *bridleway to Gleadthorpe*.

This bridleway continues for about 1½ miles through **Sherwood Forest** before you turn off. There is at least one further signpost for *Gleadthorpe*, and occasional *bridleway signs*; otherwise follow the posts marked with a *yellow horseshoe*. Eventually, you will pass round a metal barrier, and come to a crossing of wide tracks. The Robin Hood Way is signed to the left and right, but continue straight ahead along an unmarked forest track. Ignore the first significant turning off to the left, but after about ¾ mile – where the track forks – take the left-hand fork (*crossing 'NCN' Route 6*). This track, which has a hard but crumbling surface in places, meanders through the forest for about 1½ miles; ignore any minor tracks which head off at right angles, and where the track forks, keep right. Eventually, you will emerge onto a road (A6075). Go straight over into the track opposite – that may not be immediately obvious – which emerges after a short way onto a minor road, opposite the entrance to Sherwood Forest Farm Park.

Turn left, through the small settlement of **Gorsethorpe** and over a railway bridge and the River Maun. On the left-hand bend in **Old Clipstone** – shortly before the junction with the B6030 – turn right into Squires Lane. This 'no-through' road becomes a bridleway, bearing left in front of Cavendish Lodge to become Clipstone Drive, then right after a short stretch between hedged fields. The bridleway continues as a wide, rather stony, track – with woods to the right and fields on the left.

23 continued

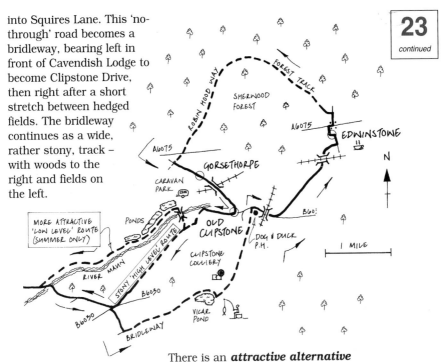

There is an **attractive alternative return route** from this point along another parallel bridleway, following close beside the River Maun. However, the surface can be muddy after wet weather, so we would only recommend it for summer use (or for adventurous mountain-bikers). To reach it from Clipstone Drive, about 400yds after the wood (Cavendish Wood) begins on the right, turn right into the wood opposite a post on the left marked with a *blue bridleway arrow*. After about 100yds, bear left downhill to cross the River Maun by a small bridge. Immediately after the bridge, with the white gateway entrance to Sherwood Forest Caravan Park on the right, turn left following *blue bridleway arrows*, leaving the River Maun on the left and a series of ponds on the right. After about 1 mile, the bridleway bears round to the right round another pond to leave the river and goes slightly uphill. 200yds further on, turn left, still following *blue bridleway arrows*, which are not very apparent in places. At a crossing of bridleways after about ¾ mile, and again at a junction of paths about 500yds further on, continue straight on, always following the *blue bridleway arrow signs*. At the end of the bridleway, turn right on New Mill Lane for about 500yds to the traffic lights at the junction with the A60.

23

continued

If you continue on the upper stony bridleway, after about 1¼ miles houses start appearing on the left, the track becomes a tarred road – still Clipstone Drive – and you're well and truly back in civilisation. From the end of Clipstone Drive, turn right into Clipstone Road East, B6030, then after about 20yds, first right again, signposted *Mansfield Woodhouse*, into New Mill Lane. (You may prefer just to walk the few yards on the right-hand pavement, rather than have to cross the B6030 twice.) Follow New Mill Lane for about a mile, then turn right, still on New Mill Lane and signed *Mansfield Woodhouse (light traffic only)*, past the point where the alternative bridleway rejoins the road, to traffic lights at the junction with the A60.

Go straight across the A60, still on New Mill Lane. After about 200yds at a second set of lights, go more or less straight ahead across the A6075 into Portland Street. Follow Portland Street round to the left; it becomes High Street, **Mansfield Woodhouse**, and then Station Street. About 200yds after it becomes Station Street, opposite Castle Street and a small green, turn right into Vale Road, then first left into Oxclose Lane. There's a bit of a dogleg where Oxclose Lane joins Grove Way at the top of the slope, but go effectively straight on, still on Oxclose Lane which becomes unsurfaced. At the steel gate just before the railway bridge, turn left to **Mansfield Woodhouse station**.

Start: Mansfield Woodhouse station (GR 534 633).

Distance: 15 miles

Terrain: Well over half this route is off-road, on bridleways and forest tracks. With the exception of parts of the River Maun alternative bridleway section, the majority of these off-road sections are well-drained, and should be ridable throughout the year, although the loose or sandy surface material makes the going a little bumpy in places. There are a few gentle slopes, but no tough climbs. The road sections are mainly on minor roads.

Refreshment opportunities: Nearly half-way round, Edwinstowe has made a virtue of its nearness to Sherwood Forest, and is well endowed with tea shops, pubs, fish-and-chip-peries and shops selling all the necessary ingredients for a picnic in the woods. The Sherwood Forest Art and Craft Centre Tea Room (almost next door to the youth hostel) is much less crowded than the Sherwood Forest Visitor Centre café. There is a café at Vicar Water Country Park, although opening hours are limited.

Ordnance Survey maps: Landranger sheet 120 Mansfield and Worksop; Explorer sheet 28 (270) Sherwood Forest

Public transport links: by rail to Mansfield Woodhouse (Robin Hood Line)

Other routes: Route 19, Ault Hucknall and Hardwick Hall, also starts at Mansfield Woodhouse station. Link route **L2** leads from the station to route **11**, the Pleasley trails, while link route **L7** joins this one at Edwinstowe to Sherwood Pines Forest Park and Center Parcs. The route follows 'NCN' **Route 6** for about 2½ miles near Clipstone and crosses it again in Sherwood Forest.

CIRCULAR ROUTES FROM 20 TO 30 MILES

Route

24

start

| 25 miles • on- and off-road • flat • Retford |

Retford round

North of Retford, Nottinghamshire takes on quite a different character. This part of the Trent valley and the neighbouring part of South Yorkshire were once marshland, not unlike the Fens of Lincolnshire and Cambridgeshire. Like the Fens, this area was drained to yield fertile grazing and arable land. In the far north of the county (touched on by route 37) the flat landscape has the same geometrical pattern of drains, large hedgeless fields and roads as the Fens, but on this route roads follow the more gentle curves of the natural landscape. There are several pleasant villages, such as Lound and Mattersey, while the little hamlet of Wiseton is well worth the detour we suggest.

It is in Wiseton that the route makes its third acquaintance with the Chesterfield Canal, originally built in the 1770s to link Chesterfield with the Trent. The route first crosses this waterway on the *Green Mile*, then meets it again at Drakeholes, about 1½ miles before Wiseton, where the canal passes through a tunnel a little over 150yds long. Unlike many canal tunnels, this one was hewn directly out of the sandstone ridge it cuts through and has no brick lining. In most low brick-lined tunnels, boats were 'legged' through: the bargee lay on his back and walked – almost pedalled – his way along the tunnel roof. This tunnel was too high, so boats had to be poled or 'shafted' through, while the horses who towed the boats in open country

24
continued

had to be walked over the top. The route crosses the canal no less than four times on its way back to Retford: just before and just after the villages of Clayworth and Hayton.

From **Retford** Square, leave the town centre via Chancery Lane and Carolgate. The first part of this is pedestrianised, so you'll have to walk, continuing straight ahead when you join the traffic as far as the traffic lights. Turn right at the traffic lights at the end of Carolgate into Albert Road, B6044, then after about 150yds first left into Thrumpton Lane and over the level crossing. About 300yds farther on, turn right after the New Inn and just before the primary school into Thrumpton Close. Follow the bridleway at the side of the school field under the railway past playing fields into Goosemoor Lane (a chicane means that tandems, trailers etc will need to make a diversion via Whinney Moor Lane – the continuation of Thrumpton Lane – turning right at the end onto London Road, A638, to pass over the railway, then first right into Goosemoor Lane). From the bridleway, turn right on Goosemoor Lane and over the bridge over the River Idle, then left into High Street. Follow High Street to a T-junction, where turn left and follow this road for about 3 miles past the airfield to **Jockey House**. Turn right, signed *Morton*.

Go by Little Morton Farm, then over the level crossing and briefly join the B6240, Mansfield Road, signed *Babworth*, then after about 150yds, go straight ahead on a minor road where the B6420 turns sharp right. This road quickly becomes a track and climbs to woods at the top of the hill, where it meets the A620. Go straight across the A620 on a minor road to **Green Mile** and Barnby Moor.

At the village of **Barnby Moor**, turn right onto the A638, the Great North Road, signed *Retford*, and then after about 600yds just after leaving the village, turn left to *Sutton-cum-Lound*. Go over the level crossing to **Sutton**. At the first T-junction turn left through the village, then right at the Gate Inn to *Lound*, following the road round to the left where the entrance to the Wetlands Waterfowl Reserve lies straight ahead. In **Lound**, go straight over the crossroads in the centre of the village on Town Street, then follow this road as it bears round to the left to a T-junction. Turn right to *Mattersey*.

In **Mattersey** follow the road round to the left by the church to a crossroads with Main Street, B6045. Turn right on the B6045 to pass over the River Idle, then take the next turning right, Eel Pool Road, still B6045, to **Drakeholes**. Bear right on a minor road, signed *Clayworth*, where the B6045 swings round to the left. (It is worth making a detour into the picturesque hamlet of Wiseton, about ¾ mile after Drakeholes. Turn left off the Clayworth road, signed *Wiseton*, and then go right in **Wiseton** to rejoin the direct route.) In **Clayworth**, go through the village to join the B1403,

24

continued

and follow this road where it bears right over the canal bridge, signed to *Hayton*. After about 2 miles the B1403 turns sharp left to cross the Chesterfield Canal again, then right into Main Street, Hayton.

At the southern end of **Hayton**, just before the junction with the A620, turn right on an unclassified road, Smeath Lane.

Follow Smeath Lane, which becomes

Smeath Road, for about 2 miles to a T-junction with Tiln Lane. Turn left on Tiln Lane, signed to *Retford Market Place*, turning right at the junction with the A620 out of Tiln Lane into Moorgate. Go down the hill, turn left at the traffic lights, then first right at another set of traffic lights into Chapelgate and Cannon Square, returning either walking via the pedestrianised section, or taking the second right into Grove Street to Market Square, **Retford**.

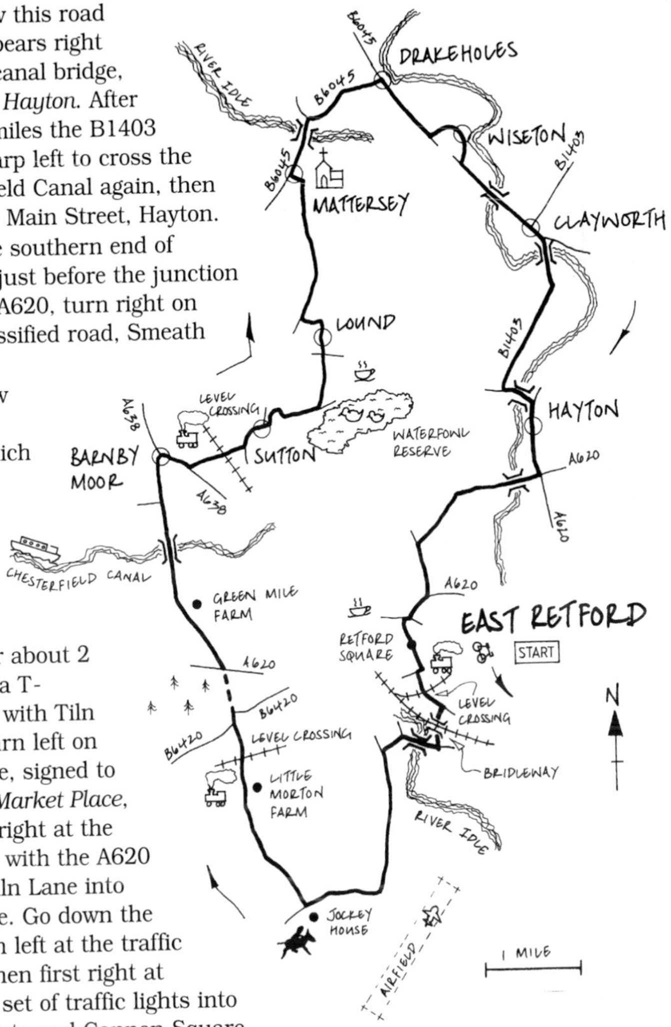

89

24

continued

Start: Market Square, Retford (GR 704 811)

Distance: 25 miles

Terrain: mostly flat on quiet roads; short section of track near Babworth.

Refreshment opportunities: there are tea shops in Retford and a tea shop/café at the Wetlands Waterfowl Reserve, between Sutton and Lound. Most of the villages also have pubs.

Ordnance Survey maps: sorry, you'll need *three* Landranger sheets – 111 Sheffield and Doncaster, 112 Scunthorpe and 120 Mansfield and Worksop; Explorer sheet 271 Newark-on-Trent (part of route only).

Public transport links: East Coast Main Line trains (well, some of them) stop at Retford, and the Arriva Trains Northern service from Sheffield to Lincoln via Worksop and Gainsborough calls at the lower station at Retford. Note that it takes about five minutes to get with a bike from the station entrance at Retford to the lower station platform, and vice versa. It also involves going up and down steps.

Other routes: Routes **16** and **29**, and the longest one in the book, **37**, also start from Retford and use some of the same roads into and out of the town.

Route

25

start

26 miles • forest track and on-road • rolling • Sherwood Pines

Laxton, Ollerton and Rufford from Sherwood Pines Forest Park

For the first few miles this route follows the same tracks and roads as the shorter version, **18**, as far as Eakring, which is described in the account of that route.

A few miles farther on, Laxton is unique – it is the last village in England to practise mediaeval strip cultivation, with strips of each of the great open fields allocated to farmers on a rotating basis by a traditional yearly meeting known as the 'Court Leet'. There is a visitor centre describing the system and its history next to the Dovecote Inn in the village.

Fine open roads lead through Egmanton to Kirton, with the little winding road from Kirton towards Walesby a further delight. In coaching days, the next village, Ollerton, occupied a very strategic position: where the Worksop to Newark road – the

Worksop to Kelham turnpike, freed from tolls in 1878 – crossed one of the London to York routes, as well as lying on the Mansfield to Lincoln route. The village's two coaching inns were the changing points for horses for the London to Glasgow coach, travelling via Newark. The Hop Pole and the White Hart still dominate the centre of the village. The name of the Hop Pole also commemorates what was another feature of the village – its hopfields; these provided the major employment until the beginning of the 20th century, when hop-growing was superseded by mining. In Ollerton village, the watermill, on the site of one mentioned in the Domesday Boke of 1086, still grinds flour and meal, the fruit of an award-winning restoration. You can see the wheel and the mill-race through a convenient viewing panel – on your way to the upstairs teashop!

25

continued

Turn left and then right out of Sherwood Pines Forest Park **Eakring Road car park** eastwards along Eakring Road for about 1½ miles to the A614. Cross the A614, and continue straight on, signed *Eakring 2¼*. After climbing a longish hill, this road becomes Bilsthorpe Road, Eakring, and then Newark Road.

Continue straight through the village of **Eakring**, following signs for *Maplebeck* and *Caunton*. After about ¾ mile, take the first left, signed *Kneesall*, for about 2 miles to the T-junction with the A616 in **Kneesall**; turn right here, signposted *Newark*. After about 150yds, turn first left just after the church into School Lane, unsigned at this junction. Follow School Lane to a T-junction just after the school. Turn right, and follow the road down the hill for about 1¼ miles to a crossroads; turn left, signed *Laxton*. Continue for about 1½ miles into **Laxton** village, climbing to a small triangular green with the Dovecote Inn and Laxton Visitor Centre on the right. Turn right just after the pub, signed *Egmanton*, for about another 1½ miles.

In **Egmanton** village, just after a bridge over a little stream, turn left into Kirton Road, signed *Kirton and Ollerton*. Follow this road for about 2½ miles to a T-junction with the A6075. Turn left on the A6075, signed *Ollerton*, down the hill into **Kirton**, and where the A6075 bears left, turn right just after the church, signed *Walesby*. At the next T-junction, after about ¾ mile, turn left (unsigned) and at the second T-junction, after about 200yds, turn left again, to pass *Walesby* village entry sign. Just past the church in **Walesby**, turn left into Main Street. Follow Main Street round to the right past the Post Office and at the crossroads with the B6387, Retford Road, go straight

25

continued

At Ollerton Mill

across into Brake Road, signed *Thoresby*, past the Carpenter's Arms. After ¼ mile there's a tea shop at Walesby Garden Centre on the right. A mile further on, at the end of the wooded section on the left, turn left (no sign). In another mile, just after the start of the built-up area of Ollerton, fork second right around a traffic island into Walesby Lane (unsigned at this point), over a rise and down a hill to the junction with Forest Road, A6075. Turn right on Forest Road for a few yards to the roundabout junction with the A616.

Bear right on Ollerton Road, signed *Ollerton village*, then shortly first left onto Main Street (no road name sign, but signed Ollerton *Watermill*).

In **Ollerton** village centre bear round to left on Market Place (the Watermill Tea Shop is on the right), following signs for *Wellow*. Pass the church on the left and leave the village uphill on Wellow Road, then take the first (very sharp) right turn into Bescar Lane. This road is blocked off at the end. Wheel your bike between the bollards, cross Kingston Drive/Hardwick Drive and go straight on, still on Bescar Lane, to pass under a railway bridge. Continue on Bescar Lane for about ¾ mile to a T-junction, at which you turn right (no sign).

Go down the hill to **Rufford**, through the ford (the 'rough ford' that gives the place its name – there is an alternative footbridge), then after about 200yds turn left, signed *Rufford Mill and Country Park*, into the car park area. Keep round to the left of the car park to join a path by the **Rufford Country Park** noticeboard. Cycling isn't permitted in the Park, so it is necessary to walk for the next section of about 800yds as far as the Old Coach House. Bear right on the lakeside path, keeping the lake on the left and at a junction of paths, bear right, signed *Rufford Abbey*. The path follows the Mouflon Sheep enclosure on the left; just opposite the information board on these sheep, turn right up a path between lines of trained trees, then follow this path round to the left (ramp beside steps) towards Rufford Abbey. Continue between shaped yew trees onto the tarred path. The second building on the left is the Old Coach House craft centre and tearooms.

To leave Rufford Park turn right into the car park: you can now start riding again. At the T-junction with the rather busy A614 there are two choices, neither ideal.

25

continued

The **first** is to turn left on the A614 for about 400yds to where a track crosses it (signed *Manor Farm* to the left).There is a pavement beside the A614 which you can walk along if you don't feel comfortable riding on the main road. Turn

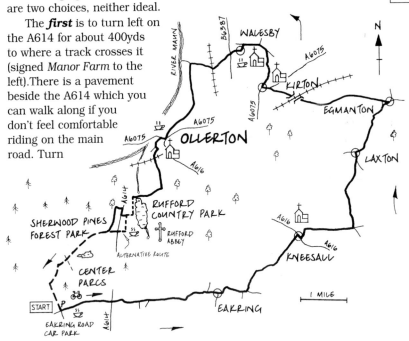

right with extreme care on to the old road, now a bridleway, for about 300yds as far as the tarred road which leads to Center Parcs Sherwood Holiday Village. Go straight on on a firm-surfaced but untarred track which is a concessionary cycle way, marked with a 'No entry sign' (for vehicles) plus *two-way blue cycle route signs* – keeping Center Parcs' perimeter fence on the left.

The **second** possibility is to turn right at the Rufford Park exit, either crossing the main road and riding up it for about 200yds or walking along the pavement on the right-hand side of the road (there isn't one the other side). In either case, turn by the Rose Cottage pub on to the B6034, signposted *Edwinstowe, Sherwood Holiday Village and Sherwood Pines.* After about 200yds take the first left, signed *Center Parcs*, for about ½ mile to a double bend at the foot of a slight slope. Turn right on the concessionary cycle way.

There is an alternative exit from the Park that may be available but we have to stress that we are uncertain how much of it is a public

25

continued

right of way. In Rufford Park continue straight on after the Coach House across the access road to a small wooden gate in the brick wall: this may or may not be locked. If it is unlocked, go through the gate onto a gravel road and bear right at the end of this on a concrete-surfaced road, then take the first left opposite Rufford Parish Council noticeboard for about 200yds. Shortly after a tennis court on the right, turn right and follow the road, signed *Robin Hood Way*, past a metal barrier, to the T-junction with A614. Cross with extreme care and go straight over on the a bridleway as in the first option to reach the tarred road which leads to Center Parcs Sherwood Holiday Village.

From this point all options follow the concessionary cycle route. After about 1¼ miles, at a cross tracks with information board marked 'Sherwood Pines', go straight on, past the green metal barrier, for about 1 mile, then left up a slight hill. (This is part of the longer waymarked cycle route in reverse: you can check that you're on the right track by the blue cycle route signs, which are mounted on short wooden posts.) Follow this track to a green metal barrier at the T-junction of tracks and car parking area. Turn left into **Eakring Road car park**.

Start: As described, the route starts from the Eakring Road car park (GR 620 616). (At the time of writing, 2004, the Eakring Road car park was closed because of a deep and persistent puddle in the middle, but it is easy to park nearby.) It would also be possible to start from either of the Rufford Abbey car parks (GR 643 647 or 646 656) or, if you are on holiday there, the Center Parcs' Sherwood Holiday Village (GR 637 640).

Distance: 26 miles

Terrain: Except for the finish section on forest tracks through Clipstone Forest and a short section which has to be walked through Rufford Country Park, entirely on-road through rolling countryside.

Refreshment opportunities: There are pubs serving food in several of the villages (the Dovecote Inn in Laxton is highly recommended), and teashops in Walesby, Ollerton and Rufford Park.

Ordnance Survey maps: Landranger sheet 120 Mansfield and Worksop; Explorer sheets 28 (270) Sherwood Forest, 271 Newark-on-Trent.

Public transport links: by rail to Mansfield Woodhouse (Robin Hood Line), then follow route 23 (either outward or return legs as described) as far as Old Clipstone, follow B6030 east for ½ or ¾ mile to the Sherwood Pines Visitor Centre, then follow link L7 to the cross-tracks west of Center Parcs' Sherwood Holiday Village to join this route.

Other routes: Route 18 is a shorter (13-mile) version of this one; link **L7** leads from Center Parcs Sherwood Holiday Village to Edwinstowe and Sherwood Forest, giving another link to route 23. Route 28, Southwell Trail and the Dumbles, overlaps this one through Eakring and Kneesall, and route 34, the northern Trent valley, touches this one at Egmanton and Laxton. 'NCN' Route 6 crosses Eakring Road (which is pretty rough here with quite a bit of loose sand in dry weather) about 1¼ miles west of the Eakring Road car park.

26 miles • on-road • almost flat • Newark-on-Trent

Route
26
start

South from Newark

This circular route from Newark meanders gently through the villages and quiet landscape of the Trent valley south of Newark-on-Trent. It's another of our routes that ventures outside Nottinghamshire: Newark is very close to the county boundary, and about seven miles of the route lie in Lincolnshire. Although the route is broadly in the Trent valley, it crosses the watershed to drop to the River Witham near Claypole and Long Bennington. Instead of joining the Trent and eventually the Humber to reach the sea at Hull, the Witham makes its way to Lincoln and then by Boston to the Wash. While not as sparsely populated as other parts of Lincolnshire, the roads on this route in both counties are remarkably quiet, passing through pleasant and sleepy, if unspectacular, villages and hamlets. One notable feature, though, is the 'Leaning Tower of Doddington' – Dry Doddington's church tower leans out several degrees from the rest of the building.

Another building to note beside the route is Sibthorpe dovecote, a large circular building prominent in a field beside the track as you approach the hamlet. It is all that's left of a mediaeval religious foundation that once stood here. The 60ft-high building had nesting places for 1260 birds: the pigeons gave food for winter and their droppings were much prized as a fertiliser.

From **Newark Castle** go south-west along Castlegate, follow this round to the left into Lombard Street, then at the traffic lights go effectively straight on into London Road, signed *Grantham* and *Balderton*. This is quite a busy link to the A1, although the footway has been converted to shared-use for pedestrians and cyclists. After 3 miles, at a roundabout just after Balderton, turn right on B6326 signed *Grantham and Claypole* to pass over the A1. Straight on at the next two roundabouts, following signs for *Claypole*. Continue for

95

26

continued

about 1 mile, then turn left, signed *Claypole*. In **Claypole**, just after the village hall on the right, turn right into Doddington Lane, signed *Dry Doddington*. At the T-junction in **Dry Doddington**, turn right on Main Street, signed *Grantham*. After passing the church with the leaning tower on the right and the Wheatsheaf pub on the left, bear left at a 'triangular' junction (no signpost) to pass to the left of the village hall. After 1½ miles at the staggered crossroads at **Westborough**, turn right, signed *Long Bennington*.

At the T-junction on the outskirts of **Long Bennington**, turn left signed *Newark*. After 300yds, turn right into Valley Lane (just before Burton's Newsagents) signed *Newark*, and almost immediately left again, signed *Staunton*. Pass over the A1, then at a fork just before power lines cross the road, bear right, signed *Staunton*. At the T-junction after ¾ mile, turn right, again signed *Staunton*. Pass by the end of the hamlet of **Staunton in the Vale** to a T-junction; turn left, signed *Kilvington*. Go through **Kilvington** (which hardly appears on the map although it's quite evident on the ground) to **Alverton**, then take the first right, signed *Flawborough*.

Go through **Flawborough**, following the road round to the left through the village, then after about ¾ mile follow the sharp bend round to the right to cross the River Smite. At the first minor cross-roads after the river bridge, go straight on, signed *Flintham*. After about another ½ mile, at a minor crossroads, turn right, signed *Sibthorpe*, on an open unfenced road through **Top Green** to **Sibthorpe**. Keep right (effectively straight on) at the end of the hamlet, signed *Elston*. About 1 mile further on at a T-junction, turn right (signpost missing), and in another 700yds, take the first left (again unsigned). After about 2 miles, take the first right, signed *Thorpe*.

The road winds through **Thorpe**, then continues, straight on, as a very straight road after the village; about 1 mile beyond the village, at a T-junction, turn

26

continued

Sibthorpe dovecote

right, signed *Hawton*. Cross the bridge over the River Devon (which the River Smite has mysteriously become), then at the T-junction in **Hawton**, bear left, signed *Newark*. You soon reach the built-up area; at a small (but not mini) five-way roundabout, continue straight on to the oblique T-junction with the B6166. Go right to the traffic lights, then left on the B6166 to **Newark Castle** or straight on (cycle bypass at 'No entry' sign) to the town centre.

Start: Castlegate, Newark-on-Trent (GR 795 540)

Distance: 26 miles

Terrain: entirely on-road, very gentle hills for the first part, almost flat for the second.

Refreshment opportunities: there are several cafés in Newark, and a coffee shop at the garden centre at Balderton. There are pubs (which may or may not supply meals) in Claypole, Dry Doddington, Long Bennington, and Staunton in the Vale, and just off the route in Orston and Elston.

Ordnance Survey maps: sorry, Newark lies at the corner of several maps and if you want to cover the whole route it takes no less than *four* Landranger sheets – 120 Mansfield and Worksop (only about a mile lies on this sheet), 121 Lincoln, 129 Nottingham and Loughborough, and 130 Grantham! Explorer sheets 260 Nottingham and 271 Newark-on-Trent cover the whole route.

Public transport links: East Coast Main Line services serve Newark Northgate. Central Trains services on Nottingham line to Newark Castle, less frequently extending to Newark Northgate as well. At its nearest point (just after Flawborough) the route is only 1½ miles from Elton & Orston station on the Nottingham–Grantham line (however, not many trains stop there, and when they do it's a request stop – and don't confuse Elton and Elston!).

Other routes: The Newark to Nottingham linear route, **40**, starts from Newark. Link route **L10** joins Newark north of the River Trent to Fiskerton and so to route **30**, while link route **L11** joins Newark to routes **28** and **34** at Norwell.

Route
27
start

27 miles • mostly on-road • gentle • Church Warsop

Clumber Park and Meden Vale

Note: do not confuse Clumber Park South Lodge (this route) with Worksop Manor South Lodge (route 14 and link L4)

This route starts by picking its way through what was part of the Nottinghamshire coalfield, with efforts now obviously being made to restore the landscape and attract visitors to local attractions and curiosities. The outward route follows the valley of the Millwood Brook, which is dammed to form the Great Lake of the Welbeck estate, emerging as the River Poulter. The highlight of the route, though, is a circuit of Clumber Park with its attractive double central avenue of lime trees – but watch out while crossing the slippery ford south of Hardwick village! (Don't worry – there's a footbridge close by.)

Clumber Park was the domain of the Dukes of Newcastle but, unlike the other large estates which form the Dukeries, the great house has now gone, demolished in 1938 with only its foundations now traceable. Other estate features, such as parts of the formal garden and vineries and the prominent Victorian Gothic Revival chapel, remain, while the clock tower now houses a welcome cafeteria and restaurant. There is also a cycle hire centre. The real attraction though is the 3800 acres of parkland – a mixture of woodland, open space and

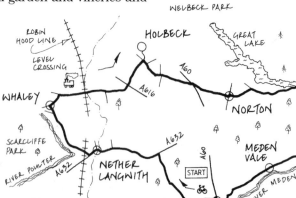

heathland surrounding an 80-acre lake. There is a network of
13 miles of tarred roads plus many other tracks and
bridleways, with cyclists able to make use of most of them.
Clumber Park is now in the care of the National Trust, which
charges motorists for access to the central area while sensibly
letting people on bicycles go in free.

27

continued

The route returns to Church Warsop by the valley of the River
Meden. The name of the last village on the route, Meden Vale, is
very recent: for half a century after it was built to service the
colliery the settlement was known as Welbeck Colliery Village –
it was officially changed to Meden Vale only in 1975 and many
local people still use the old name.

Link route **L12** has been specially devised to allow you to join
this route and so reach Clumber Park from the Robin Hood
Line station at Langwith-Whaley Thorns. Bikes go free on these
trains, so you can leave the car at home!

The church which gives **Church Warsop** its name lies at the junction
of Bishops Walk, B6031, and Church Road, A60: head west along
Bishops Walk, signed *Shirebrook*.
After about ½ mile turn right
into Wood Lane for
Nether Langwith, and
after 1½ miles, at the
T-junction with the
main road (A632 but
unsigned), turn left. Follow
the A632 (a relatively quiet road,
despite its A-road status) into
Nether Langwith and just before
the traffic signals controlling
traffic through the tall railway
bridge, turn right for *Whaley*. This
is a delightful little road which
follows a tributary of the River
Poulter.

Just before the village of **Whaley**,
where the road bears round to the
left, take the first turning to the right. At the
T-junction about 300yds later turn right, and
right again at the next T-junction a further 400yds on: these
junctions are not signposted. Cross the railway line at the gated level

99

The Victorian Gothic chapel at Clumber

crossing, and bear left (effectively straight on) at the next junction 500yds later, again unsigned, to reach the A616. Go straight over the main road for *Holbeck*, and bear right on passing the **Holbeck** village sign, for *Norton*. Take care as you meet an unexpected oblique minor cross roads – no signs or indications of priority – continuing straight ahead until you reach the A60 after about 1 mile. Cross the main road into Norton Lane, and after 1 mile go left at the T-junction in **Norton** village for *Carburton*. This road skirts the southern edge of the **Great Lake of Welbeck Park**, and towards the eastern end of the lake look out for the heronry on the far shore. After about 2½ miles you reach the staggered crossroads with the B6034; the Carburton Old School tea shop is on the right.

Go right and left across the B-road to follow signs for *Clumber Park*, passing by the hamlet of **Carburton** with its odd little church before reaching the entrance to the park. Stay on the wide tree-lined avenue for 2½ miles (*crossing 'NCN' Route 6 after about 1¼ miles*), then turn right at the minor crossroads signed for *Hardwick Village*. Go through **Hardwick**, and through the ford across the weir over the River Poulter – there is a footbridge if you don't want to tempt fate!

Where the road bears round to the left at the top of the slope, continue straight ahead round a low wooden barrier onto a firm path, then past a second barrier, after which the path becomes a firm track. After about 300yds the track emerges, past yet another low barrier, onto a tarred minor road; turn right and follow this road westwards for about 1½ miles.

27
continued

Just before the road passes over the handsome arched bridge at the western end of **Clumber Lake**, turn left onto a 'No-through road' signed for *South Lodge* ('*NCN' Route 6 joins again here*). Just before the barrier approaching the firmly-closed lodge gates, turn left to follow the *cycle route sign* along a path which comes to a T-junction with a bridleway. Turn right signed *RUPP to Duncan Wood*, still on the cycle route, and follow this firm-surfaced path for just over a mile to the B6034. Cross straight over, following NCN Route 6 for ¾ mile to the A616. Again, straight over, continuing on Route 6 for ¾ mile to emerge on an unclassified road, opposite a sign for the *Severn Trent Budby* works, turn right. This road follows the line of the River Meden, passes just south of the village of **Meden Vale** and then on into **Church Warsop**. At the junction with the A60, turn right – back to the start of the route.

Start: Church Warsop, Parish Church of St Peter and St Paul (GR 568 688) (Link **L12** to the Robin Hood Line starts at Langwith-Whaley Thorns station and follows the same roads as this route from soon after Whaley Common to Clumber).

Distance: 27 miles (29 miles including link route L12 going out-and-home from Langwith-Whaley Thorns station).

Terrain: Mostly on quiet roads, but includes a couple of stretches of bridleway in Clumber Park, and some off-road sections of NCN Route 6. There are also several main road crossings, and a mile or so of A-road, but these don't seem particularly busy at weekends. While undulating in places there are no hills to speak of.

Refreshment opportunities: There is a tea shop near Carburton – about half-way round – and another a little further on in Clumber Park (slightly off the actual route). This ride does not otherwise pass through many villages, nor by many pubs.

Ordnance Survey maps: Landranger sheet 120 Mansfield and Worksop; Explorer sheet 28 (270) Sherwood Forest.

Public transport links: Robin Hood rail line to Langwith-Whaley Thorns (no Sunday service).

Other routes: Route **17** meets this one at Clumber, and route **39** gives a largely off-road link from Hardwick village to route **25** at Ollerton. Link route **L8** is an on-road link from Clumber to route **25** at Walesby; the first part of link route **L12** leads from Langwith-Whaley Thorns station to join this route near Whaley Common. The route crosses '**NCN' Route 6** about halfway along the lime tree avenue in Clumber Park and later follows the line of it for about 4 miles from Clumber Bridge on the way back.

Route

28

start

The Southwell Trail and the Dumbles

The first few miles of this route make use of part of the Southwell Trail – a disused rail line converted to a shared-use path for walkers, cyclists and horse riders. This is flat, and while the hedges on both sides obscure distant views, they also give shelter from the prevailing westerly winds and contribute to the trail's attraction as a wildlife corridor. The route then follows the very attractive leafy lanes of Hexgreave Park, through the former mining village of Bilsthorpe, and out into rolling farmland crisscrossed by minor rivers and streams and their valleys ('dumbles').

Head north-west from the start at the **Southwell Trail car park** along the Trail towards *Farnsfield*. Here the route leaves the Trail – after about 4½ miles (or possibly half an hour's riding or more). While there are no signs, the point where you leave the Trail is where it crosses a minor road (as opposed to going under or over them at bridges), at GR 648 572. This means negotiating two wooden 'squeeze gates' in quick succession and going down a ramp to the minor road (the continuation of the trail goes up a similar ramp on the other side). Turn right on the minor road, which is soon signed as a *private road* – it nevertheless incorporates a bridleway. At the T-junction, turn right where Cockett Barn Farm is signed off to the left, then first left after about 200yds along a tree-lined avenue. This lovely lane winds through **Hexgreave Park**, and eventually, after descending gently through a second, more shady, avenue, curves right to join the A617.

Turn left on the A617 and first right after about 175yds, then after about 500yds turn left at the T-junction, signed *Eakring* and *Ollerton*, into **Bilsthorpe**. At the T-junction with Kirklington Road, turn right through the village (past a warning sign 'ducks crossing'!), straight on at the roundabout, and soon after the former Bilsthorpe Colliery turn right. Turn right again at the next T-junction after about 400yds, and

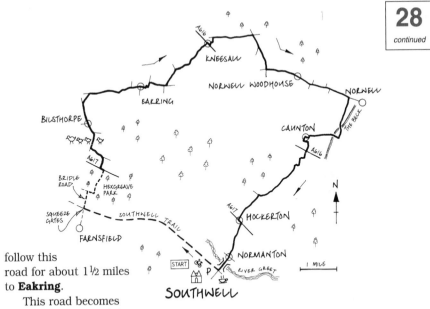

follow this road for about 1½ miles to **Eakring**.

This road becomes Bilsthorpe Road and then Newark Road. Continue straight through the village, following signs for *Kneesall*. After about ¾ mile, take the first left, signed *Kneesall*, for about 2 miles to the T-junction with the A616 in **Kneesall**; turn right, signposted *Newark*. After about 150yds, turn first left just after the church into School Lane. Follow School Lane to the T-junction just after the school. Turn right, follow the road gently downhill for about 1½ miles to a crossroads; turn right, signed for *Kersall*. Take the first left turn (unsigned) after ½ mile, then left again at the next crossroads, just over ½ mile further on and through the rather straggling hamlet of **Norwell Woodhouse**.

Shortly before the village of **Norwell**, with a prominent plantation of willows on the left, take the right turn signed for *Caunton*. Turn right at the T-junction after about 1 mile, immediately crossing a stream known as 'The Beck'. Follow this road as it winds through **Caunton**. Just after a public telephone box turn left, signed *Hockerton*, into Main Street, continuing past the Plough Inn and the church. At the southern edge of Caunton, go straight over the A616, again signed *Hockerton*, which you reach after 3 miles. In **Hockerton**, turn left at the junction with the A617, and shortly right for *Southwell*: this road will bring you to where the route started, just past the converted mill buildings on the outskirts of **Southwell**.

28
continued

Start: Southwell Trail car park, Station Road, Southwell (GR 706 545)

Distance: 25 miles

Terrain: Predominantly on quiet country roads, with a five-mile section of the Southwell Trail at the beginning. In this area of rolling farmland there are inevitably one or two slopes, although these are generally fairly short and ridable with low gears.

Refreshment opportunities: Most of the villages en route have pubs serving food, many also have a number of shops. Southwell, where the ride starts and finishes, has several tea shops.

Ordnance Survey maps: Landranger sheet 120 Mansfield and Worksop; Explorer sheets 28 (270) Sherwood Forest, 271 Newark-on-Trent.

Public transport links: The nearest rail station to Southwell is Fiskerton on the Nottingham to Newark Castle line (Central Trains), about 2½ miles south-east of Southwell. Fiskerton is a request stop: trains stop there if you tell the conductor when you get on, or give a hand signal as the train approaches. Not all trains on this route will stop at Fiskerton.

Other routes: Route **18** joins this one briefly between Bilsthorpe and Eakring; route **22** uses the same section of the B6386 over Oxton Bank to Oxton; route **25** overlaps it through Eakring and Kneesall. Route **30** comes out from Nottingham to Southwell. The very short link route **L1** joins this route to route **34** at Norwell.

Route
29
start

29 miles • on- and off-road • mostly flat • Retford

Retford and Harworth

This circuit north and west of Retford is in a way a cycling pilgrimage. The mining village of Harworth has a claim to cycling fame as, sadly, the burial place of Tom Simpson, who grew up here. A former World Champion and the first British rider to wear the coveted 'yellow jersey' in the Tour de France, he collapsed and died on the baking slopes of Mont Ventoux in Provence in the 1967 event. He was only 29. His grave is a few yards in front and to the right of the entrance to Harworth cemetery, which is signposted from the centre of the village. The route passes not only close to the Sutton-cum-Lound Wetlands Waterfowl Reserve (see route 16) but also by the Daneshill Lakes Local Nature Reserve and Wildlife Sanctuary – 120 acres of woodland and lakes with public access. Admission is free.

About three miles farther on the route follows a fine bridleway above the valley of the River Ryton – through open woodland which is a riot of bluebells in late spring – before crossing the river just beyond Serlby. The return route from Harworth passes through Scrooby village with its Pilgrim Fathers links (see route **37**), and then offers the option of an off-road section through to the pleasant village of Mattersey. From here the route back to Retford follows the same roads as route **24**.

29	
continued	

Leave **Retford** Market Square at the northern end, turning left at the mini-roundabout by the White Hart into Bridgegate to cross the River Idle. At the next roundabout take the second exit, signed *Bawtry A638*; this is the old Great North Road, the original coaching route from London to York and Edinburgh. After about 1½ miles, just before the main road begins to climb to a railway bridge, fork right at an oblique cross-roads onto a minor road, Sutton Lane, signed *Sutton and Wetlands Wildfowl Reserve*. Follow the road round through **Sutton**, continuing on Mattersey Road. After about 1 mile, turn left into Daneshill Road, signed *Torworth*. Some 2 miles further on, go over the level crossing, then just before the junction with the A638, turn right into **Torworth** by way of Low Street which runs parallel to the main road. Take the third left into the narrow Blacksmith Lane (the sign is behind you as you turn) to cross the main A638 just south of the Huntsman Inn, onto a minor road, signed *Blyth*. After about 1 mile, just over the brow of a gentle climb and where the road you are on bears left, fork right (unsigned) on to a very minor road. This joins the B6045 at a T-junction after about ½ mile.

Turn right on the B6045 (unsigned) for about 200yds. Turn left into what appears at first to be signed as the driveway of Blyth Cottage. Keep to the right of Blyth Lodge, following the signed *bridleway*. After about 1 mile the bridleway crosses a private tarred access road. Continue straight on on the (still unsigned) bridleway for about ½ mile past a golf course to the left, passing to the left of a metal gate to reach a tarred road.

Turn left (unsigned) between two white posts through **Serlby** to cross the River Ryton, following the road round to the left to the A614. Go straight over the main road, signed *Harworth*, past the glassworks and colliery. At the next T-junction, turn right (unsigned) to pass the colliery entrance. At the first mini-roundabout on the outskirts of **Harworth**, turn right into Scrooby Road, signed *Bircotes*. (*Go straight ahead if you want to visit Harworth village, then retrace to this roundabout.*) Some 2 miles later this road reaches the A614

29
continued

(unsigned), again at a T-junction.

Turn left on the A614 for about 500yds uphill, then take the first minor road turning on the right into Gibbet Lane, signed *Scrooby*. In about 300yds this road reaches the old Great North Road, A638 (also unsigned at this point). Go straight across on a minor road, Mill Lane, and cross two streams into **Scrooby**, where Mill Lane becomes Low Road. At the crossroads by the church, if you don't want to negotiate stiles, go straight on to rejoin the A638 to the outskirts of **Ranskill**, turning left about 500yds after passing the very decayed-looking Scrooby Top House on the right, into Folly Nook Lane. At the T-junction at the end, turn left on the B6045 over a railway bridge to the centre of **Mattersey** village.

The *alternative off-road route from Scrooby to Mattersey* turns left in **Scrooby** into Station Road to the level crossing. There are two stiles to negotiate to go over the crossing when the gates are locked. Beyond the crossing follow the well-defined track that runs parallel to the railway, then just before a metal gate, turn left over a very narrow bridge (or follow the path across the field to a third stile). Bear round to the right at the corner of the field, then almost immediately left over another footbridge over a second stream. Continue on this path beside a wetland area to the right, then across an open field. After some 400yds the path joins a firm-surfaced track. Bear right down this track, which is bordered on both sides by a tall hedge, then 200yds later left, following this track for about 1 mile until it becomes a tarred road. After about ½ mile there is a T-junction; this is **Mattersey Thorpe**. Turn left, signed *Mattersey*, and then follow the road round to the right for about ½ mile to a crossroads with the B6045 in **Mattersey** and go straight across.

Both routes now follow this road, signed *Sutton-cum-Lound and Mattersey Priory*. After about 150yds, just after the Barley Mow and just before the church, turn left into Church Lane which passes between the two, to cross a narrow bridge over the River Idle then on

Tom Simpson's grave at Harworth

to a T-junction with the B6045. Pass through the cycle gap in the fence and turn right on the B6045 (unsigned) to **Drakeholes**. Just before the Griff Inn on the left, turn right, signed *Wiseton, Clayworth and Hayton*, leaving the canal basin and the entrance to Drakeholes canal tunnel on

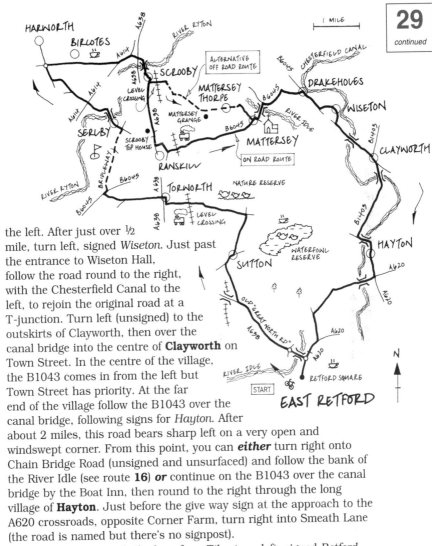

29 continued

the left. After just over ½ mile, turn left, signed *Wiseton*. Just past the entrance to Wiseton Hall, follow the road round to the right, with the Chesterfield Canal to the left, to rejoin the original road at a T-junction. Turn left (unsigned) to the outskirts of Clayworth, then over the canal bridge into the centre of **Clayworth** on Town Street. In the centre of the village, the B1043 comes in from the left but Town Street has priority. At the far end of the village follow the B1043 over the canal bridge, following signs for *Hayton*. After about 2 miles, this road bears sharp left on a very open and windswept corner. From this point, you can *either* turn right onto Chain Bridge Road (unsigned and unsurfaced) and follow the bank of the River Idle (see route **16**) *or* continue on the B1043 over the canal bridge by the Boat Inn, then round to the right through the long village of **Hayton**. Just before the give way sign at the approach to the A620 crossroads, opposite Corner Farm, turn right into Smeath Lane (the road is named but there's no signpost).

At the junction with the lane from Tiln, turn left, signed *Retford Market Place*. This soon enters the built-up outskirts of Retford and after about ¾ mile joins the A620, Moorgate. Turn right downhill, turn left at the traffic lights at the foot of the hill onto Arlington Way, then right at the next set of lights into Chapelgate to return via the short pedestrianised section to **Retford** Market Place.

29
continued

Start: Market Square, Retford (GR 704 811)

Distance: 29 miles

Terrain: mostly flat on quiet roads with some bridleway sections; optional section of gravel track along Chain Bridge Road.

Refreshment opportunities: there are tea shops in Retford, a café in Harworth, and a café at the Waterfowl Reserve at Sutton-cum-Lound, just off the route. Most of the villages also have pubs.

Ordnance Survey maps: sorry, you'll need *three* Landranger sheets – 111 Sheffield and Doncaster, 112 Scunthorpe and 120 Mansfield and Worksop.

Public transport links: East Coast Main Line trains (well, some of them) stop at Retford, and the Arriva Trains Northern service from Sheffield to Lincoln via Worksop and Gainsborough calls at the lower station at Retford. Note that it takes about five minutes to get with a bike from the station entrance at Retford to the lower station platform, and vice versa. It also involves going up and down steps.

Other routes: Routes 16 and 24, and the longest one in the book, 37, also start from Retford and use some of the same roads into and out of the town.

Route
30
start

30 miles • on-road • some hills • Daybrook

Daybrook Square to Southwell

This route starts in a north-east suburb of Nottingham but – once you are over the considerable lump of the misleadingly-named Mapperley 'Plains' – is soon out into gently rolling countryside, passing through some of the most attractive of Nottinghamshire's villages. Just over half way, the route passes through Southwell, with its impressive Minster and numerous refreshment places. Heading back towards Nottingham, the route climbs up onto a ridge – Oxton Bank – which affords grand views over the surrounding valleys, which have been shaped by numerous small rivers or 'dumbles'. The route finally takes in Calverton, a large former mining village whose colliery closed in 1999.

Once across the main A6097, the route passes through the long attractive village of Epperstone, then down a delightful open lane to Gonalston, another pretty village. Gonalston is one of

several Nottingham villages to have an elaborate forge with a large horseshoe-shaped entrance of black brick. The next two villages, Hoveringham and Thurgarton, lie on the flat flood plain of the now-tamed River Trent. Although Thurgarton lies astride the busy main Nottingham to Southwell road, several of the little side roads are quiet attractive backwaters. One of them, Beck Lane, leading from Hoveringham up to the main road, runs beside the small

30

continued

Gonalston Smithy

and surprisingly clear stream that gives it its name, the houses that line it being approached by a series of small bridges. And if you need to know the time, the village clock on the main road appears – at least when we've passed by – to be a model of accuracy. It was originally above Platform 4 at Nottingham station and was installed here by a lifelong railwayman when he retired.

The route reaches the River Trent at Fiskerton, at one time quite an important inland port – the name is a Danish version of an Anglo-Saxon one meaning 'the settlement of the fishermen'. In the early days of the Industrial Revolution roads were very poor, railways had not been invented and most goods traffic was by water. Convenient deep-water riversides such as Fiskerton were valuable for exporting Nottinghamshire's mineral wealth, and bringing in other goods in exchange. The river frontage still has substantial piling and wharfage.

It's only two or three miles from here to the pleasing little town of Southwell which figures on several of our routes, not least as it offers a variety of refreshment opportunities! (There's more on Southwell in the description of route 8.)

After Oxton and its cobbled ford, the last village on the route before the built-up area of Nottingham is Calverton. Expanded from its former modest size – around a thousand inhabitants at the turn of the 19th century – when mining came here as late

30

continued

as 1952, it has a much earlier industrial history. In 1589 William Lee of Calverton invented the stocking-knitters' frame, later to become the nucleus of a cottage industry throughout the county. The operators of these frames needed good light to work by and several of the old cottages have the characteristic long windows of frame-knitters' homes. A particularly fine example in Calverton is Windles Square, almost opposite the foot of Bonner Hill from Lambley, where the run of brick cottages has recently been expertly restored. It was the threatened displacement of these village hand industries by mechanised factories in the towns that sparked off the Luddite riots of the early 19th century.

With the Grove in **Daybrook Square** behind you, cross over the main – A60 – road into Nottingham Road. Take the second exit, effectively straight on, at the mini-roundabout by McDonalds, still on Nottingham Road. At the first set of traffic lights, turn right into Arnot Hill Road, then very soon left at the mini-roundabout into Hallam's Lane. Continue along this road, which becomes Gedling Road, then Brookfield Road. At the T-junction at the end of Brookfield Road, turn left opposite a parade of shops – this is Rolleston Drive. After 600yds, at the signal-controlled crossroads, turn right up the hill – this is Coppice Road. There is a mini-roundabout at the end of Coppice Road where you turn left onto Mapperley Plains, B684, signed to *Woodborough*. Before long you pass Brookfields Garden Centre (and coffee shop) on the left.

   When the road bears round to the left after about 1 mile, turn right, again signed *Woodborough*. This attractive descent brings you to the western end of **Woodborough**; turn right at the T-junction, signed Lowdham, and continue to the eastern end of the village. Where the road bears to the right, turn left up Shelt Hill – opposite the Nags Head, for *Epperstone*. Follow this road for about ¾ mile until it reaches the A6097, where you turn right and immediately left for Epperstone.

110

Keep on this road for some 2½ miles, through **Epperstone** to Gonalston. In **Gonalston** look out for the old forge on the left, then cross straight over the A612, signed *Hoveringham*, and on over a railway level crossing into **Hoveringham**. Just beyond St Michael's church, turn left at the T-junction signed *Thurgarton* and *Southwell*. Cross back over the railway at a level crossing by Thurgarton station, then, where the road bears left, turn right into **Thurgarton**.

Helping to create the
GREENWOOD

30
continued

COMMUNITY
FOREST

At the junction with Main Road, the A612, turn right and right again after about 150yds – just past the Coach and Horses – into Bleasby Road, signed *Bleasby* and *Staythorpe*. A mile or so further on the road swings round to the right and there is a short descent into **Bleasby** village: look out for the Manor Farm Tea Shoppe on the left. The Waggon and Horses in Bleasby dates back to the 17th century, and just beyond the sign for this, turn left at a minor crossroads into Gypsy Lane. This lane meanders between hedged fields; at the far end turn left, no sign post.

Just past the Bromley Arms in **Fiskerton**, turn left into Station Road, signed *Southwelll 3*. Go over the level crossing at Fiskerton Station, through Brinkley, past

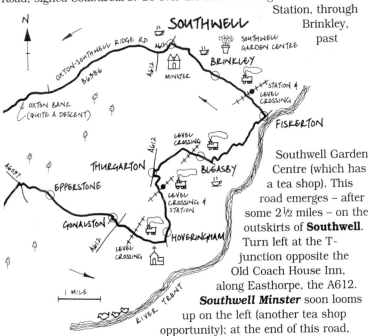

Southwell Garden Centre (which has a tea shop). This road emerges – after some 2½ miles – on the outskirts of **Southwell**. Turn left at the T-junction opposite the Old Coach House Inn, along Easthorpe, the A612. **Southwell Minster** soon looms up on the left (another tea shop opportunity); at the end of this road,

30
continued

Southwell Minster

turn left at the mini-roundabout, opposite the Saracen's Head (still the A612). Continue on this road (ignoring the turn where the A612 is routed off to the left) as it becomes Oxton Lane (B6386), and leaves Southwell.

Climbing gradually over about 4 miles, the road comes out at the top of a fairly steep descent, known as Oxton Bank. Swoop down and continue along the valley bottom, taking the second turning on the right – Sandy Lane – into **Oxton** to go through a little cobbled ford (there is a footbridge you can wheel your bike over if you prefer). Just beyond the ford, turn left along the aptly named Water Lane, a narrow and quite pretty little road beside a stream which emerges opposite Ye Olde Bridge Inn. Turn left and immediately right into Nottingham Road, B6386 (effectively straight on from Water Lane). Go straight over at the roundabout, across the A6097, and along the B6386 signed to *Nottingham.* Continue on for about 1 mile, and at the minor crossroads, turn left for *Calverton,* past a Scout camp site. After about 300yds, turn right into Flatts Lane, by the '*Borough of Gedling/Calverton*' sign on the right-hand side of the road. After about 400yds, Flatts Lane crosses Park Road in a dog-leg, right-and-left crossing. Continue on Flatts Lane for another 400yds to a T-junction with Collyers Road (not signed at this point) by the Co-op shop. Turn right, then almost immediately left into Mews Lane, in front of the

Cherry Tree, a large roadhouse-style pub.

Where Mews Lane meets Main Street, **Calverton,** turn right and in about 30yds turn left into George's Lane, signed *Arnold 3*, to go up George's Hill. This is quite a tough climb, but with fine views to the left. At **Dorket Head** crossroads at the top of the climb go straight on at the traffic lights, over the B684, into Calverton Road (not named at this point), signed *Arnold 1¼* to go down a quite steep hill. Just after the Longbow Inn on the right towards the foot of the hill there is a 'speed table' – a long brick-paved road hump to slow traffic outside the school – so take it steady! Calverton Road becomes Church Street shortly after this. At the end of Church Street, by the Robin Hood and Little John pub and facing the County Library, turn right at the mini-roundabout into Cross Street, then after about 100yds at the traffic lights by Arnold Leisure Centre take the filter lane to turn left into High Street, **Arnold**, signed *Nottingham* (A60). Continue along High Street then, at the traffic lights by the Ernehale pub and Wilkinson's, go straight on on Nottingham Road. Take the first exit at the mini-roundabout by McDonalds, effectively straight on, to complete the circuit at the Grove, **Daybrook Square**.

30
continued

Start: Daybrook Square, north-east Nottingham (GR 579 446)

Distance: 30 miles

Terrain: Entirely on-road, mainly quiet country lanes except for the first and last couple of miles which are urban. For the most part gradients are fairly gentle, although the ridge of Mapperley 'Plains' presents quite a stiff climb both at the start and towards the finish of the route

Refreshment opportunities: Tea shops at Brookfields Garden Centre, Mapperley Plains; Manor Farm, Bleasby; Southwell Garden Centre; and Southwell Minster Refectory. There are other places in Southwell but just off the route. Most of the villages en route have at least one pub and a shop.

Ordnance Survey maps: Landranger sheets 120 Mansfield and Worksop, and 129 Nottingham and Loughborough; Explorer sheets 260 Nottingham, 28 (270) Sherwood Forest.

Public transport links: The nearest rail station to Southwell is Fiskerton on the Nottingham to Newark Castle line (Central Trains), about 2½ miles south-east of Southwell. Fiskerton, and Thurgarton and Bleasby on the same line and also on the route, are request stops: trains stop there if you tell the conductor when you get on, or give a hand signal as the train approaches. Not all trains on this route will stop at Thurgarton, Bleasby or Fiskerton.

Other routes: Route **20**, Lambley and Lowdham, overlaps this one between Epperstone and Hoveringham, and route **22**, Blidworth and Halam, crosses at Westhorpe and in the centre of Southwell. Route **28**, Southwell Trail and the Dumbles, starts and finishes at Southwell. Link route **L10** joins this route, from Fiskerton, to Newark-on-Trent.

CIRCULAR ROUTES LONGER THAN 30 MILES

Route

31

start

31 miles • on-road • gently rolling • Bingham

Bingham and the Vale

This route shares for its first few miles the often surprising delights of the shorter circuit from Bingham, route 13. The charming little hamlet of Tithby (or 'Tythby' – see later), approached through wide open fields, seems very remote. The road through the next village, Cropwell Butler, leads eventually out out onto a tiny open hedgeless road crossing corn-covered open wolds, and then crests the brow to reveal one of the most attractive views in south Nottinghamshire, across the village of Shelford, nestled in a bend of the Trent.

From here the route follows for a few miles the top of the 'cliff' marking the south-eastern limit of the Trent's floodplain, through East Bridgford. The next hamlet of Kneeton, just off the route, seems peaceful enough now but was the scene of a vicious engagement in the English Civil War of the 1640s when no more than a handful of the losing side managed to reach the opposite bank and safety.

About four miles later the route crosses the Hawksworth to Scarrington road on its way to Thoroton. A two-mile detour from the described route at this point leads to the village of Scarrington. One of the most striking features here is a 17ft-high column of some 50,000 used horseshoes, beside the road that leads to Aslockton. For all its historic look, the stack is in fact quite recent, having been accumulated by the local smith in the twenty years leading up to his retirement in 1965. At one time at risk of being sold to America, this curiosity now belongs to Nottinghamshire County Council.

31
continued

After Thoroton the route crosses the River Smite to reach Orston. This village had, surprisingly, an illustrious industrial past going back to the Middle Ages as a source of gypsum for plaster (still a major local industry). At one time the Royal Plaster Works in the middle of the village were described as the best in the land. The pits were worked up to 1873; all that is now left are hollows and hummocks in the ground.

In Cropwell Butler

When you are in quiet Granby, one of the last villages on the route, it seems strange to think that this village is honoured up and down the whole of England in a common pub name – the Marquis of Granby. The wide spread of the pub name is attributed to the large number of soldiers who had served under the Marquis in battle in the Seven Years War in the 1750s and 60s. In the days before there were pensions for common soldiers it was the practice for commanders to buy inns for men who had served them well, to give them a continuing income, and the Marquis of Granby was one of the most generous in rewarding his troops. The name was further spread by his grandson, a rather eccentric enthusiast for pubs.

From **Bingham** station go south on Station Street, then right along the edge of Market Place to Market Street, where you turn left. At the T-junction opposite the Wheatsheaf Inn, turn right into Long Acre, unsigned at this junction. After a short distance, turn left at the signalled cross-roads into Tithby Road, signed *Tithby* and *Langar*. There is now quite a steep climb up to the A52. Cross the A52 at a staggered crossroads, right and left, still on Tithby Road. (The hamlet appears as 'Tithby' on the OS map and the signs in Bingham but generally as 'Tythby' on the ground. We use the spelling you'll see on the actual sign.) Head southwards and after about 1¼ miles take first right, signed *Tithby*. The road bears round to the left into the hamlet of **Tythby**. At a minor crossroads by the church, turn right, signed

115

31
continued

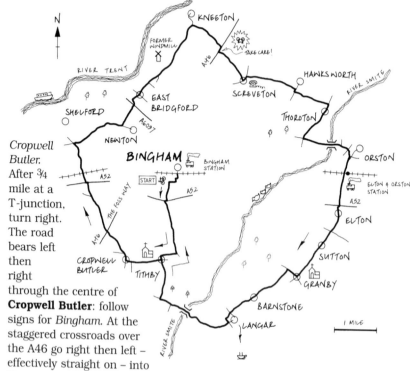

Cropwell
Butler.
After ¾
mile at a
T-junction,
turn right.
The road
bears left
then
right
through the centre of
Cropwell Butler: follow
signs for *Bingham*. At the
staggered crossroads over
the A46 go right then left –
effectively straight on – into
Henson Lane. After nearly 1 mile at Upper Saxondale, a new housing
development on the site of a former hospital, turn right and almost
immediately left – effectively straight on – still on Henson Lane. Pass
to the right of a wooden gate which bars access to motor vehicles.
Then, about 100yds before the junction with the A52, the road is
again blocked to cars but a cycle gap has been left. At the A52 go left,
then almost immediately right, signposted *Shelford*. Follow this open
unfenced road with its fine views over the Trent valley for about 1 mile
to a crossroads. Turn right, signposted *Newton*, and after about 1½
miles on the outskirts of **Newton**, turn left, signed *East Bridgford*, to
the junction with the A6097. Go straight over the main road,
signposted *East Bridgford*.

At the crossroads by the church in **East Bridgford** go straight on
on Kneeton Road past a former windmill for about 2¼ miles to a
junction, where the road to Kneeton goes straight on. Turn right,
signed *Newark and Nottingham*, for about 1 mile to a T-junction with
the A46. Turn right (care!) on the A46, signed *Leicester*, then after
about 200yds turn left just after the Red Lodge, signed *Screveton 1*.
Continue for about 1 mile to a T-junction in Screveton opposite a

31
continued

telephone box and bus shelter; turn left (no signpost). After about 200yds, take the first right, signed *Hawksworth*. About 1¼ miles later, at a T-junction, turn right, then first left – in effect a very staggered crossroads, with the signpost, to *Thoroton*, somewhere in the middle. After about 1 mile at a further T-junction, turn right, signposted *Thoroton*. Continue through **Thoroton** for about 1 mile to a crossroads, then turn left, signposted *Orston*. Cross the River Smite into **Orston**. At a T-junction after the church, turn right on Mill Lane, signed *Elton*. Mill Lane becomes Hill Road and bears left, signed *Elton Station*. Follow this road up a short steep climb and keep right at both junctions at the top by the triangular green to cross over the railway at Elton & Orston Station. At the junction with the A52, go straight across the main road into **Elton**, signposted *Granby*, and straight on at the next crossroads, about ¾ mile after Elton, signed *Sutton and Granby*.

Continue through **Sutton** to **Granby**, then at the crossroads by the church, turn right into Main Street, signed *Barnstone*. Just after leaving the village, at the foot of a small hill, turn left, again signed *Barnstone*. Continue through **Barnstone**, a long straggling settlement, to a crossroads about ½ mile past the village. Go straight on on Musters Road into **Langar** village. The road bears round to the left through the village, past the Post Office to a T-junction by the Unicorn's Head. Turn right, signed *Colston Bassett*. After nearly 2 miles take the first right turn, unsigned.

In **Tythby**, go straight on by the church, signed *Bingham*. The road bears round to the right to a T-junction after about ½ mile. Turn left, signed *Bingham*, for 1¼ miles to a T-junction with the A52. Turn right, then left into **Bingham**. The road descends steeply to the traffic lights in Bingham, where you go straight on into Fairfield Street. After 150yds turn right into Newgate Street, signed *Library and health centre*. Just after the road bears round to the right, turn left

Barnstone Church

31
continued

along the edge of Market Square, then first left by two telephone boxes into Station Street; sure enough the **station** is at the end of this road.

Start: Bingham station (GR 705 401)

Distance: 31 miles

Terrain: entirely on-road, gently rolling

Refreshment opportunities: the tea rooms at Langar Airfield Parachute Club and the Wildflower Farm both lie just off the route at Langar.

Ordnance Survey maps: Landranger sheet 129 Nottingham and Loughborough; Explorer sheet 260 Nottingham.

Public transport links: Central Trains services to Bingham and Elton & Orston on the Notting-ham–Grantham line (not all services on this line stop at Bingham and only 2–3 per day stop at Elton & Orston)

Other routes: Route **13** is a shorter (11-mile) version of this one, also starting and finish-ing in Bingham. Route **35** uses a stretch of the same roads as this one between Cropwell Bishop and Elton, while route **36** also briefly overlaps south of Tithby. Route **40**, the linear route from Newark to Nottingham, crosses this one at Screveton and East Bridgford.

Route
32
start

32 miles • on-road • gently rolling • Nottingham

Sutton Bonington and the Soar valley

Although quite long, this is an easygoing route, fairly flat with only the occasional incline. It goes right down to the south-western corner of Nottinghamshire, making use of the good network of cycle routes in the south-west sector of Nottingham to leave and re-enter the city, where this route starts and finishes. One of the features which struck us as we rode round this route was the very large number of roadside seats, many with pleasing countryside or river views – ideal picnic stops. Once it leaves the built-up area the route crosses a remarkable piece of open landscape – Clifton Pasture and Barton Moor – on its way to Gotham. Famed in the nursery rhyme, the Three Wise Men of Gotham may not have been as daft as they seemed as they tried to fence in a cuckoo to ensure perpetual

32

continued

springtime. Their foolery is sometimes claimed to have been part of an ingenious plot to hoodwink the authorities responsible for taxation, conscription, paying for compulsory roadbuilding and other such unpleasantnesses, into giving this obviously sadly afflicted – and probably highly infectious – village a wide berth.

The route first meets the valley of the River Soar which it is to follow for some way at the pretty hamlet of Kingston on Soar, though the water under the hamlet's picturesque bridge is not the Soar itself but the Kingston Brook. The River Soar marks the very edge of Nottinghamshire. The next valley village, Sutton Bonington, is a long, straggling place – partly because it used to be two separate hamlets: Sutton and Bonington. In the nineteenth century a thriving centre of the local hosiery industry, it is now largely a residential and commuter village. It also houses the School of Agriculture of Nottingham University, the latest name for an agricultural college that began life in 1895 as the Midland Dairy Institute.

Normanton on Soar too straggles along the bank of the River Soar, with several pathways cutting between the houses to the river – and several more of those roadside seats.

Eventually the route climbs away from the Soar. Its final return towards Nottingham follows an old trackway from Plumtree through the lost village of Flawford or Flawforth, now commemorated only in the names of a couple of farms. Where this track meets a tarred road again, about two miles east of Ruddington, is the site of Flawforth church. Now all that remains are a few gravestones set in a grassy lawn. A variety of finds from archaeological digs here are

Detail on one of the Flawforth gravestones

32

continued

housed in an old house now a museum – The Hermitage in Ruddington village. Ruddington is one of many villages – now grown into a small town – around Nottingham to have been very much a centre of the hosiery trade. Here as elsewhere the long windows on many of the houses show their origins as the homes of frame-knitters, and one of the village's no less than three museums depicts a hosiery complex.

Turn left outside **Nottingham Midland Station**, and almost immediately right to join the cycle route on Queens Bridge Road, signed Meadows, *Wilford*, and *Clifton*. After a short distance, use the double set of cyclists' traffic lights to cross Waterway Street and Meadows Way, and continue along the tree-lined Queens Walk cycle track. At the far end go straight on at the roundabout, over Wilford Toll Bridge – spanning the River Trent – following the

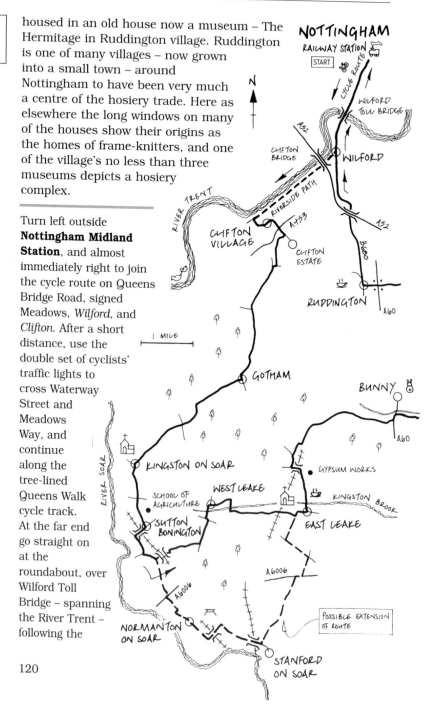

32
continued

cycle route signs for Wilford. Continue ahead at the far side of the bridge along Main Road through **Wilford** village, and at the signalled crossroads bear right onto the cycle track signed *Clifton Village.*

Soon after passing under the A52 Clifton bridge, just beyond a signalled cycle crossing, turn right down a short slope into a 'river users' car park' to join a path, signed *River Trent Greenway, Clifton Village, Barton-in-Fabis.* Cross the bridge over Fairham Brook to join a firm-surfaced path which bears round to the left to follow the southern bank of the River Trent. Continue on this path, keeping more or less to the waterside for some 2 miles as far as a metal access gate, just past which the route turns left, away from the river, up a wide but fairly steep track. At the top this emerges onto a minor road by Clifton Hall; bear left and follow this road (Village Road) as it winds through **Clifton village** to join the main road, A453.

Cross straight over the busy A453 (there is a signal-controlled pedestrian crossing which can be helpful), bearing slightly right, into Green Lane, signed *Ruddington.* Take the second turning on the right, Waterdown Road, go up a slight rise and second right again into Bransdale Road. Turn right at the mini roundabout at the far end of Bransdale Road, into Farnborough Road, and left at the T-junction signed *Gotham.* This road sweeps down across the broad open spaces of Clifton Pasture, Barton Moor and Gotham Moor and into **Gotham** village. Turn right just before the centre of the village into Kegworth Road, signed *Kingston.* In **Kingston on Soar**, after about 3 miles, turn left opposite the church into Station Road, past Nottingham University's School of Agriculture to bear right over the railway bridge and down Marlepit Hill into **Sutton Bonington**.

You pass through this straggling village along Main Street. About two-thirds of the way along, bear left opposite the Old Plough, still on Main Street (the straight-on road now becomes Park Lane). The turning is marked as *Main Street leading to Hungary Lane* and shortly passes under a railway bridge and climbs gently for about 1 mile to a T-junction with Trowell Lane. Turn left, signed *West Leake* and *Nottingham,* gently downhill towards a prominent line of willows. At the foot of the slope take the second turn right, just after the left bend in the road and just before the Star Inn, signed *West Leake, East Leake and Nottingham.* In **West Leake** the road bears round to the right, signed East *Leake and Costock.* This road follows the pleasant shallow valley of the Kingston Brook and after about 2 miles comes

121

32
continued

into **East Leake** by the church at a T-junction opposite the Three Horseshoes. Turn left on Brookside, signed *Costock and Gotham*.

Just beyond the village hall, turn left into Gotham Lane, signed *Gotham*. (Just after this turn there are public toilets and a tea shop-cum-bakery (not Sundays) on the right.) Continue along Gotham Lane out of East Leake, passing the British Gypsum works and, after crossing the rail line, take the first turning on the right, signed for *Bunny*. After about 2 miles the route comes into the outskirts of **Bunny** and meets the A60: turn left, signposted *Nottingham*, and first right after about 150yds into a very minor, unsigned, lane which it is quite easy to miss.

Follow this lane, which runs along the banks of a stream, for about a mile and then turn left at the T-junction, signed *Bradmore*. After ¾ mile, turn right at the minor staggered crossroads, into Bunny Lane for *Keyworth*. Left at the T-junction in **Keyworth**, signed *Plumtree* (although if you want a break, a right turn leads into the centre of the village where, just beyond the church, there is The Coffee Shop on the right). The road winds through Keyworth for about 1 mile and soon after leaving the village the route passes under a high railway bridge to come into **Plumtree**; continue straight on through the village, signed *Tollerton*.

On leaving Plumtree, just before a wooden bus shelter on the left, turn left, passing through two metal five-barred gates onto a signposted stony but firm-surfaced *bridleway* – which passes back under the railway and becomes grassy to follow the edge of a hedged field before emerging, after 1½ miles, onto a minor road near the site of **Flawforth** church (there are a few gravestones on a preserved turfed area on the right). Turn left (effectively still following the direction you have been following on the track), then – after a mile or so – continue straight on at the signalled crossroads with the A60 into Kirk Lane, B680, signed *Ruddington*. At the T-junction in **Ruddington**, turn right onto High Street, still B680, signposted *Wilford* (the Village Coffee Shop is on the left soon after this turn).

Follow the B680 out of Ruddington and, after about 2 miles, pass

32

continued

under the A52 for a further mile into **Wilford**. On reaching the signalled cross roads – which you should recognise from earlier on in the route – go straight over from Ruddington Lane into Main Road, following *cycle route signs for the city centre*. Cross Wilford Toll Bridge, and retrace the outgoing route along Queens Walk back to **Nottingham Midland station**.

*It is possible to lengthen the rout*e by a little over 3 miles to take in the attractive village of Normanton on Soar and the little hamlet of Stanford on Soar by continuing straight ahead at the Old Plough in **Sutton Bonington** along Park Lane where the main route goes left. At the T-junction with the A6006, turn right, signposted *Ashby*, and first left after a short distance into Moor Lane, signed for *Normanton*. Continue through **Normanton on Soar**, following signs for *Stanford on Soar*. Pass over the Midland Main Line railway and then over the preserved Great Central Railway, before turning left at the T-junction – just before Stanford village – for *East Leake*. Go up the steady climb of Firdeal Hill for about 1½ miles to join the A6006, turn right, signed *Rempstone* and *East Leake*, then first left after about 150yds, signed *East Leake*. Turn left at the first minor crossroads, again signed for *East Leake* and first right after ½ mile down the hill into **East Leake**. Turn right at the T-junction into the village centre. (This doesn't exhaust all the possibilities: the Landranger map shows plenty of other alternatives from the Soar valley to East Leake.)

Start: Nottingham Midland Station (GR 574 393)

Distance: 32 miles (increased to 35 with the Normanton and Stanford extension)

Terrain: Predominantly on-road, but using several off-road links – including a Trent-side cycle path and a bridleway.

Refreshment opportunities: There is a a good variety of pubs serving food en route, together with a number of village shops. The large villages of East Leake, Keyworth and Ruddington also boast tea shops – although none of these is open on Sundays. Manor Farm Animal Centre and Donkey Sanctuary, south of East Leake, has a coffee shop open all week. The Cosy Teapot Café is close to the station in Nottingham.

Ordnance Survey maps: Landranger sheet 129 Nottingham and Loughborough; Explorer sheet 260 Nottingham.

Public transport links: Midland Main Line, Robin Hood Line and Central Trains services go to Nottingham Midland Station.

Other routes: City routes **6** and **10**, and longer routes **33** and **36** also start and finish at Nottingham station. Route **40**, the linear route from Newark, finishes here. Link route **L5** joins Nottingham station to the short route round the Attenborough Nature Reserve, route **1**.

Route

33

start

35 miles • on-road • undulating • Nottingham

Villages beginning with 'W'

Although it starts near the centre of Nottingham, this route takes you very quickly into open rolling country south of the city. It passes through a variety of villages, with more than what seems a fair share starting with 'W': Wysall, Wymeswold, Willoughby-on-the-Wolds (two for the price of one there!) and Widmerpool. Most of the villages are worth a stop to look round the church and fine old buildings, the names of cottages – 'The Old Post Office', 'The Old Forge', 'Bakehouse Cottage' – often testimony to the self-sufficient nature of these settlements in the past. The route dips into Leicestershire to take in the refreshment opportunities at Six Hills – a good enough reason for breaching the frontier!

The first settlement on the route, Ruddington – now grown into a small town, is one of many villages around Nottingham which was once very much a centre of the hosiery trade and the village houses a knitting museum. Ruddington is another village where the long windows on many of the houses show their origins as the homes of frame-knitters.

The route soon enters rolling countryside, the foothills of the higher wolds of south Nottinghamshire and Leicestershire. Many of the names of villages in this area betray their Danish origins: this was near the edge of the Danelaw – the area of England ruled by the Danes at the end of the 9th century. A village sign without a village on the next stretch of road proclaims 'Thorpe in the Glebe', a now-lost village, its name derived from the old Danish word *thorp*, a farmstead, often one dependent on a nearby larger village. Many villages in the Vale of Belvoir and on the surrounding wolds, end in the Danish -*by*, meaning a hamlet or homestead. Our W-rich Willoughby, which welcomes you back to Nottinghamshire after a ten-mile foray into Leicestershire, was the 'hamlet or homestead among the willows'.

Sometimes the place-names seem to have got a bit mixed up:

124

the first part of Widmerpool means the 'wide or willow-fringed mere or lake', so you don't really need the extra 'pool' at the end. Widmerpool has been an 'estate' village since the thirteenth century, giving rise to a Widmerpool family, although the place-

33
continued

name is a good deal older. Nowadays the pool is much smaller and the quiet village nestles in a hollow between rolling hills.

Cross over the main road outside **Midland Station**, bearing left to join the cycle route on Queen's Bridge Road signed to *Meadows, Wilford* and *Clifton.* Use the two parallel sets of cyclists' traffic lights to cross Waterway Street and Meadows Way, and continue on the segregated cycle path down Queen's Walk. Straight on at the roundabout at the far end, to cross the River Trent by Wilford Toll Bridge – which is closed to all traffic except those on foot and bike, and whose toll charges disappeared long ago, although there's a reminder on a board at the old toll-house.

Once over the river, go straight on following the cycle route signs towards *Clifton.* After about 1 mile cross Wilford Lane using the traffic lights at the staggered crossroads, into Ruddington Lane. Follow this road as it leaves the outskirts of Nottingham, for some 2 miles to **Ruddington** village. Along the High Street, turn left just after the Bricklayers Arms into Kirk Lane; continue to the traffic lights and right on to the A60 – signed *Bunny.* Continue on this main road – which does not carry too much traffic outside peak periods – for about 1½ miles; just beyond **Bradmore**, take the second left turning, Pendock Lane, towards *Keyworth* and *Wysall.* Stay on this road, following signs to *Wysall*, which you will reach after about 2½ miles – plus a climb up Windmill Hill!

At the T-junction as you reach the outskirts of Wysall, turn right for *Widmerpool* and *Wymeswold.* Through **Wysall** village turn left opposite the church, signposted *Wymeswold.* Pass through the site of the lost village **Thorpe the Glebe** before you reach **Wymeswold** after some 2 miles, turn right at the T-junction along East Road, then almost immediately left down Church Street. At the next T-junction, turn left along Brook Street, which is bordered by a willow-lined

33
continued

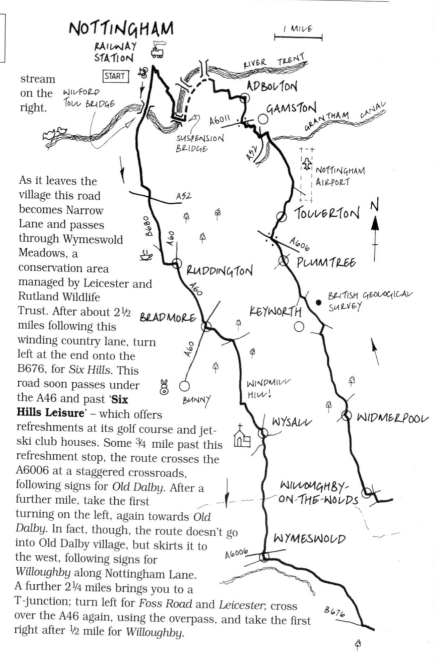

stream on the right.

As it leaves the village this road becomes Narrow Lane and passes through Wymeswold Meadows, a conservation area managed by Leicester and Rutland Wildlife Trust. After about 2½ miles following this winding country lane, turn left at the end onto the B676, for *Six Hills*. This road soon passes under the A46 and past '**Six Hills Leisure**' – which offers refreshments at its golf course and jet-ski club houses. Some ¾ mile past this refreshment stop, the route crosses the A6006 at a staggered crossroads, following signs for *Old Dalby*. After a further mile, take the first turning on the left, again towards *Old Dalby*. In fact, though, the route doesn't go into Old Dalby village, but skirts it to the west, following signs for *Willoughby* along Nottingham Lane. A further 2¼ miles brings you to a T-junction; turn left for *Foss Road* and *Leicester*; cross over the A46 again, using the overpass, and take the first right after ½ mile for *Willoughby*.

126

33

continued

At the crossroads in the centre of **Willoughby-on-the-Wolds**, go right for *Widmerpool*, for about 1½ miles. In **Widmerpool**, turn right at the T-junction signed for *Keyworth* and *Nottingham*. Go up the hill, and follow this road for about 1½ miles. Just as you enter **Keyworth** turn right into Willow Brook, signed for *Stanton* and *Plumtree*. At the end of Willow Brook, go left onto Nicker Hill, then down the hill, past the British Geological Survey; after this it's right at the T-junction for *Plumtree* and *Nottingham*. Follow this road for about 1 mile, through **Plumtree**, and when it meets the A606, turn left and first right after a short distance at the traffic signals, into Tollerton Lane. This lane skirts Tollerton to the east and Tollerton Airport to the west.

After about 2½ miles this road crosses the Grantham Canal; about 100yds further on turn right before you meet the busy A52, down a minor road signed to *Bassingfield*. As this bears round to the right after about 200yds, turn left to use the cycle and pedestrian lights to cross the A52. Go straight on at the other side, into the **Gamston** housing estate, where you join a minor residential road – Kirkstone Drive – which meanders through the housing development, to emerge eventually at an unsigned T-junction. Turn right, up to the traffic lights, then use the dedicated cycle crossing of the A6011 to reach the shared-use path along Regatta Way, signed for *Holme Pierrepont*. Take the first left, after ½ mile, down Adbolton Lane, then first right – Adbolton Grove – as you enter the built-up housing area. Left at the bottom of Adbolton Grove, into Holme Road, and after about 600yds follow the cycle route signed for the *Meadows* and *City Centre*, which bears off to the right across open ground.

This cycle route meets the River Trent, where you turn left along the bank, and follow it under Lady Bay Bridge, past Nottingham Forest football ground, and under Trent Bridge. Cross the river using the cycle/pedestrian suspension bridge, just past County Hall. At the other side turn right on the road and then bear left into Bunbury Street, past the bus garage, following cycle route signs for *City Centre via Arkwright Walk*. This route takes you aross Bathley Street, then second right into Radcliffe Street, left along Arkwright Walk, left and right through the Meadows shopping centre, under the subway below Meadows Way, and eventually back to **Midland Station**.

33
continued

Start: Nottingham Midland Station (GR 574 393)

Distance: 35 miles

Terrain: On-road, using quiet country lanes for the most part, with cycle routes to get in and out of the city of Nottingham. The countryside is generally gently rolling, with the occasional hill up to the Wolds.

Refreshment opportunities: Most of the many villages this route passes through have pubs and shops (the latter not usually open on Sunday). About halfway round there are refreshment opportunities at the Six Hills Leisure Park.

Ordnance Survey maps: Landranger sheet 129 Nottingham and Loughborough; Explorer sheets 246 Loughborough and 260 Nottingham.

Public transport links: Midland Main Line and local services to Nottingham Station; Wymeswold, at the southern end of the route, is only 5 miles from Loughborough (Midland Main Line, local services (including Ivanhoe Line to Leicester)) and Barrow upon Soar (Ivanhoe Line) stations.

Other routes: City routes **6** and **10**, and longer routes **32** and **36** also start and finish at Nottingham station. Route **40**, the linear route from Newark, finishes here. Link route **L5** joins Nottingham station to the short route round the Attenborough Nature Reserve, route **1**.

Route
34
start

36 miles • on-road • gently rolling • Tuxford

The northern Trent Valley

This ride follows the valley of the River Trent towards the northern end of the county. Starting and finishing at the small town of Tuxford, the route first heads south-east, then turns north – meandering through the minor lanes which link the numerous villages of this part of the Trent Valley. However, aside from a brief touch at Carlton-on-Trent, this is not a riverside route: the cooling towers of the power stations which are a feature of the waterway are kept at a comfortable distance, where they can make an imposing skyline. The route eventually turns west and soon south, when the terrain becomes more undulating, yet the reward is some fine views over the county and its neighbours.

Now quiet and bypassed, Tuxford was once a bustling market

Above: the west wall of Old Newstead Abbey

Right: in the Japanese garden, Newstead Abbey grounds

Above: Greasley church

Left: Nottingham Canal

*Above: Blidworth
Woods in Autumn*

*Right: The Herb
Garden near
Hardstoft*

Above: Hardwick Hall

Below: Detail in Rowthorne

Above: Looking towards the chapel in Clumber Park

Right: A mile post on 'NCN' Route 6 at Hazel Gap

Above: Hexgreave Park

Left: Detail in Norton village

Above and right: Sherwood
Pines Forest Park

Above: North Wheatley

*Left: Detail in Rufford
Abbey Sculpture Park*

town on the Great North Road from London to York and
Edinburgh, boasting nine hotels, inns and taverns. There must
have been an unruly element among the travellers, since in
1823 a town lock-up was built to allow drunks and villains to
cool off overnight. The building is still preserved, beside the
Egmanton road by which the route leaves Tuxford.
In Carlton-on-Trent, just south of the route on the old Great
North Road, lies Carlton's smithy, one of several to be marked
with a giant horseshoe emblem in black brick surrounding the
entrance. There is another at Gonalston, on routes 20 and 30.
A footpath leads to the bank of the River Trent – a matter of
yards – from the corner of Carlton Lane in Carlton-on-Trent. At
this point the river is just below the lock which marks the
upper limit of the tidal section.

34

continued

Follow Newcastle Street, between the Newcastle Arms and the Sun Inn
at the southern end of the town, out of **Tuxford**, signposted
Egmanton. Go straight on in **Egmanton** after 1½ miles, signed for
Laxton, which you reach about 1½ miles later. In **Laxton**, turn left at
the T-junction by the Dovecote Inn. There is a visitor centre next to
this pub, with an exhibition of the mediaeval strip cultivation that is
still – uniquely in England – practised in the village. At the far end of
Laxton at the foot of the slope, turn left – signed *Moorhouse* – where
the road bears round to the right for Kneesall. Follow this pleasant
little lane for about 2 miles to the hamlet of **Moorhouse**. At the T-
junction, turn right, signed *Ossington*, and in **Ossington** turn left at
the T-junction signed *Carlton-on-Trent*. After about ¾ mile, turn right,
signed *Norwell*, and on reaching Norwell, turn left at the T-junction
(no sign post here when we researched the route).

Follow this
pleasantly winding
minor road for
about 2½ miles to a
T-junction. Turn
right, signed
Carlton-on-Trent, to
cross the East
Coast main railway
line at a level
crossing and the A1
via a bridge, then
straight on at the

Headon Church

34
continued

cross-roads with the B1164, the old Great North Road, in **Carlton-on-Trent** into Ferry Lane. As the road bears right, turn left into an unnamed 'No-through road', signed *'No vehicular access to River Trent'*, then very shortly left again into Carlton Lane. This mile-long lane is impassable to motor vehicles as there is a narrow bridge over a stream about halfway along – but cyclists can go straight on into **Sutton on Trent**.

At the T-junction in Sutton, turn right (effectively straight on) and go through the village on Main Street, which becomes Church Street and, just beyond Sutton-on-Trent primary school, turn right into Ingram Lane. Follow this little lane for nearly 2 miles until, about ½ mile beyond a sweeping left bend it reaches a T-junction in the hamlet of **Grassthorpe**, opposite Corner Farm. Turn right and then first left after a short distance for *Normanton*. Continue as the road meanders through **Normanton on Trent**, and turn left at the T-junction by the church, signed *Tuxford*. After approximately ½ mile, turn right for *Skegby* and, at the end of this mile-long road and just after passing through the hamlet of **Skegby**, go left and right at an unsigned junction – effectively straight on.

On the River Trent

Follow this open road as it winds through farmland for about 2½ miles then, at the junction with the main A57 in **Dalton**, turn left and in about 100yds first right for *East Drayton*. Go straight on at the cross-roads in **East Drayton**, signed *Stokeham*. After about a mile, in **Stokeham**, go right at the T-junction, signed *Rampton* and *Treswell*, and left at the next – after about 100yds – for *Treswell*. After a further mile take the second turn on the left into **Treswell** and, at the T-junction in the village, turn left, signed *Grove*. There is a steady 3-mile climb into **Grove**.

Carry straight on through Grove, and about ¾ mile past the village, go left at a T-junction signed *Rampton*. After about a further mile at the foot of a slight slope, take the first right for *Headon*. This minor road winds through **Headon** village – or villages, since half of it is Nether Headon. Shortly after passing the squat but prominent church, turn right at the T-junction signed *Askham*. In the next village, **Upton**, turn left at the T-junction, signed *East Drayton*, then first right after about 100yds into Askham Road, signed *Askham*. Continue straight through the attractive village of **Askham** and on following the sign to *East Markham*.

On the approach to **East Markham** you cross directly over the A57, then go straight on at the first minor cross roads in the village – over High Street into Farm Lane – then at the next minor cross-roads, after a short climb, turn right into Priestgate, signed *West Markham*. This road climbs over a bridge to take you back over the A1 to join its predecessor, B1164, the old Great North Road. Turn left at the T-junction on the B1164 for *Tuxford*, on the approach to which you pass a working windmill which is sometimes open to the public. Climb Eldon Street, **Tuxford**, which becomes Newark Road, then Market Place. On the right are the two pubs marking the start of the route.

34
continued

Start: Newcastle Arms, Tuxford (GR 736 710)

Distance: 36 miles

Terrain: Entirely on-road, gently rolling, save for a couple of more challenging hills near the start and towards the end of the ride.

Refreshment opportunities: Many of the villages this ride takes in have pubs serving food and small shops selling basic groceries.

Ordnance Survey maps: Landranger sheet 120 Mansfield and Worksop; in theory, you need sheet 121 Lincoln, too, to cover the 4 miles or so between Carlton-on-Trent and Grassthorpe, but we think the route description is clear enough that you can manage without the map. The whole route is covered by Explorer sheet 271 Newark-on-Trent.

Public transport links: although the East Coast main line passes through the outskirts of Tuxford there is no longer a station there. The nearest rail link to any part of the route is by way of route L11 (below) from Norwell to Newark.

Other routes: Route 25 overlaps this one between Egmanton and Laxton. Link route L1 is a very short link in the village of Norwell between this route and route 28; link route L3 joins this route to route 24; link route L11 is a route from this route to Newark.

Route

35
start

36 miles • largely on-road • rolling • Nottingham, Trent Bridge

The Vale of Belvoir

This route, longish but across gentle countryside, travels almost the length of the Vale of Belvoir – dominated at its south-east end by Belvoir Castle itself. The route begins by climbing up to the low ridge which separates the valley of the Trent from the broader Vale of Belvoir. We choose an off-road route for this, but one that can be tackled with any bike. Once at the top and across the old Roman Foss (or Fosse) Way, the road swoops down to a crossroads, the left-hand limb of which leads to the tiny hamlet of Owthorpe up a dead-end road. Owthorpe has an attractive little church, set in the fields, and one other claim to fame: the village hall can seat 102 – nearly five times the hamlet's total population of 22!

Another couple of miles brings you to Colston Bassett, passing

132

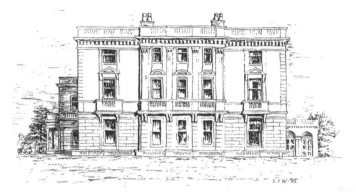

Colston Bassett Hall

the impressive Colston Bassett Hall on the left before crossing
the River Smite. The now-peaceful village had a turbulent past,
with a number of Civil War skirmishes and visitations of the
plague. In mediaeval times, Colston Bassett was a large and
prosperous wool village, but the trade declined and the village
with its old church on the hill was abandoned. Later, the
place's fortunes revived and the new village and eventually a
new church grew on the present site.

Colston Bassett has another important role: as a producer of
delicious Stilton cheese, which you can buy direct from the
dairy (Mondays to Fridays 9am–12.30pm and 1.30–4pm;
Saturdays 9–11.30am) or from the village shop. The famous
blue cheese was never actually made at Stilton – which is just
south-west of Peterborough – but in Vale of Belvoir villages like
this. In fact, Stilton is the only British cheese which has to be
made in a closely defined area to qualify for its name – like fine
wines in wine-growing countries. It gained its name by being
transported eastwards and then sold at the inn at Stilton to the
many passing travellers on the Great North Road.

After Colston Bassett, villages turn up at two- or three-mile
intervals for the rest of the route. If one of them, Granby,
sounds familiar it could well be because this village is honoured
up and down the whole of England in a common pub name –
the Marquis of Granby. Presumably the village's own inn of this
name in the middle of the village is the original. The wide
spread of the pub name is attributed to the large number of
soldiers who had served under the Marquis in battle and then
retired to wayside inns provided for them by their generous

133

35

continued

commander! It's also believed to owe something to the promotional zeal of his grandson.

The final stretch of way back into Nottingham passes the impressive red brick Holme Pierrepont Hall and then skirts the National Water Sports Centre, with its long straight 2000-metre rowing course – a landmark that makes it instantly recognisable from the air, should you find yourself flying over the East Midlands on a clear day.

Leave **Trent Bridge, Nottingham** by the riverside cycle path on the south side of the river past Nottingham Forest FC ground, signed *Cycle Route Lady Bay*. Continue along the path to pass over the Grantham Canal and under Lady Bay road bridge, between cast iron bollards, with playing fields on the right and river on the left. At the end of the playing-field fencing on the right, turn right on a path (no sign) leading to Holme Road (not named at this point); turn left signed *Cycle Route Lady Bay*. Follow the road round to the right, becoming Adbolton Road. At the T-junction at the end , turn left on Adbolton Lane, signed *Cycle Route Holme Pierrepont*. At the next T-junction,

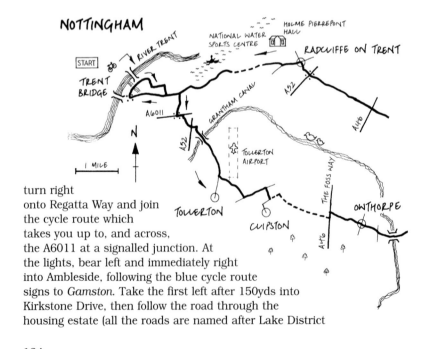

turn right onto Regatta Way and join the cycle route which takes you up to, and across, the A6011 at a signalled junction. At the lights, bear left and immediately right into Ambleside, following the blue cycle route signs to *Gamston*. Take the first left after 150yds into Kirkstone Drive, then follow the road through the housing estate (all the roads are named after Lake District landmarks), bearing right into Old Tollerton Road, which becomes Bassingfield Lane. Go straight on at *No through* road signs, then across the A52 using the toucan crossing.

35
continued

On the far side, turn right onto a minor road. At the next T-junction, unsigned, turn left into Tollerton Lane, over the Grantham Canal. Continue to pass the airfield and after about 1¼ miles, in **Tollerton**, turn left on Cotgrave Lane, signed *Cotgrave*. Follow this road for about ¾ mile to a T-junction, then turn left, again signed *Cotgrave*. After about ½ mile, take the first right, Gilliver Lane, signed *Clipstone on the Wolds*. Where the road bears right near the top of the hill, where the road bends right take the track to the left (a RUPP, although not signed) through the edge of a wood, round a metal gate, then go straight on. The track becomes a path with a hedge immediately on the right; follow the path round to the right up the slope. At the end of the hedge, turn left on a wide gravel track. After about 1 mile at a crossing of tracks, go straight on along a narrow track through woodland for 1 mile or so to its T-junction with the A46. **(Beware the ford, hidden in a dip, shortly before the main road!)**

Turn left on the A46 for some 200yds, then right at the crossroads onto a minor road, signed *Owthorpe*. Go down the hill past the end of the hamlet of **Owthorpe**, continue straight on signed *Colston Bassett*, then go straight on at the next crossroads, still signed *Colston Bassett*. After about 1 mile at a T-junction, turn right on Hall Lane, signed *Colston Bassett*. Follow the road as it winds through **Colston Bassett**, leaving the church on the right, then follow the road round

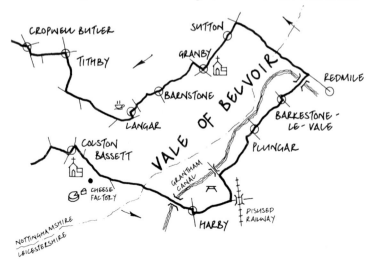

135

35

continued

to the right,
Harby Lane,
signed *Hose* and
Harby. Go past
the Stilton
cheese 'factory'
(Colston Bassett
Dairy) and
continue straight
on for 3½ miles
following signs
for *Harby*. At the
T-junction in
Harby opposite
the Nags Head,
turn right,

Primitive Methodist chapel at Sutton

signed *Waltham*, then take the first left, Stathern Lane, signed
Stathern and *Bottesford*. Follow this road for about 1 mile then, just
before railway bridge, turn left signed *Dove Cottage*.

Just before the hump-backed bridge over the Grantham Canal,
follow the road round to the right (picnic spot) and continue to follow
it as it winds through **Plungar**, following signs for *Barkestone and
Redmile* along Barkestone Lane. Go through **Barkestone**, then follow
signs left and right to *Redmile*; the road becomes Redmile Lane. At the
T-junction turn left, signed *Whatton*, then at the next crossroads after
about 2 miles turn left, signed *Sutton*. Go through **Sutton** and on to
Granby. At the crossroads in **Granby** by the church, turn right onto
Main Street, signed *Barnstone*. Leave Granby down hill and at the foot
of the hill, turn left, signed *Barnstone*. Follow the road through
Barnstone to **Langar** where you go straight on at the crossroads,
signed *Langar village*. The Wildflower Farm, off to the left at this
crossroads, has a tea shop. Follow the road round to the left past the
Post Office, then at the T-junction at the Unicorn's Head, turn right
signed *Colston Bassett*. After nearly 2 miles, turn right, unsigned. In
Tithby, turn left at the minor crossroads just before the church,
signed *Cropwell Butler*. At the T-junction on the outskirts of **Cropwell
Butler**, turn right (signed *Radcliffe*, visible on the right only after you
have turned). Follow the road round to the right past the Plough Inn,
then at the walled village green, by the pump, turn left, signed
Radcliffe (the sign is just past the junction). Go straight on at the
crossing of the A46, into a minor road, signed *Radcliffe*.

On the outskirts of **Radcliffe-on-Trent**, go straight on on Cropwell
Road at the traffic light-controlled crossing of the A52, then turn left

at the crossroads in the centre of Radcliffe, signed *Nottingham*. This is Main Road. After about ½ mile, just after passing the Cliffe Inn on the left, turn right into The Green (marked as a '*No through road*'); this bears round to the left and becomes Holme Lane. Continue straight on through **Holme Pierrepont** – the road is rough for a stretch before Holme Pierrepont Hall on the right, and there are some sharp traffic-calming humps on the tarmac section. Pass the National Water Sports Centre and camping site after about 1½ miles, then take the first turn right into Adbolton Lane, signed *Adbolton*. Continue along Adbolton Lane which becomes Trent Boulevard. At the traffic lights, go straight on on Radcliffe Road, signed *Trent Bridge* to return to **Trent Bridge, Nottingham**.

35

continued

Start: Trent Bridge, south side (GR 582 382) (This has been a starting-point for cycle outings for well over a century: the CTC Monthly Gazette of 1894 mentions rides starting there!)

Distance: 36 miles

Terrain: the route has three short off-road sections of which one, the RUPP from Clipston to the A46, can be very muddy. This section can be avoided by keeping to surfaced roads via Cotgrave. The countryside is never more than gently rolling, although there is a steepish little pitch up towards Clipston-on-the-Wolds.

Refreshment opportunities: most of the villages have pubs that serve food. The Wildflower Farm at Langar has a tea shop.

Ordnance Survey maps: Landranger sheet 129 Nottingham and Loughborough; Explorer sheet 260 Nottingham.

Public transport links: Midland Main Line, Central Trains and Robin Hood Line trains serve Nottingham station, just under 1 mile from Trent Bridge.

Other routes: This is the only route that starts and finishes at Trent Bridge. However, several start from Nottingham Midland Station, which is just under a mile away. The outward leg of route **6**, which starts and finishes at the station, crosses the A612 about 200yds north of Trent Bridge – just turn right to cross the bridge. Probably the most pleasant way to reach the station from Trent Bridge is to join the riverside path a short distance towards the boathouses (or continue on it at the end of this route), pass back under Trent Bridge and cross the suspension bridge to The Embankment. Turn left on the Embankment as far as the roundabout by the north side of Wilford Bridge. (This roundabout has unusual priorities: take care.) Take the fourth exit (including the bridge) into Queens Walk, a shared pedestrian and cycle route to the station. In the other direction, turn left at the station exit and follow the outward section of route **6** to the suspension bridge; cross the bridge and continue along the riverside path which is the outgoing leg of this route. City route **10**, and longer routes **32**, **33** and **36** also start and finish at Nottingham station. Route **40**, the linear route from Newark, finishes at Nottingham station. Link route **L5** joins Nottingham station to the short route round the Attenborough Nature Reserve, route **1**. Route **36** overlaps this one for part of the outgoing and return route near the start and for a mile or two near Colston Bassett.

45 miles • mostly on-road • fairly flat • Nottingham

The Grantham Canal

This route follows the towpath of the Grantham Canal as far as Hickling, then continues on country roads which cross this waterway from time to time. The Grantham Canal was opened over 200 years ago, in spring 1797, and ran from the River Trent at Nottingham to Grantham. The canal thus linked Grantham to a major waterway and the sea, a valuable connection at a time when land transport was slow and laborious. Despite the coming of the railways, which killed off many canals, this one carried commercial traffic for 132 years before being closed in 1929. Subsequently most of the humpback bridges were demolished and replaced by concrete culverts, effectively putting paid to continuous navigation. A restoration society has ambitious plans to re-open it as a navigable waterway but faces many difficulties since not only bridges but locks have been concreted in. Nevertheless, some locks at least have been restored. The abandoned canal has become a wildlife haven, some of it even designated a Site of Special Scientific Interest, and re-opening will need to be sympathetic if this is not to be endangered. Parts of the towpath, including the section used for this route, have been improved with a crushed stone surface making it eminently suitable for cycling, which is specifically permitted with a free permit (see p198) over the whole length of the canal.

The first part of the towpath from West Bridgford is scenic but ends rather ignominiously where it meets a supermarket car park, while the canal suffers the indignity of being in a pipe under the A52. Beyond the main road, there is a fine stretch of towpath, which the route follows for around ten miles. Although it is all easily ridable, don't expect towpath riding to be particularly fast. The towpath goes through Cotgrave Country Park, an attractively landscaped area with a lake and woodland, formerly the site of Cotgrave Colliery. It then passes near the village of Cropwell Bishop, which, like Colston Bassett on the

138

return leg of the route, is a producer of delicious Stilton cheese, which you can buy direct from the dairy. (There are others in the Leicestershire villages of Harby, on route 35, and Hose nearby.) The famous blue cheese was never actually made at Stilton – which is just south-west of Peterborough – but in Vale of Belvoir villages like this. In fact, the cheese has to be made in a closely defined area to be allowed to bear the Stilton name – similar to *appellation contrôlée* wines in France – and is the only

36
continued

Grantham Canal mile post

British cheese to enjoy this status. It gained its name and fame by being transported eastwards and then sold at the inn at Stilton to the many passing travellers on the Great North Road. Before reaching Kinoulton the towpath leads round a sharp bend somewhat imaginatively named the Devil's Elbow. Here it crosses a bridleway bordered by a striking avenue of poplars (currently being replanted because of disease) leading from Vimy Ridge Farm. Until the end of the first world war, the farm was known as Pasture Hill Farm, but was renamed by the owner in memory of his son, killed in action in 1916 during the fighting at Vimy Ridge in northern France. He also planted the avenue of some 188 poplars, supposed to be one for every officer killed in the same action.

In the next village, Hickling, the most prominent feature is the large basin of the Grantham Canal, now cleared and restored. It has 'resident' flocks of ducks and swans and makes a fine summer picnic spot.

Shortly after this, the route leaves the flat country (and – for about ten miles – Nottinghamshire) to climb up to the Belvoir ridge. Before taking up the reward for your earlier efforts by swooping down the open hill to Long Clawson, pause to take in the stunning view out over the Vale of Belvoir – extending right across to Lincoln Cathedral on a clear day. From here, after crossing the Grantham Canal once again between Long Clawson and Colston Bassett, it's a mainly gentle run in through vale villages to return to Nottingham beside the Trent.

36

continued

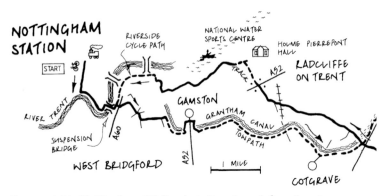

From outside Nottingham Midland station, turn left and
then almost immediately right to cross the road and
join the signed cycle route on Queens Bridge Road. Use
the double set of cyclists' traffic lights to cross Meadows
Way and Waterway Street, then proceed straight on along Queen's
Walk cycle track. At the roundabout near Wilford Toll Bridge, take the
second exit, passing through the gates and along The Embankment
for about ¾ mile. Keep the river on your right and then turn right
over the pedestrian and cyclists' suspension bridge to cross the River
Trent, bearing very sharp left at the far side of the bridge to continue
along the river bank for a short distance. Turn right, through the gap
between houses marked by a cycle route sign for *West Bridgford Town
Centre*, and use the cyclists' traffic-lights to cross the dual
carriageway into Millicent Road. Go straight on at the crossroads,
continuing along Millicent Road, then right at the T-junction with
Bridgford Road. As you approach **West Bridgford** town centre, go
straight ahead at the mini-roundabout where Bridgford Road becomes
Central Avenue. Straight on again at a second mini-roundabout after
a short distance, into Gordon Road. Take the third turning on the left,
Eltham Road, and straight on where this crosses Abbey Road. At the
end, where Buckfast Way bears off to the right, go straight on to join
the **Grantham Canal**.

Turn right along the towpath for ¾ mile, until the path rises up to
meet a road – the canal itself passes through a culvert under the A52.
Turn left on the service road running parallel to the A52 and right
after 400yds into Windermere Close, at the end of which a bridleway
passes through a gap in a fence onto a tarred road: bear right on this
road, continuing straight on at the end to cross the A52 with the aid
of a toucan (shared-use, signalled) crossing. Turn right on the far side
of the main road, to a T-junction after about 300yds where you turn

left onto Tollerton Lane. A short distance along this lane leave the road, bearing left to rejoin the Grantham Canal towpath. Follow the towpath for approximately 10 miles, crossing several minor roads, passing through **Cotgrave Country Park** and under the A46 Fosse Way, until you reach **Hickling**, where the canal widens to form **Hickling Basin**.

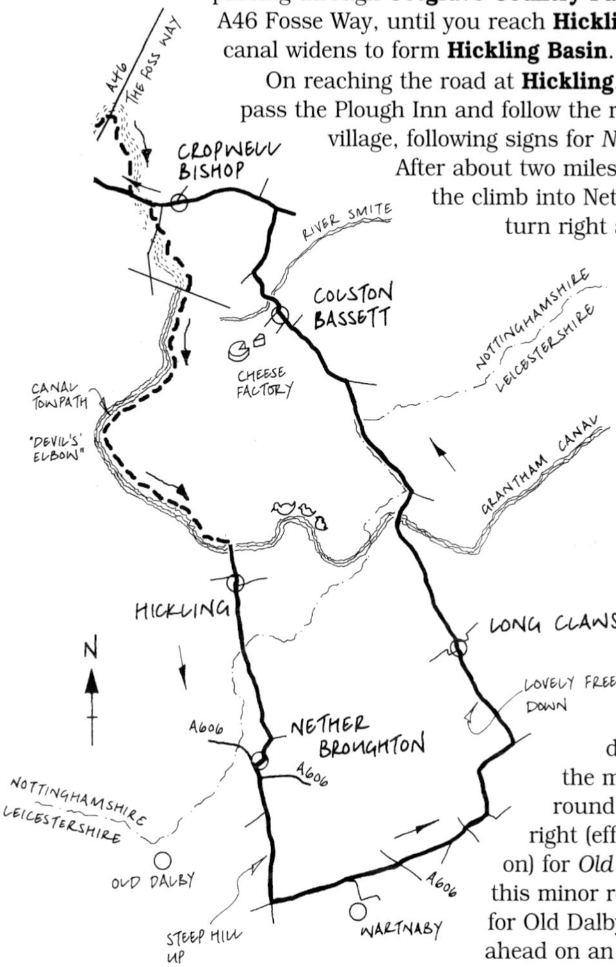

36
continued

On reaching the road at **Hickling**, turn right to pass the Plough Inn and follow the road through the village, following signs for *Nether Broughton*. After about two miles, at the top of the climb into Nether Broughton, turn right at the T-junction near the church, signed *Village Centre*. Turn right again in the centre of **Nether Broughton**, up Chapel Lane – following signs for the *A606*. Turn left at the T-junction with the A606 and, after a short distance where the main road bears round to the left, turn right (effectively straight on) for *Old Dalby*. Where this minor road bears right for Old Dalby, carry straight ahead on an even more minor road, signed as a left turn for *Saxelbye*. Climb the main hill of the route – quite a steep one – then turn left at the crossroads signed *Wartnaby*. Continue along the ridge for 1½ miles, to go straight across the A606, signed *Eastwell*, then bear left at the shallow T-junction for *Long Clawson*. Do not take the first turning on the left for Long Clawson, but the second one, after a

141

36

continued

further 1¼ miles, which is also signed for *Long Clawson*.

On reaching **Long Clawson** at the foot of this superb downhill swoop, turn right at the junction, onto Hose Lane, and first left after a short way (effectively straight on), signed *Colston Bassett*. Continue along this lane for some 2½ miles, crossing the Grantham Canal after 1½ miles, following signs for *Colston Bassett*, then left at the T-junction and on into **Colston Bassett**. Go past the Stilton cheese creamery, then turn right where the road bears left into Church Gate. Go down the hill and over the River Smite and up Spring Hill, then right at the T-junction signposted *Cropwell Bishop*, and left at the next T-junction, again signed *Cropwell Bishop*.

Passing through the village of **Cropwell Bishop** you cross the canal again, but continue on the road to the A46 (Fosse Way). Cross straight over the A46 (with the aid of traffic signals), then over the canal again at Mann's Bridge after a short distance. Proceed straight on along the road, eventually to meet the A52 at a signalled junction. For the last half mile a shared pedestrian and cycle route runs beside the road. Just before the lights a blue sign directs the cycle/pedestrian path to the right-hand side of the road. Follow the direction signs and use the push-button 'toucan' crossing to cross the main road. Do not follow the cycle route sign on the far side but go straight on onto a mainly unsurfaced farm track, which is quite bumpy in places and brings you out near Holme Pierrepont Hall. Turn left opposite the gates to the Hall, past the National Water Sports Centre and campsite, then right into Adbolton Lane. Take the first right – Adbolton Grove – as you enter the built-up housing area. Turn left at the bottom of Adbolton Grove, into Holme Road, and after 600yds follow the cycle route signed for the Meadows and City Centre, which bears off to the right across open ground. This cycle route meets the River Trent, where you turn left along the bank, and follow it under Lady Bay Bridge, past Nottingham Forest football ground, and under Trent Bridge. Cross the river using the cycle/pedestrian suspension bridge, just past County Hall, and retrace your route to Nottingham Midland station via the Embarkment and Queen's Walk cycle track.

Start: Nottingham Midland station (GR 574393)

Distance: 45 miles

36
continued

Terrain: Fairly flat but with one significant hill, and mostly on-road but there is one fairly lengthy off-road section – on the towpath of the Grantham Canal – and a couple of other shorter ones.

Refreshment opportunities: The route also passes through a number of villages with pubs and small grocery shops.

Ordnance Survey maps: Landranger sheet 129 Nottingham and Loughborough; Explorer sheets 246 Loughborough, 260 Nottingham..

Public transport links: Midland Main Line, Robin Hood Line and Central Trains services go to Nottingham Midland station

Other routes: City routes **6** and **10**, and longer routes **32** and **35** also start and finish at Nottingham station. Route **40**, the linear route from Newark, finishes here. Link route **L5** joins Nottingham station to the short route round the Attenborough Nature Reserve, route **1**. This route overlaps route **35** near the start and finish and also near Owthorpe and Colston Bassett.

Route

37
start

45 miles • on-road • mostly flat • Retford

Retford and the far north

As we saw on route 24, north of Retford, Nottinghamshire takes on quite a different character. This route probes further into the geometrical landscape of the drained marshland. Here the great square arable fields are separated by straight drains, while the dead flat straight roads turn apparently inexplicable right-angle bends: maybe they are tacking their way across the often windy landscape, like a sailing boat beating into the breeze. That's not to say there aren't some slight rises on the route: at Gringley-on-the-Hill the route reaches a dizzy 70m – enough to give broad views over the flatter country to the north and west.

The early part of the route follows part of the former Great North Road, passing through several workmanlike but not really picturesque villages. One of these, Scrooby, has a claim to fame for its connection with William Brewster, one of the

143

37
continued

Pilgrim Fathers. Born in the village, he travelled first to Holland with other members of his Separatist church to escape religious persecution, and then on to America on the Mayflower in 1620, to found the state of New England. The connection is commemorated in the 'Pilgrim Fathers' inn but there remain few other links with Brewster. Sturton le Steeple, later on on the route, also has connections with early Separatist church members.

The route leaves Nottinghamshire for rather over two miles to pass through the little coaching town of Bawtry in South Yorkshire. Bawtry may no longer lie astride the artery to the north but there is a fine broad market square with some handsome buildings – and shops and places to eat.

From Bawtry, the route heads north-east – as far as the right-angle bends in the marshland road allow – and after about seven more miles, and the village of Misson, reaches the northernmost point of all our routes. The extreme northern pointed tip of the county lies about a mile from the junction after Beech Hill Farm, just to the left of the track straight ahead which becomes a bridleway. The 'hill' in Beech Hill must be pretty relative, since this is also about the lowest point on any of the routes, at a mere two metres above sea level.

The route continues on its geometrical way to the high levée bank of the River Trent at Heckdyke, then follows the river upstream through West Stockwith, where the River Idle joins the Trent, and on to the fringes of Misterton. Misterton provides a link with one of the great names in Fenland engineering – Cornelius Vermuyden, the Dutch engineer who was brought over in the mid-17th century to drain many of eastern England's marshland areas. The drained land proved immensely fertile and laid the base for the agricultural prosperity of settlements such as Misterton. Later its strategic position close to where the River Idle and the Chesterfield Canal meet the Trent made it a centre for local trade.

From the flatlands of Misterton the route actually does climb, to Gringley on its hill, then runs down to Clayworth. After Clayworth the route climbs again (only a few feet!) away from the marshlands into a more rolling countryside, passing through several villages, including Sturton le Steeple, which – like Scrooby – has Pilgrim Fathers connections. Oddly, the church at Sturton le Steeple has a prominent tower – but at least it's crowned by a dozen miniature steeples! The most notable feature of the next village, North Leverton, is the windmill, dating from 1813, which lies to the west of the village, and is one of the country's relatively few remaining working mills. It's open to visitors at certain times and you can buy stone-ground flour milled on the spot.

37
continued

From the Market Square in **Retford** go north-west along Bridgegate to a roundabout. Go straight ahead (second exit) into North Road, A638, for about 4 miles to **Barnby Moor**. Continue on A638 – the old Great North Road, relatively quiet now that it's bypassed by the new A1 – for another 6 miles through **Torworth**, **Ranskill** and **Scrooby**. (There is a coffee shop at Bawtry Garden Centre, ¾ mile beyond Scrooby.) Soon after the A638 is joined from the left by the the A614, go straight on at the traffic lights to **Bawtry** town centre. At the north end of the Market Place, turn right in front of a prominent red-brick chapel on Station Road, A614, signed *Thorne*. (Jayster's cafe is on the right soon after this turn.) On the outskirts of **Austerfield**, where the A614 bears left, go right, effectively straight on, on Newington Road through **Newington** to **Misson**. (There is a cafe open weekdays at Misson Mill, a small industrial estate on the right as you enter the village.)

At the crossroads in the village centre, turn left on Station Road, following the road for about 4 miles, first round a succession of right-angle bends and then over a level crossing, to join the B1396. Turn right on the B1396, signed *Westwoodside, Haxey* and *Misterton*. At the next crossroads after about 1½ miles turn right to recross the railway at another level crossing. Bear left with the road soon after the railway by Fountain Farm, and continue for a little over 3 miles to a crossroads with the A161. Go straight ahead, on what is signed as a *no through road*, but appears to be a de facto bridleway, to use the swing gates over another level crossing. Continue for about 2 miles – straight ahead at a minor crossroads, signed *Gunthorpe* – to a T-junction with the River Trent bank at **Heckdyke**.

145

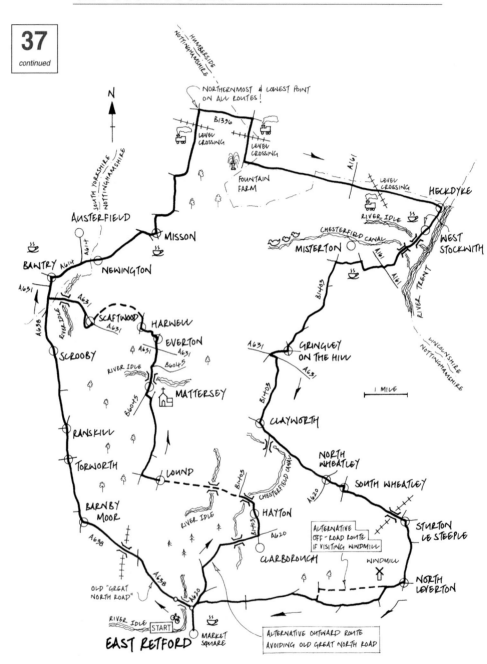

It is possible to avoid the 9 miles of the old Great North Road, to Bawtry by the following alternative, which involves off-road riding and adds about 4½ miles to the total distance:

37
continued

From Market Square, **Retford**, go into Cannon Square, then fork right into Chapelgate, then left into Arlington Way, A638. Turn right at the traffic lights, still on A638, to go up Moorgate. At the top of the hill bear left on a minor road, Tiln Lane, signed *Hayton*. After about ¾ mile this bears round to the right as Smeath Road, which becomes Smeath Lane to cross the **Chesterfield Canal** and reach a crossroads with the B1043 and the A620. Turn left on the B1043, Main Street, **Hayton**, and go through the village past the Boat Inn and over the **Chesterfield Canal** at the far end. After about 400yds, the B1043 turns sharp right; go straight ahead onto a track and follow this over the **River Idle** for about 2½ miles to **Lound**. In Lound, go straight over at the first crossroads (with Town Street) and at the second 700yds further on, turn right, signed *Mattersey*.

On the outskirts of **Mattersey**, turn first left, Job Lane, and then right on Main Street, B6045, through the village. After crossing the bridge over the **River Idle**, bear left where the B6045 goes right uphill, to *Everton*. Cross A631 onto High Street to the centre of **Everton**. Take the second left, Brewery Lane and follow this where it bears round to the right; this is Old Post Office Street. At the end, turn left into Ferry Lane, then in about 100yds, turn right into Chapel Lane. Follow this lane, which becomes Harwell Lane, round to the left to **Harwell**. Turn right, then after about 400yds where the road forks, bear left onto a track, signed *Pasture Farm*. Follow this track for about 1½ miles until it meets the A631. Cross the dual carriageway *(care!)* onto Theaker Lane into **Scaftworth**. At the end of the lane, turn right to rejoin the dual carriageway A631. Turn left on the A631 and follow it over the **River Idle** into **Bawtry**; turn right at traffic lights onto High Street, A638, to rejoin the main route.

Turn right, signed *West Stockwith*, through **West Stockwith** and over the **River Idle** and the **Chesterfield Canal** to a T-junction (almost a staggered crossroads) with the A161 again. Turn right on the A161, then immediately left into Fox Covert Lane. Follow the road round to the right, where it bocomes Grove Wood Road, and past a school. Take the first turning on the left after the school, opposite The Dovecote Cafe, into Gravelholes Lane to its T-junction with the B1403, Gringley Road (unsigned at this point). Turn left on the B1403,

37

continued

towards Gringley on the Hill. At the top of Beacon Hill after just under 3 miles, turn right on High Street into **Gringley on the Hill** village, then at the cross, Cross Hill, follow the road round to the left and then right to the dual carriageway A631. Turn left on the A631, signed *Gainsborough*, then first right (*care!*) on the B1403 to **Clayworth**. Turn left on Town Street, still B1403 signed *Retford* and *Hayton*, but after 300yds at a fork where the B1403 goes over a canal bridge, bear left on Wheatley Road, signed *North Wheatley*, which follows the canal for about ½ mile. Just before North Wheatley cross the dual carriageway A620, signed *North and South Wheatley* and *Sturton le Steeple*, to **North Wheatley**. At the far end of North Wheatley, follow the road round to the right, signed *Sturton, North Leverton* and *Littleborough* into **South Wheatley** and continue for about 2 miles, crossing over the railway, on to **Sturton le Steeple**.

Bear right with the road in Sturton on Cross Street, which becomes Leverton Road and continue to **North Leverton**. At the crossroads in the centre of the village, turn right on Main Street, which becomes Retford Road – leaving the working windmill on the right – and continue for about 6 miles to **Retford**. (An alternative for the first part of this, if you visit the windmill, is to continue on the road past the mill which becomes a broad grassy track, then at a T-junction of tracks by a wood, turn left to rejoin the road into Retford.) At the traffic lights go straight ahead to Cannon Square and subsequently into Market Square by way of the pedestrianised area.

Start: Market Square, Retford (GR 704 811)

Distance: 45 miles (nearly 50 using the alternative route to Bawtry)

Terrain: entirely on road, including some relatively quiet stretches of A-road, and almost flat, except for climbs to Gringley on the Hill and North Wheatley. (The alternative route to Bawtry involves quite a bit of bridleway riding.)

Refreshment opportunities: There are tea shops in Retford, Bawtry, Misson, Misterton and at the Doll Museum in West Stockwith, while many of the villages have pubs serving food.

Ordnance Survey maps: sorry, you'll need three Landranger sheets – 111 Sheffield and Doncaster, 112 Scunthorpe and 120 Mansfield and Worksop

Public transport links: East Coast Main Line trains (well, some of them) stop at Retford, and the Arriva Trains Northern service from Sheffield to Lincoln via Worksop and Gainsborough calls at the lower station at Retford. Note that it takes about five minutes to get with a bike from the station entrance at Retford to the lower station platform, and vice versa. It also involves going up and down steps.

Other routes: Routes 16, 24 and 29 also start from Retford and use some of the same roads into and out of the town.

LINEAR ROUTES

9 miles • largely off-road • gentle • Hardwick or Ollerton

Linear route: Hardwick village and Ollerton by bridleways

Although essentially a link route – joining route 27, Clumber Park and Meden Vale, with route 25, Laxton, Ollerton and Rufford from Sherwood Pines – this largely off-road route is of interest in its own right. It is described in both directions.

Hardwick village to Ollerton: From the telephone box in the centre of **Hardwick** village go south, downhill, and at the end of the houses on the left of the road there is a gate, marked with a low wooden post engraved 'BW' (for bridleway) with an arrow to the left. Go eastwards along this bridleway. The path is well marked with *bridleway blue arrows* on a firm earth-based track. The route first crosses open farm land, then goes through a swing gate with a chain fixing into a short wooded section, to emerge through another swing gate onto the A614 at a layby. *(Do not follow the National Trust cycle route signs in the wood where they bear left up hill.)* Cross the A614, still on the bridleway marked with a *blue bridleway arrow.* The route follows the river valley for about 1½ miles past ***Crookford Farm*** to reach a minor tarred road.

Turn right down a gentle hill for about 200yds and, where the tarred road bears sharply round to the left, continue straight ahead on a broad track with a '*Ford*' road sign. There is a footbridge, which is as well since the ford – of the ***River Poulter***, which has already formed the lakes in Welbeck and Clumber Parks – is quite deep. Continue along this track and after about 400yds the main track bears round to the left. A minor track, which you follow, passes through a wooden barrier and bears round to the right towards a gate marked '*Private – keep out*'. Just before the gate, a bridleway bears left

149

38
continued

following a line of telegraph poles along a fire break. Where the path emerges from the woods it continues as a well-defined path across open fields. About 350yds after the end of the woods it reaches a minor road; continue straight across, signed *Public bridleway*. This is a well-defined compacted track which continues for a little over ½ mile to a point where two well-defined tracks diverge to right and left underneath some overhead power lines (the right-hand track leads to a small enclosure by the road with a 'nodding donkey' oil-well pump.) Follow a narrower path which goes straight ahead to the road, keeping a hedge to your right-hand side.

At the tarred road, turn left for about 300yds to a T-junction with another minor road. Turn right, signed *Thoresby* and *Warsop*. After about ¾ mile, the bridleway version of the Robin Hood Way crosses, about 400yds short of the main road which you can see in the distance; turn left at the wooden 'Public Bridleway' finger post along the edge of a field, keeping the hedge to your right. At the far end of the field the path crosses the **Rivers Meden** and **Maun** by two wooden bridges, again following *blue bridleway arrows*. At the far side of the second bridge, bear right and left, following *bridleway arrows* through a wood. There are occasional clearings to the left then, after about ½ mile, where the main path bears left, bear right round a wooden barrier to emerge from the woods and cross a gravel road. Continue with the **River Whitewater** and a (very) miniature rocky gorge on the right. It is waymarked throughout by *blue arrows*. Keep to the wide sandy track for 1 mile or so to reach a three-way minor road junction.

Turn left on the road and then almost immediately right onto an unsigned, unnamed road with woodland to your left. After about 1 mile, just after the start of the built-up area of Ollerton, fork second right into Walesby Lane (unsigned at this point), over a rise and down hill to the junction with Forest Road, A6075. Turn right on Forest Road for a few yards to the roundabout junction with the A616. Bear right (second exit) on Ollerton Road, signed *Ollerton village*, then shortly first left onto Main Street, **Ollerton** (no road name sign, but there is a sign to the *Watermill Tea Shop*).

Ollerton to Hardwick village: From **Ollerton** Watermill turn left on Main Street up to Ollerton Road. Turn right for about 200yds to a roundabout junction, continuing straight on on Forest Road, A6075 for a few yards. Turn left into Walesby Lane and climb through the built-up area to an oblique T-junction. Bear left for about 1 mile to a further T-junction; turn left and then almost immediately right through a gap in the fence which is signed *Public bridleway* and *Walesby Scout Camp*. Follow the broad sandy track, keeping the

Whitewater stream to the left. The path, marked throughout by *blue bridleway arrows*, goes into a wood, with occasional clearings to the right. At the end of the wood bear right and left, then over two bridges over streams (the **Rivers Meden** and **Maun**). Follow the path round a field, keeping the hedge to your left and following *blue bridleway arrows*.

When the path reaches a minor tarred road, turn right (unsigned). After about ¾ mile, turn left, signed *Clumber*. About 300yds after the T-junction turn right at a *bridleway sign* onto a path through a gap in the hedge. Follow the path beside the field, keeping the hedge to your left, to a meeting of paths and tracks. Continue straight ahead on a now broader path, going slightly uphill still with a hedge on the left, towards some buildings. At a minor road, continue straight across, signed *Public bridleway*, and follow this across an open field towards some woods. In the woods, the path follows a line of telegraph poles along a fire break. At a gate on the left marked 'Private – keep out', bear right onto a path and after about 50yds go round a wooden barrier to reach a more substantial path where you bear left to a ford. This is quite deep but there is a footbridge. Go uphill from the ford to reach a minor tarred road.

Go straight on up this road for about 200yds, then turn left onto a firm track signed *Public bridleway*. Go past **Crookford Farm**, past a 'Private road' sign, with occasional reassuring *blue bridleway arrows*. The path emerges after about 1½ miles onto the A614. At the A614 go straight over into the layby, then through a swing gate with a chain fixing, following *blue bridleway arrows*, through the woods to **Hardwick** village.

151

38
continued

Start: either (Old) Ollerton (GR 653 674) or Hardwick village in Clumber Park (GR 638 756)
Distance: 9 miles
Terrain: mainly off-road and mostly easily ridable with any type of bike, although some short sections near the Walesby Scout Camp are very loose and sandy in dry weather.
Refreshment opportunities: Clumber Park and Ollerton
Ordnance Survey maps: Landranger sheet 120 Mansfield and Worksop; Explorer sheet 28 (270) Sherwood Forest
Public transport links: none really
Other routes: This route links routes **25** and **27**; link route **L8** is an on-road alternative. Route **17** also visits Clumber Park and passes about 400yds north of Hardwick village, while link route **L12** offers a direct route from Langwith-Whaley Thorns station to Clumber Park. **'NCN' Route 6** passes through Clumber Park about 1 1/2 miles south-west of Hardwick village.

Route
39
start

9 miles • mainly off-road • flat • Basford

Linear route: Leen Valley Path from Basford to Newstead

A great deal of work has been put in over the last few years to create 'green corridors' out of the city, following waterways. The River Leen rises just above Newstead Abbey and is dammed to form the lakes in the Abbey grounds. It then flows through Papplewick, Bulwell and Basford until, at Radford, it is ignominiously culverted for much of the remainder of its journey to the River Trent, about 300yds west of Wilford Bridge. At the Basford and Bulwell end a riverside path has been constructed. This route continues this path as far as Newstead Station.

Part of this route follows paths constituting 'National Cycle Network' Route 6 – which didn't exist when the first edition of this book was prepared in 1996 – and might even be thought to have been superseded by it. We have left it in because in places it offers an alternative to Route 6 (see pp29-32) and would

make a pleasant outward route from Bulwell, returning by the
Robin Hood Line or by Route 6.

39
continued

At the T-junction by Saint
Leodegarius' church,
Basford, turn
north (right) into
Church Street,
and then first right again
by the White Swan, still
marked Church Street
although it is a definite
turn. Church Street becomes
Lincoln Street. Shortly after the
left turn of Cowley Street,
opposite Lincoln
Street children's
playground, turn
left round metal
barriers onto a cycle and
pedestrian path (unsigned at
the time of checking), uphill
to emerge into Academy
Close. Turn left at the T-
junction and first right
into Arkers Close, then at
the end of the short close
continue along a cycle path
signed 'NCN' Route 6', down a
dropped kerb, then straight
on across Bramble Close (not
signed at this point). Bear
round to the right when you
have passed **Old Basford Community
Centre**, then past a
concrete bollard
down a path which
runs between a brick wall and black metal railings,
following 'NCN Route 6' signs, towards the B6004. At the
foot of the path (another concrete bollard), keep straight on on the
cycle path which leads you to a light-controlled crossing of the B6004.
    Once across the road, jog right and left to join the path signed

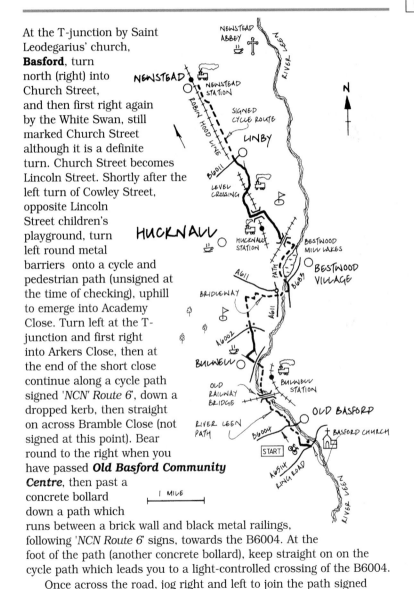

153

39

continued

Bulls' head castings, Bulwell

'*NCN Route 6*' *Bulwell* and *Bestwood village*. Continue on this unsurfaced path, following '*NCN Route 6*' signs, first through a housing area, then joining the **River Leen**. Where '*NCN Route 6*' is signed off to the right, over the river, continue straight on a signed cycle route to *Bulwell Town Centre*. Continue on the path which switches from the left-hand to the right-hand side of the **River Leen**. The path emerges by **Bulwell Station** (Robin Hood Line) opposite the Horseshoe Inn in **Bulwell**, soon after having passed a children's playground with mini-Sheffield cycle stands.

From Bulwell Station turn left opposite the Horseshoe Inn to cross the bridge over the **River Leen**, then bear right across the road into Bulwell Market Square. Cross the square diagonally and bear left up Marketside, leaving Boots to the left and Nottingham Building Society to the right. Pass under Bulwell High Road at the underpass (with black cast-iron decorative bulls' head bollards), following cycle route signs to *Blenheim Ind. Estate* and *Hucknall*, to join Commercial Road. After a short distance turn right at the T-junction, still Commercial Road. Take the first right after about 200yds, Latham Street (the entrance is closed to cars but there is a cycle gap), then at the next T-junction turn left into Ravensworth Road (no sign post at this point) which becomes Squires Avenue. Cross the A6002, Camberley Road/Sandhurst Road, at the traffic lights into Norwich Gardens, and go straight on into Bulwell Hall Park where Norwich Gardens bears left. At the car parking area on the left, where the tarred traffic-calmed road bears left to the golf course, bear right (effectively straight on) on a tarred path past some football pitches. After a short distance the path forks: ignore the spur off to the left and continue straight on.

After Bulwell Hall Wildflower Meadows on the left, and the football pitches on the right, go over a tiny bridge across a minute but very clear stream, then, at the end of the tarred path, go right on a bridleway (no sign post in evidence when the route was checked). Leave an open field to the left, trees to the right, then enter a stretch with trees on both sides. Where the trees on the left stop, bear left on a path to the gap in the old railway embankment, once through the gap you bear right onto a firm-surfaced track. When the bridleway meets Hucknall Lane, A611, turn left on the cycleway marked beside

39

continued

the road, then cross the A611 by the central island, just before the roundabout, onto a path signed *To Bestwood* (***caution: cross tram tracks and railway with care at the swing gates***), then go straight on past a disused mill into Old Mill Close.

Turn left out of Old Mill Close at the T-junction with the B683, Bestwood Road (not signed). After about 200yds, on the outskirts of **Bestwood**, just after you pass under a pedestrian and cycle bridge (part of 'NCN Route 6', in fact) turn left off B683, at the brown *Mill Lakes* sign. Wheel your bike up the concrete channel beside steps (on the wrong side if you're right-handed!) onto a stone-surfaced path in the ***Leen Valley Country Park*** (although everybody calls it Bestwood Mill Lakes). Follow the path straight on through the park, keeping Mill Lake to the right, then through two metal chicane-style barriers either side of a surfaced path to carry straight on on a stone-surfaced path. At the top of a slight rise, bear left with the path (signed 'NCN Route 6') to pass under a railway bridge, then over a wooden bridge across a stream. Through another metal barrier then continue along the path between wooden fences, which emerges into Wigwam Lane (not signed), with a golf course on the reclaimed pit spoil heap to your right. After about a mile, at the top of Wigwam Lane, turn left at the mini-roundabout onto Station Road over the railway bridge, then first right at the next mini-roundabout into Linby Road, signed *Linby*.

(For **Hucknall Station** (Robin Hood Line and NET terminus), turn left at the roundabout at the top of Wigwam Lane, over the railway bridge, and left at the next mini roundabout. This is marked as a no-through road, but there is a gate and ramp at the bottom which enables pedestrian and cycle access to the station and tram stop, avoiding a long detour via the car park.)

After about ½ mile Linby Road passes over a level crossing, then after another 500yds bear left onto a cycle/pedestrian path, signed 'NCN Route 6' to *Linby* and *Worksop*. This passes through a fairly modern housing estate and brings you – after around ½ mile – to the B6011, just to the right of a roundabout. Cross the B6011, jog left and right, onto the cycle path signed 'NCN Route 6'. Passing a wooden barrier you join the ***Linby Trail***. After about a mile, when 'NCN Route 6' bears sharply to the right, bear left to a further wooden access control barrier by a metal gate. Continue straight ahead to pass **Newstead Station** (Robin Hood Line) on the left. For access to the station, continue to the level crossing, turn left over the crossing, then left again to the station.

Helping to create the
GREENWOOD
COMMUNITY
F O R E S T

39

continued

Start: St Leodegarius' church, Basford (GR 553 428). It would also be possible to start at Bulwell station (GR 540 449)

Distance: nearly 9 miles in total; Basford–Bulwell, 2 miles; Bulwell station–Hucknall station, 31/2 miles; Hucknall station–Newstead station, 3 miles

Terrain: the route follows a considerable distance of firm-surfaced cycle track and bridle-way, with some small urban roads.

Refreshment opportunities: the route passes several pubs and shops. There are several weekday cafés in Bulwell and Hucknall and a teashop at Newstead Abbey, about 1 ½ miles east of Newstead station (see route 15) (there is a charge to enter the Abbey grounds).

Ordnance Survey maps: Landranger sheets 120 Mansfield and Worksop, and 129 Nottingham and Loughborough; Explorer sheets 260 Nottingham, 28 (270) Sherwood Forest.

Public transport links: Robin Hood Line to Bulwell, Hucknall and Newstead stations (no Sunday service).

Other routes: The Hucknall–Newstead Abbey–Papplewick circuit, route **15**, follows the same line between Hucknall station and Newstead. Route **2**, Bestwood Park, overlaps for a short stretch at Bestwood Mill Lakes. As noted in the preamble, this route reaches the same destination as **'NCN' Route 6** and in places follows the same line.

Route

40

start

27 miles • on-road • almost flat • Newark-on-Trent

Linear route: Newark to Nottingham – south of the Trent

This linear route links Nottingham to Newark-on-Trent, travelling to the south of the River Trent by quiet minor roads and two short stretches of track. So that you can make a two-way trip, in one of the route information boxes we suggest four ways in which parts of other routes in the book can be combined to make up a similarly quiet route north of the river. Although it's never very far from the Fosse Way, the first part of this route passes through a surprisingly unpopulated countryside. Hamlets and villages are not infrequent but outside these and the isolated farms set in their broad fields

Newark Castle

there is little habitation.

After about five miles a mile of firm-surfaced track leads to the hamlet of Sibthorpe. Prominent in a field beside the track as you approach is a large circular building – a dovecote, the only remnant of a mediaeval religious foundation on the site. The 60ft-high building had nesting places for 1260 birds: the pigeons were used for winter food and their droppings much prized as a fertiliser.

A further five miles on, Car Colston is notable for its two large open greens, the larger – not illogically called the Large Green – covering some 16 acres. The greens were left open for villagers to graze their stock when the rest of the fields were enclosed around 1598, rights which are still exercised. The green also forms a fine setting for the village cricket club's matches on summer weekends. The 'Car' part of the name comes from the old Scandinavian word for 'church'.

The route now heads towards the Trent. One of the most attractive views in Nottinghamshire is to look down northwards from the Malkin Hills, the ridge road linking Radcliffe-on-Trent and East Bridgford, to see the village of Shelford with its prominent church tower nestling in its bend of the River Trent (see routes **13** and **31**). Like Rufford, Shelford is another of those almost unchanged place-names, relatively rare in

157

40
continued

England: it simply means the 'shallow ford' – though the now-managed Trent doesn't look particularly shallow today. Until relatively recently a ferry linked Shelford – where it's still signposted – to Stoke Bardolph on the opposite bank (and it would be very useful to cyclists if somebody would reinstate it). The *Domesday Boke* records the village as having had 250 inhabitants in 1086. At a guess it's about the same today! The now-quiet village had, like many in this length of the Trent valley, its times of turbulence in the Civil War when over two hundred men were slaughtered following a siege of the church tower. The route's final run in to Nottingham is through Holme Pierrepont and then

Nottingham to Newark north of the River Trent

Option A: route 6 as far as Manvers Street, where turn right and follow the marked cycle route out to Netherfield. From Netherfield follow Chandos Street under the Colwick Loop Road (A612) and under the mineral railway line bridge. This road becomes Emerys Road. At the T-junction with the level crossing to the left, turn right through Stoke Bardolph to return to the A612 in Burton Joyce. Go straight across into Main Street, then take the third right, Meadow Lane to join route 20. Follow this route in reverse past Gunthorpe Bridge to Hoveringham, then turn right to follow route 30 to Fiskerton. From here use link route L10 to Newark.

Option B: route 20 as far as Fiskerton, then link route L10.

Option C: route 30 to Mapperley Plains, then right on route 5 (road version) to Lambley. Continue straight on on Main Street, Lambley to join route 20 to Fiskerton, then L10.

Option D: route 30 in reverse via Southwell to Fiskerton, then L10.

onto the cycle route along the south bank of the Trent.

From **Newark Castle** go

158

south-west along Castlegate, follow this round to the left into Lombard Street, then at traffic lights turn right and almost immediately left, signed *Hawton* 1¼. At a small (but not mini) five-way roundabout, continue straight on, signed *Hawton*; this road is now Hawton Road. In **Hawton** go straight on at the church, signed *Cotham*. Continue for about 3 miles through **Cotham**, then at the far end of the village, turn right, signed *Shelton*. At a junction after ¾ mile keep straight on, signed Shelton and Elston, then after a further ¾ mile, just after crossing the bridge over the **River Devon**, turn right at a T-junction, signed *Elston*.

40
continued

Continue for about ¾ mile, then, just after Elston Grange Farm on the right, turn left by the sign for *Firs Farm* on an unsigned bridleway (tarred surface where it leaves the road) which follows a line of electricity poles. Continue past the farm buildings, where the track becomes stony-surfaced. On reaching the tarred

NEWARK ON TRENT

road at **Top Green**, turn right for about ½ mile through **Sibthorpe** (mediaeval dovecote in field on right). At a right-hand bend in the road at the far end of Sibthorpe, turn left, signed *Flintham*. Shortly after a very sharp left-hand bend (a T-junction with a roughly tarred track) there is a further T-junction; turn right, signed *Flintham*.

In **Flintham**, just after the Boot and Shoe, turn left, signed *Screveton*. Continue straight on for about 1½ miles into **Screveton**, following the sign for *Car Colston*. At the T-junction in **Car Colston**, facing the wide village green and cricket pitch, turn right, signed

159

Holme Pierrepont Hall

Fosse Way. At the T-junction with the A46 (which is the Fosse Way), turn left, signed *Leicester*, then after about 300yds, turn right (care!), signed *East Bridgford*. (It is possible to avoid these 300yds of the A46 by going almost straight across at the main road on a bridleway into East Bridgford, but this track is inclined to be sticky in anything other than very dry weather.) At the crossroads in the centre of **East Bridgford** by the church, continue straight on down Trent Lane. The road emerges by the south bank of the Trent, to meet the A6097 by Gunthorpe Bridge.

Go straight across the A6097 (care!), signed *Shelford*, still on the south side of the river. Continue through **Shelford**, then uphill to a crossroads. Turn right, signed *Radcliffe*. After about 2 miles, at the junction in **Radcliffe on Trent**, turn right, signed *Nottingham*, for about 400yds, leaving the church on the left. Just after passing the Cliffe Inn on the left, turn right into The Green, signed as *no through road*. The Green becomes Holme Lane which continues to **Holme Pierrepont Hal**l, where there is a short section of unsurfaced road. About ½mile past the exit from the Water Sports Centre on the right and the campsite on the left, turn right into Adbolton Lane. Take the first right as you enter the built-up area, following the blue and white cycle route signs for the *Meadows* and *City Centre*. This is Adbolton Grove. Turn left at the bottom of Adbolton Grove, into Holme Road, and after 600yds follow the cycle route signed for the *Meadows* and *City Centre*, which turns off to the right round a metal gate and across open ground. This cycle route meets the **River Trent**, where you turn left along the bank, and follow it under Lady Bay Bridge, past Nottingham Forest football ground, and under Trent Bridge. Cross the river using the cycle/pedestrian suspension bridge, just past County Hall. At the road, The Embankment, on the north side of the bridge, turn left to the small roundabout by the entrance to Wilford cycle-and-pedestrian bridge. Go round the roundabout and take the third exit into Queen's Walk cycle track. Continue straight on, crossing two sets of cycle traffic lights to **Nottingham Midland Station**.

40
continued

Weather vane in East Bridgford

Start: Newark Castle (GR 796 540)

Distance: 27 miles

Terrain: nearly all flat, except for the unexpectedly sharp climb up from Shelford, between Gunthorpe Bridge and Radcliffe on Trent, and almost entirely on-road.

Refreshment opportunities: there is a teashop at Gunthope Lock, while most of the villages have pubs, some of which serve food. There are several cafés in Newark.

Ordnance Survey maps: Landranger sheets 120 Mansfield and Worksop, and 129 Nottingham and Loughborough; Explorer sheets 260 Nottingham and 271 Newark-on-Trent.

Public transport links: East Coast Main Line from London Kings Cross and Doncaster to Newark Northgate, Central Trains services from Nottingham to Newark Castle, calling also at Carlton, Burton Joyce and Lowdham (not all services on this line call at these smaller stations, and on some services they are 'request' stops – you ask the conductor when you get on or make a hand signal to the driver if you are waiting at the small station).

Other routes: Route **26** explores some of the villages south-east and south-west of Newark. Routes **13** and **31**, the Bingham circuits, join this route at Shelford crossroads; route **20**, the half off-road route from Lambley and Burton Joyce, virtually joins this one at Gunthorpe Bridge and offers an alternative route back to the eastern suburbs of Nottingham. Link route **L10** joins Newark north of the River Trent to Fiskerton and so to route **30**, while link route **L11** joins Newark to routes **28** and **34** at Norwell.

LINK ROUTES

Note: the figures in brackets after the route title are numbers of the primary routes 1–40 linked; 'RHL' indicates a direct link to a Robin Hood Line station

Route L1 start

³⁄4 mile • on-road • flat • Norwell

Link: Norwell village (28 and 34)

This very short link joins together two circular routes, **28** Southwell Trail and the Dumbles, and **34** the northern Trent Valley, so that they can be combined to make a larger circuit or part of a linear route from north to south of the county. It is described in both directions.

East to west: from the junction by the former Wesleyan Chapel in **Norwell**, turn right, signed *Caunton* and *Ollerton*. Continue through the village, sweeping round to the right, signed *N (for Norwell) Woodhouse* and *Kneesall*. After about 500yds, turn left to rejoin the Southwell Trail route, signed *Caunton* and *Southwell*.

West to east: from the T-junction about 2 miles after Caunton, where the road from Caunton joins the Norwell to Kneesall road, turn right, signed *Norwell* and *Cromwell*. Bear round to the left in **Norwell**, signed *Cromwell* and *Newark*. At the junction just past the former Wesleyan Chapel on the left, turn left, signed *Ossington* and *Carlton on Trent*.

Start: in Norwell village, either at GR 773 618 or GR 765 618

Ordnance Survey maps: Landranger sheet 120 Mansfield and Worksop; Explorer sheet 271 Newark-on-Trent

Other routes: 28 Southwell Trail and the Dumbles, and 34 the northern Trent Valley. Link route L11 joins Norwell, and hence both these routes, to Newark.

162

1¹/2 miles • on-road • flat • Mansfield Woodhouse

Link: Mansfield Woodhouse to Pleasley Vale (RHL and 11)

From **Mansfield Woodhouse station**, walk down the ramp at the northern end of the eastern platform (the one for Nottingham-bound

trains) and turn left, following blue cycle route to town centre sign, to exit beside a steel gate at the north end of the station car park into Oxclose Lane (unsurfaced and unnamed at this point). Turn right on Oxclose Lane then, after a short distance, at a diagonal crossroads where the road bears round to the right, sharp left and left again into Thoresby Road. When we surveyed this route Thoresby Road was being redeveloped and there were no signposts in evidence. Towards the end of this road, just before the railway embankment, turn right into Manor

Mansfield Woodhouse station

Road. At a T-junction, turn left into Vale Road (not signed at this point). Where the road bears round to the right and continues as Brown Avenue, turn left – effecively straight on – on Vale Road. After a short distance you pass under a low railway bridge, where the road becomes Common Lane (not signed at this point). Follow this road for about 1½ miles to join *Pleasley Trails route 11*.

Start: Mansfield Woodhouse station (GR 534 633).

Distance: about 1½ miles

Terrain: flat, on-road

Ordnance Survey maps: Landranger sheet 120 Mansfield and Worksop; Explorer sheet 28 (270) Sherwood Forest.

Public transport links: by rail to Mansfield Woodhouse (Robin Hood Line)

Other routes: Route 11. Routes 19 and 23 also start at Mansfield Woodhouse station.

2 miles • on-road • flat • North Leverton or Treswell

Link: North Leverton and Treswell (24 and 37)

This short route provides a link between routes **24**, Retford round, and **37**, Retford and the far north, so that they may be combined or used to form part of a linear route from north to south of the county – or vice versa. It is described in both directions.

North Leverton windmill

From North Leverton to Treswell: Leave **North Leverton** south on Southgore Lane, signed *Rampton, Newark* and *Cottam*; this becomes Station Road. In **South Leverton**, follow the road as it bears round to the right, becoming Church Street, then round to the left past the church. Continue straight on on this road, ignoring all minor road crossings, to **Treswell**.

From Treswell to North Leverton: In **Treswell**, turn right just after the Red Lion hotel on the left, signed *South Leverton* and *Gainsboro'*. Follow this road into South Leverton, where it becomes Church Street. Follow this where it bears round to the right after the church, then round to the left, becoming Station Road into **North Leverton**.

Start: either Treswell (GR 782 792) or North Leverton (GR 785 822)

Distance: 2 miles

Terrain: on-road, flat

Ordnance Survey maps: Landranger sheet 120 Mansfield and Worksop; Explorer sheet 271 Newark-on-Trent.

164

2¹/2 miles • mostly off-road • gentle • **Worksop Manor South Lodge or Creswell Crags**

Link: Worksop Manor South Lodge and Creswell Crags/Creswell Station (spur off 14)

*Note: do not confuse **Worksop Manor South Lodge** (this link and route 14) with **Clumber Park South Lodge** (route 27).*

This route is a spur off route 14 allowing a visit to the Creswell Crags archaeological site. It is described in both directions.

The route follows a public bridleway which skirts the well-kept grounds of Welbeck Abbey. Welbeck is one of the places which earned the area the title of the Dukeries: it is the country seat of the Dukes of Portland, whose influence in north Nottinghamshire in particular is shown by the frequency with which Portland Roads and Portland Arms pubs crop up in the nearby towns and villages. Most of the current building dates from the middle of the 19th century and is set in a vast park. Creswell Crags lie half in Nottinghamshire and half in Derbyshire, on either side of a small lake. Remains have been found in the caves and rock shelters beside the lake indicating that they were lived in at least as early as late Palaeolithic times – some 10 000 years ago. The caves are not generally open to the public, although guided cave tours are arranged from time to time; there is also an extensive display in the nearby visitor centre, which can also give information on the guided trips. The opening times of the Creswell Crags Visitor Centre – which offers some refreshments (vending machine) – are February to October, daily, 10.30am to 4.30pm; November to January, Sundays only, 10.30am to 4.30pm. On a warm day the lake shore by the crags makes a very pleasant picnic spot.

L4

continued

From the Worksop Manor South Lodge to Creswell Crags: From the **Lodge** follow the bridleway signed *Public Bridleway, Welbeck Abbey*. Pass through two wooden gates, then follow the grassy bridleway downhill across a field. (There are occasional *Robin Hood Way bow-and-arrow* signs.) At the foot of the slope go through the opening in the wooden fence to cross a broad bridge between two lakes to emerge on a tarred road by **Welbeck Abbey**. Turn right, following *bridleway* signs. After about 250yds, at the end of the woodland on the left, turn left on a wide grassy track following the wooden *bridleway* fingerpost. This track follows the edge of a wood and past a playing field, emerging after about 500yds onto a concrete road. Turn right, still following *bridleway* fingerpost, first down a sweeping open concrete road, then along a tree-lined access road for ¾ mile to emerge, once you've negotiated the barrier near the end, at the A60. Go straight across and round another barrier onto a compacted but untarred track signed as *bridleway* and *Robin Hood Way*. At a gate across the path, the official bridleway bears off to the right. Go straight ahead through the side swing gate beside a cream-coloured barrier: this is now a footpath, leading to the **Creswell Crags Visitor Centre**, which is about 200yds down the path.

From Creswell Crags to Worksop Manor South Lodge: From the **Visitor Centre** head east from the far end of the car park to the vehicular access on a footpath for 200yds, passing through a swing gate beside a cream-coloured barrier onto a bridleway. Continue straight on to the A60, around another barrier as you approach the main road. Go straight across, negotiating another barrier, onto a minor road signed as a bridleway, following *bridleway blue arrow* signs and fingerposts. Straight on where another track crosses, and up the hill, now on a more bumpy concrete road. At the top of the incline turn left off the concrete road onto a grassy track, still following *bridleway* signs for about 500yds, past playing fields on the

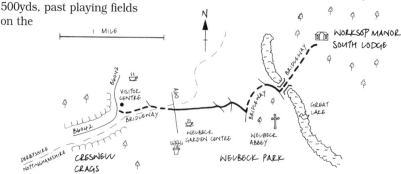

right. At a tarred road on the edge of the wood, turn right and follow *blue bridleway arrows* along the left fork in the road for about 250yds. Where the road ahead is marked as a private entrance to **Welbeck Abbey**, turn left following the *blue bridleway arrows* and *Robin Hood Way bow-and-arrow* signs across a broad bridge between two

Creswell Crags

lakes. Go through the opening in the wooden fence at the far side and up a grassy track across an open field. At the top of the incline at the edge of the wood go through a wooden swing gate, then follow the path to the right parallel to the fence to a second swing gate to emerge at **Worksop Manor South Lodge**.

Start: either Worksop Manor South Lodge (GR 568 754) or Creswell Crags Visitor Centre (GR 537 744)

Distance: 2½ miles

Terrain: almost entirely off-road, some up-and-down

Refreshment opportunities: light refreshments at the Creswell Crags Visitor Centre. There is also a café at Welbeck Garden Centre, ¼ mile south of where the route crosses the A60.

Ordnance Survey maps: Landranger sheet 120, Mansfield and Worksop; Explorer sheet 28 (270) Sherwood Forest

Public transport links: Creswell station on the Robin Hood Line is about 1 mile west of Creswell Crags Visitor Centre – see below

Extension from Creswell Crags to Creswell Station (about 1 mile)

From Creswell Crags Visitor Centre: take the exit road north and at the end turn left on B6042 through the light-controlled section by the Crags themselves. At the junction with A616, turn right (signed *Clowne*) and after about 300yds turn left into Elmton Road (signed *Town Centre, Station* as well as several other places). The station is about 300yds up the road, by the railway bridge. Take the road just before the bridge for Mansfield and Nottingham trains; take the one after it for Worksop trains.

From Creswell Station: go down the exit ramp and road to the junction with Elmton Road (unsigned at this point) and turn left. After about 300yds, turn right on A616 (signed *Cuckney, Newark*) and in a further 300yds, turn left on B6042 (signed *Creswell Crags*) and follow signs to the *Visitor Centre.*

Other routes: Link route **L9** joins Creswell Crags to route **27** at Whaley, and so could be used to reach Langwith-Whaley Thorns station on the Robin Hood Line, though obviously Creswell is nearer.

Route

L5

start

4 miles • on- or off-road cycle route • flat • Beeston

Link: Beeston and Nottingham (1 and 6, 10, 32, 35, 36, 40, L6)

T his route provides a link between the centre of Nottingham and route **1** to the Attenborough Nature Reserve. Link route **L6** continues from Beeston to join route **4**.

From **Beeston Square**, follow cycle route signs to *University* and *Nottingham*, across Wollaton Road/Station Road at traffic lights into Beeston High Road, signed '*Cyclists dismount for Beeston High Road*'. (Cycling is not permitted from 10am to 4pm, Monday–Saturday.) At the far end of pedestrianised section of the High Road, turn right into City Road, with cycle route sign to *Highfields, Lenton, City Centre*. Halfway along City Road pass through the cycle gap in the road closure. At the foot of City Road, turn left following cycle route signs to *Highfields, Lenton, City Centre* along the contraflow cycle lane on Middle Street. At the end of Middle Street, at the junction with Humber Road, cross by the central island to go straight on into Fletcher Road, still following

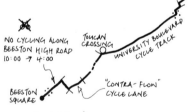

cycle route signs to *Highfields, Lenton, City Centre*. Towards the end of Fletcher Road, bear right on a segregated shared-use cycle track with the *blue pedestrian-plus-cyclist* sign but no direction sign. This runs between fences and winds round gardens to emerge on a road (Lower Road but not signed at this point). Go straight on and, just before this road joins the main road, turn right, following the cycle route signs to a toucan pedestrian-plus-cycle light-controlled crossing over the A6005, Queens Road East, just south of a roundabout.

Beyond the crossing, turn left onto an unsegregated shared-use cycle track along the south side of University Boulevard, with

168

occasional cycle route signs now reading *Tennis Centre, Dunkirk Industrial Estate, Wilford, Clifton.* ('NCN' Route 6 runs parallel, on the north side of University Boulevard.) Follow the cycle track as far as the entrance to Highfields Science Park, then follow the cycle route directions, which are to join the traffic stream leaving the Science Park to cross the dual carriageway of University Boulevard at the traffic lights. At the University South Entrance, bear right on a segregated cycle track now along the north side of University Boulevard. Take the first left into Greenfield Street, with cycle route sign now reading *QMC, Lenton, City Centre,* then first right into City Road, still following cycle route signs. At the end of this road use the double set of cycle/pedestrian traffic lights to pass under the Dunkirk flyover, and at the far side turn right on the shared-use segregated path, which bears round to the left into Abbey Street.

L5
continued

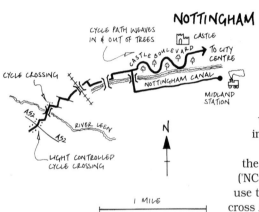

Follow the cycle path over the bridge over the River Leen ('NCN' Route 6 leaves here), then use the pedestrian/cycle lights to cross Abbey Street. At the far side, go left and right into Priory Street, with the cycle route signs now reading, *City Centre, Meadows, West Bridgford.* Just before the dead end of Priory Street, turn left, still following the cycle route signs to *City Centre, Meadows, West Bridgford,* through a gap between fenced gardens, then straight on to a T-junction. Turn right following the cycle route signs onto a segregated shared-use footpath, then after 200yds, again follow cycle route signs to cross by an advisory crossing, signed *Castle Boulevard, City Centre.* Continue straight on between the BT depot on the right and iron railings on the left, under a low railway bridge and between bollards to emerge onto a minor road, with more cycle route signs to *Castle Boulevard and City Centre.* Continue straight on along Grove Road, taking the second on the right, Alderney Street, following cycle signs. At the end of Alderney Street, turn left alongside the Nottingham Canal (more cycle route signs) to go under a road bridge. Immediately after this bear left away from the canal along the cycle path to join Castle Boulevard. For the city centre, bear right along Castle Boulevard and after some 400yds cross by the lights and follow

169

L5

continued

the famous cycle path that weaves in and out of the trees, and then follow cycle route signs to the *Castle and City Centre.*

For the station, turn right along the shared-use path on the south side of Castle Boulevard, then just beyond the HSS Hire Shop take the footbridge on the right over the canal. Follow the curve of the footbridge round to the right, then turn right on reaching the canal towpath and continue along it, keeping the canal on your left, for about ½ mile, leaving at the ramp just after the new Magistrates' Court building up to Carrington Street, almost opposite **Nottingham Midland Station.**

Start: Beeston town centre (GR 528 369)

Distance: 4 miles

Terrain: Mostly on signed cycle route, a mix of on-road and tarred off-road paths, plus a length of improved canal towpath; flat

Refreshment opportunities: Nottingham, Beeston

Ordnance Survey maps: Landranger sheet 129 Nottingham and Loughborough, or Explorer sheet 260 Nottingham. The whole route is also on the AZ Premier Street Map of Nottingham and on the cycle route map produced by Nottingham City Council.

Public transport links: Midland Main Line, Robin Hood Line and Central Trains services go to Nottingham Midland station. Central Trains services and Midland Main Line Turbostar services call at Beeston.

Other routes: City routes **6** and **10**, and longer routes **32**, **35** and **36** start and finish at Nottingham station. Route **40**, the linear route from Newark, finishes there. Link route **L6** joins Beeston to the short, largely off-road, route **4**. This route follows **'NCN' Route 6** along University Boulevard to the Leen Path turn-off.

Route

L6

start

3½ miles • on- and off-road • gentle • Beeston or Strelley

Link: Beeston and Strelley village (1 and 4, L5)

This route is a link between Beeston town centre and the short off-road route **4** to Strelley and Cossall.

Beeston to Strelley: From **Beeston** Town Centre, head south-west on Chilwell Road following *blue cycle route* sign for *Bramcote.* Just before

170

L6

continued

its junction with B6464, Middle Street, and opposite the church, turn right on Devonshire Avenue, passing Broxtowe Borough Council offices on the right. At the head of Devonshire Avenue turn right on Glebe Street and then almost immediately sharp left into Bramcote Road. Cross straight over the busy Park Street and continue to the end of Bramcote Road, which is quite uphill. Go diagonally across Bramcote Drive following the blue cycle route sign for *Bramcote* (and a green *Public Bridleway* sign) to join a walled path which becomes a well-surfaced fenced bridleway between trees across a golf course.

At the far side of the golf course, follow the cycle route signs for *Bramcote* to turn onto a tarred cut-through between houses. Turn right just before the bollards at the end of the cut-through, still following cycle route signs for *Bramcote*, on Claremont Avenue (not named at this point). Claremont Avenue curves round to the left to come to a T-junction; turn right and almost immediately left into Beeston Fields Drive, marked with blue cycle route sign to *Bramcote*. After about 100yds, go straight across Cow Lane into Bridle Road and continue on this road until it meets the A52.

The route goes, or would go, straight ahead but there is no gap in the central reservation of the A52, so turn left for a short distance to a light-controlled pedestrian crossing and cross the A52 on foot, then turn right back to the junction with Moor Lane opposite Bridle Road, and turn left into Moor Lane. Continue on Moor Lane leaving schools to the left. Go straight on onto a well-surfaced bridleway which goes through a cutting, then through a wooded area. This path can become quite muddy after wet weather. Shortly after crossing a humpbacked railway bridge, turn right between bollards in a metal rail fence into Beverley Close (not signed at this point). At the T-junction at the end of this short close, turn left up Teesdale Drive (not signed at this point), then right at the end of Teesdale Drive into Farndale Drive. Ignore the first left turn (Monmouth Close) and then follow Farndale Road round to the left to its junction with Wollaton Vale (not signed at this point).

Turn left on Wollaton Vale, passing Spices Indian restaurant on the left, then bear left across traffic lights onto Nottingham Road, A609. Immediately after the traffic lights, turn right (***care!***) into a minor road, The Moor, signed *Bridleway to Cossall* and *Public footpath to Strelley*. At the entry to Moor Farm on the left, continue straight on, passing to the right of metal barrier onto a well-surfaced track. After about 300yds you reach a junction of bridleways at GR 501 409 *(Route 4: Strelley and Cossall, joins here)*. Turn right, a signed *Bridleway*, to pass a small wood on the left and go through several gates. After about ½ mile at a T-junction of tracks, turn left and

L6
continued

STRELLEY

STRELLEY
CHURCH

BRIDLEWAY

THE MOOR A6002

MOOR
FARM

BUSY JUNCTION –
TAKE CARE!

A609

GONDOLA
PUBLIC
HOUSE

HUMP-BACKED
RAILWAY BRIDGE

BRIDLE ROAD

SCHOOL

A52

SIGNALLED
CROSSING

GOLF
COURSE

BRIDLEWAY

GOLF
COURSE

TOWN HALL

BEESTON
SQUARE

BEESTON

Barton

| MILE

follow this bridleway between hedges until it bears round to the right and reaches a tarred road. **N** Turn left for about 300yds to **Strelley** church.

Strelley to Beeston: From **Strelley** church head south-east (towards Nottingham) for about 300yds, then at the sharp left bend in the road, turn onto a bridleway on the right (where the grass verge has a line of posts with red and white markers). Go through the gap at the side of the metal gate. The bridleway, between hedges, bears round to the left. Ignore the first wide track on the right after about 150yds. About 300yds farther on turn right by the *bridleway* sign with step-over bars at the gateway. Continue straight on for about ½ mile through several more gates and past a small wood on the right to a junction with a wide hard-surfaced track at GR 501 409 *(this is where route 4: Strelley and Cossall turns off to the right).*

For this link route, turn left to head south-east on a firm well-surfaced track, passing to the left of a metal barrier where the track from Moor Farm comes in from the right. Continue straight on to join a tarred road by the entrance to Spring Farm on the left. Follow this road, Moor Road, to its oblique T-junction with the A609, Nottingham Road. Turn left on A609 to the traffic lights where the outer ring road, A6002, crosses. Bear right at about 45° at the lights into the fifth arm of the junction, Wollaton Vale, to pass Spices Indian restaurant, then take the first right, signed as *Farndale Drive leading to Wheeldale Close* etc, then go left into Dentdale Drive which runs parallel to Wollaton Vale, then immediately first right into Farndale Drive. Take

172

the second left into Teesbrook Drive, then first right into Beverley Close, signed as *No through road*. At the end of this short close, pass between some bollards to join a bridleway. Turn left on the bridleway over the railway bridge, and continue straight on at all crossing tracks. Go through a set of barriers at the end of the wooded section and continue straight on on this well-surfaced track until it becomes a tarred road, Moor Lane (not signed at this point), which passes some schools on the right.

L6
continued

At its junction with the A52 the route goes straight on but as there is no gap in the central reservation, go right to a light-controlled pedestrian crossing, cross the road on foot, and then come back to turn right into Bridle Road, which is signed as *No entry* with an exemption for cycles. At the end of Bridle Road, go straight across Cow Lane into Beeston Fields Drive, signed as cycle route to *Beeston Town Centre*. After about 100yds, turn right and almost immediately left, following cycle route signs into Claremont Avenue, which curves round to the right. At the apex of the bend, turn left, still following blue cycle route signs to *Beeston* past a bollard onto a tarred cut-through between houses, then onto a fenced well-surfaced path between trees across a golf course.

At the end of the path go diagonally across Bramcote Drive into Bramcote Road, still following blue cycle route signs for *Beeston*. Follow Bramcote Road downhill, still following occasional blue signs, cross Park Street (give way), then continue on Bramcote Road to its junction with Glebe Street. Turn right, then first left into Devonshire Avenue past Broxtowe Borough Council offices to the junction with Chilwell Road, just before that road meets the B6464, Middle Street. Turn left, following the cycle route sign for **Beeston Town Centre**. The town centre is about 300yds along this road.

Start: junction of bridleways at GR 501 409 (on route 4: Strelley and Cossall) or Beeston town centre(GR 528 369).

Distance: 3½ miles

Terrain: fairly gentle, with a mixture of bridleway and minor roads

Refreshment opportunities: Beeston.

Ordnance Survey maps: Landranger sheet 129 Nottingham and Loughborough; Explorer sheet 260 Nottingham. The whole route is also on the AZ Premier Street Map of Nottingham

Public transport links: Central Trains services (and Midland Main Line Turbostar trains – but see p207) call at Beeston station, about ½ mile south-east of Beeston town centre.

Other routes: Route 1, Attenborough Nature Reserve, starts and finished at Beeston. Link route **L5** gives a route from Beeston to Nottingham city centre. **'NCN' Route 6** passes through the south of Beeston: see route **L5**.

Route

L7

start

2¹/2 or 5 miles • on- and off-road • gentle • Sherwood Pines

Link: Sherwood Pines and Edwinstowe (23 and 7,18, 25)

This route links Sherwood Pines Forest Park to route **23** at Edwinstowe, with an extension to or from Center Parcs' Sherwood Holiday Village, hence giving a fairly traffic-free route from there to Sherwood Forest. By combining this link route with either outward or homeward legs of route 23 it is possible to follow a largely traffic-free route to Mansfield Woodhouse station; the route is described in both directions.

Sherwood Pines to Edwinstowe: From **Sherwood Pines Visitor Centre** car park ignore cycle waymarking and follow *Exit* signs until you reach a tarred road, where *Exit* is signed to the right. Turn right down the slope for about 400yds to the B6030. Turn left on the B6030 and then after about 100yds turn right onto a minor road, signed *Edwinstowe.* After about 1 ½ miles at a T-junction on the outskirts of Edwinstowe, turn left (red stop sign but no direction sign) over the river bridge to the foot of the High Street. Follow the one-way system round to the left up West Lane, signed *Sherwood Forest Visitor Centre.* At the traffic light-controlled junction with Mansfield Road, A6075, turn right, signed *Ollerton* and *Budby* and still signed for the *Visitor Centre.* After about 150yds at the next set of traffic lights either turn right for **Edwinstowe** High Street or left on Church Street, B6034, to follow signs for *Sherwood Forest Visitor Centre.*

Edwinstowe to Sherwood Pines: At the foot of the High Street in **Edwinstowe**, head straight on over the river, then take the first turning on the right, Mill Lane, signed *Clipstone.* Follow this road for about 1½ miles to a T-junction with the B6030. Turn left, then after about 100yds take the first right, signed *Sherwood Pines Forest Park.* Follow the road steadily uphill for about 400yds to a point where the road divides, the right-hand turning being signed *Forest Office.* Go straight on, following the pictorial signs for *Toilets, Picnic area,*

174

Information, past a green barrier used to close the car park at night. Follow this road down to the car park and **Sherwood Pines** Forest Park **visitor centre** (toilets, café, picnic area, children's playground, cycle hire).

L7

continued

Center Parcs to Sherwood Pines: Leave Center Parcs **Sherwood Holiday Village**, and at the S-bend at the foot of a slight slope bear left on a firm-surfaced but untarred track – a concessionary cycle way (there are *No Entry* signs, but these only apply to cars) – keeping Center Parcs perimeter fence on the left. After 1¼ miles, at a cross tracks with an information board marked *'Start of cycle route'*, turn right on a broad forest road, passing beside a green painted barrier and follow the blue and green *cycle route waymark* signs to the **Sherwood Pines** Forest Park **Visitor Centre** area.

Sherwood Pines to Center Parcs: From the **Visitor Centre**, follow the *waymarked cycle route* in reverse as far as the entrance to the car park (which is at the far end of the car park from the visitor centre). Continue on this path, which runs almost parallel to the main access road, to a T-junction of tracks. Turn right, following the obviously more used track (there is a *cycle-route marker* at the junction). Follow this track for about 400yds down a slight slope between tall pines to a crossroads of tracks. (If you are returning from Edwinstowe to Center Parcs and don't want to call in at the Visitor Centre, turn left before the Visitor Centre/Forest Office junction, just after the *20mph speed restriction* sign, across a short stretch of grass to pass between some boulders placed to stop car traffic onto a gravel path. Continue on this path for about 200yds to join the *waymarked cycle route* in reverse. Continue straight on for about 400yds down a slight slope between tall pines to a crossroads of tracks.)

From either route, turn left on a sandy but firm-surfaced broad track (there is a *cycle-route marker* just to the left of the junction on the far side of the track). After about 300yds, at the top of a slope at a T-junction of tracks, turn right (there is a *cycle-route marker* immediately to the right, and there are plenty of cycle-route repeater signs later). Follow this track for about 500yds down a slight slope and pass to the left of a green painted barrier. Almost immediately after the barrier, turn left at a crossroads of tracks (by the cycle route information board) along the concessionary route. This reaches a tarred road after about 1¼ miles. Turn right up the slope to Center Parcs **Sherwood Holiday Village**.

L7

continued

Start: Sherwood Pines Forest Park Visitor Centre (GR 612 642) (extension to/from Center Parcs' Sherwood Holiday Village (GR 637 640))

Distance: 2½ or 5 miles

Terrain: a mix of forest track and minor road; gently rolling

Refreshment opportunities: Sherwood Pines and Edwinstowe

Ordnance Survey maps: Landranger sheet 120 Mansfield and Worksop; Explorer sheet 28 (270) Sherwood Forest.

Public transport links: by rail to Mansfield Woodhouse (Robin Hood Line), then follow route **23** (either outward or return legs as described) as far as **Old Clipstone**, follow B6030 east for ½ or ¾ mile to join this link route, **L7**, to the **Sherwood Pines Visitor Centre**.

Other routes: Route **7** is a short off-road forest circuit and routes **18** and **25** are mainly on-road circuits, all from the Eakring Road car park and using some of the same forest roads. Route **23** is joined by this link at Edwinstowe.

Route

L8

start

4 miles • on-road • undulating • Hardwick or Walesby

Link: Clumber Park and Walesby (25 and 27)

This link joins route **27**, Clumber Park and Meden Vale, with route **25**, Laxton, Ollerton and Rufford from Sherwood Pines Forest Park. It is described in both directions.

From Walesby to Clumber Park: From the Carpenter's Arms in **Walesby**, head north on the B6387, signed *Bothamsall* and *Retford*, then straight on at the next crossroads, signed *Gamston* and *Retford*. After about 1½ miles, shortly after a double bend by the railway and bridges over the **Rivers Maun** and **Meden**, where the B6387 goes right, turn left on a minor road signed *Bothamsall* and *Thoresby*.

In **Bothamsall**, by the church, follow the road round to the left, signed *Thoresby* and *Warsop*. About ¾ mile after the village, and about ½ mile after climbing past a prominent mound on the left (marked on the map as 'Motte' – the mound on which a castle was built) and then

176

L8

continued

going down a gentle slope, turn right onto a minor road, signed *Clumber*. After about 1½ miles this meets

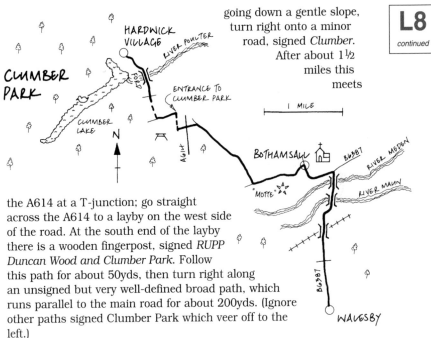

the A614 at a T-junction; go straight across the A614 to a layby on the west side of the road. At the south end of the layby there is a wooden fingerpost, signed *RUPP Duncan Wood and Clumber Park*. Follow this path for about 50yds, then turn right along an unsigned but very well-defined broad path, which runs parallel to the main road for about 200yds. (Ignore other paths signed Clumber Park which veer off to the left.)

The path emerges onto a minor tarred Park entrance road just before two gateway portals. Turn left between the portals and past the barrier into **Clumber Park**. After about 400yds there is a substantial low timber pole barrier on the right. Turn right (no sign) to pass by the barrier and between two five-barred gates onto a firm track flanked by fences. Continue along this track for about 350yds, passing another low wooden barrier about halfway along, to emerge by yet another barrier on a minor tarred road at a bend. Go straight ahead on this road, downhill, passing a metal barrier that closes access to the Park from 9pm to 8.30am. At the bottom of the hill there is a ford – with a footbridge for the wary. Cross this and climb gently to **Hardwick** village.

From Clumber Park to Walesby: Go south from **Hardwick** village, gently downhill to a ford – which has an alternative footbridge if you don't want to ride through. At the top of the rise from the ford on the other side, pass a metal barrier, and where the road bends left, go straight ahead round a low wooden pole barrier on a firm-surfaced but untarred track for about 350yds, passing another low timber barrier part way along. The track reaches a tarred minor road at a

L8
continued

third low timber barrier. Pass round the barrier and turn left on the road to one of the gateways to the Park. Pass between the gateway portals and immediately after, and before reaching the main road, turn right onto a well-defined but unsigned path which runs through the woods parallel to the main road. After about 200yds turn left onto a bridleway path which emerges onto a layby on the west side of the A614 (unsigned).

Go almost straight across the main road onto a minor road with 7.5T limit sign, signed *Bothamsall*. After about 1½ miles, at a T-junction, turn left, signed *Bothamsall*. In **Bothamsall** follow the road round to the right, signed *Gamston* and *Retford*. After about ½ mile this road meets the B6387 at a bend on the B-road. Turn right on the B6387, signed *Walesby* and *Ollerton* to the Carpenter's Arms at **Walesby**.

Start: Hardwick village in Clumber Park (GR 638 756) or the Carpenter's Arms crossroads, Walesby (GR 680 705)

Distance: 4 miles

Terrain: almost entirely on-road; flat except for the up-and-down just south of Hardwick village and around Bothamsall.

Refreshment opportunities: Clumber Park, Walesby

Ordnance Survey maps: Landranger sheet 120, Mansfield and Worksop; Explorer sheet 28 (270) Sherwood Forest

Public transport links: Link route **L12** gives a pleasant route from Langwith-Whaley Thorns station (Robin Hood Line – no Sunday service) to central Clumber Park, while route **17** gives most of the rest of the link to Hardwick village as well as supplying the link from Worksop station.

Other routes: This route links routes **25** and **27**; route **38** is an off-road alternative. Route **17** also visits Clumber Park and passes about 400yds north of Hardwick village. **'NCN' Route 6** passes through Clumber Park about 1½ miles south-west of Hardwick village.

Route

L9
start

4 miles • on- and off-road • flat • Whaley Common or Creswell Crags

Link: Whaley Common and Creswell Crags (27 and L4)

This link is a spur from route **27** Clumber Park and Meden Vale at Whaley Common to the Creswell Crags Visitor Centre. Combined with route **L4** Worksop Manor South Lodge to Creswell Crags, it provides a route into Worksop and an alternative route to and from Clumber Park. The route is described in both directions.

For details of the Creswell Crags archaeological site, see the description for route **L4**.

L9
continued

Whaley Common to Creswell Crags: About 150yds east of the T-junction at **Whaley Common**, turn north (that is, left if you are following the instructions for route **27**, Clumber Park and Meden Vale) along a well-defined firm-surfaced track that runs between hedges. (There is a bridleway *horseshoe* sign at the junction.) After a little over ½ mile the track joins a minor tarred road (Frithwood Lane, but unsigned at this point), at a minute triangular grass green, near a farm (**Frithwood Farm**). Turn left on the road (effectively straight on) for about ¾ mile to a T-junction. Turn right (no sign) gently downhill into **Creswell**, and just after the Black Diamond pub on the left, turn right into Model Village, just before a village shop. Go straight across the grassy oval centre of the Model Village to the large Clubhouse, now sadly derelict. At the T-junction go right and immediately left to pass by the side of the Clubhouse on a little, unsigned road. Immediately behind the building turn left along a path that skirts two sides of a playing field (keeping the field on your right) to reach a railway footbridge at the opposite corner of the field. Go over the footbridge and then down a residential street (Morven Street – not named at this point – which becomes Duchess Street) gently downhill to a T-junction with the A616 (not signed at this point). Turn left and almost immediately right on the B6042, signed *Creswell Crags Visitor Centre*. Continue on the B6042 for about ½ mile to **Creswell Crags** Visitor Centre.

Creswell Crags to Whaley Common: Turn left from **Creswell Crags** Visitor Centre on the B6042 for about ½ mile to a T-junction with the A616. Turn left, signed *Newark*, then after about 50yds, turn right into Duchess Street, and continue uphill, continuing ahead where the road bears round to the right, to a railway footbridge. Cross the bridge, and then follow a path that skirts two sides of a playing field, keeping the field to your left, to reach the opposite corner of the field. The path emerges beside the derelict Clubhouse of Creswell Model Village. Turn right along the side of the building, and then right and immediately left to cross the central grass oval of the Model Village to reach the main street at a T-junction. Turn left (unsigned), passing the Black Diamond pub on your right, and go gently uphill. About

L9
continued

400yds after the end of the built-up area, turn left into Frithwood Lane (otherwise unsigned) and follow this road for about ¾ mile until it reaches a minute triangular grass green, just before some farm buildings (**Frithwood Farm**). Turn right on a firm-surfaced but untarred track, with a bridleway *horseshoe* sign, for about ½ mile. At the end of the track, at a T-junction with a tarred minor road about 150yds east of **Whaley Common**, turn left towards the level crossing visible about 600yds away to continue on route **27**.

Start: either Whaley Common (GR 520 720) or Creswell Crags Visitor Centre (GR 537 744)

Distance: 4 miles

Terrain: a mix of on- and off-road, the latter firm-surfaced track and path

Refreshment opportunities: Creswell Crags Visitor Centre (light refreshments)

Ordnance Survey maps: Landranger sheet 120, Mansfield and Worksop; Explorer sheet 28 (270) Sherwood Forest

Public transport links: Creswell station on the Robin Hood Line is about ½ mile north-east of the Model Village.

Other routes: Route 27. Link route **L4** also goes to Creswell Crags.

Route
L10
start

6 miles • on-road • flat • Newark or Fiskerton

Link: Newark and Fiskerton (30 to 26, 40, L11)

This link joins Newark to route **30** Daybrook to Southwell, which makes possible a north-of-the-Trent route from Nottingham to Newark or vice versa. Other Nottingham to Newark suggestions are give with route **40**. The route description of this link is given in both directions.

From Newark to Fiskerton: Leave **Newark** northwards on the B6326 over the level crossing by Newark Castle station. This road reaches a large and rather unpleasant roundabout junction with the A46, A616 and A617. Unfortunately there is no alternative, but there are shared-use cycle and pedestrian paths which cross each arm of the roundabout individually. Take the second exit from the roundabout,

L10

continued

A617, signed *Kelham* and *Mansfield*. The A617 is quite a busy road but – once again – there is really no alternative. There is, however, a parallel cycle path between the roundabout and the river crossing. Cross the western arm of the **River Trent** and continue through **Kelham** on the winding A617. After about 1 mile, fork left onto a minor road, Staythorpe Road, signed *Averham village only* with a brown *Robin Hood Theatre* sign, into **Averham**. At the next T-junction, after a short distance, turn left, still on Staythorpe Road, signed *Staythorpe*, *Rolleston* and *Fiskerton*. Ignore the turning to the Robin Hood Theatre and continue to a T-junction. Turn left, signed *Staythorpe* and *Rolleston*, still on Staythorpe Road, through the hamlet of **Staythorpe** over the level crossing and past the now-closed power station (but still lots of switchgear, transformers and pylons) to Rolleston. In **Rolleston** bear round to the left, signed *Fiskerton*. After about a mile the road reaches the banks of the **River Trent** at a popular picnic spot and joins route **30**, Daybrook to Southwell, which comes in from the right on a road signed *Railway station* and *Southwell*, in **Fiskerton**.

From Fiskerton to Newark: From Southwell on route **30** at the T-junction in **Fiskerton**, turn

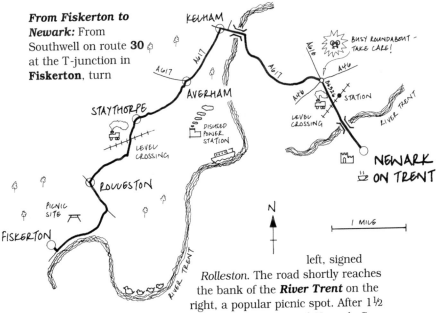

left, signed *Rolleston*. The road shortly reaches the bank of the **River Trent** on the right, a popular picnic spot. After 1½ miles, in **Rolleston**, bear right, signed *Staythorpe* and *Newark*. Go past the now-closed power station (but still lots of switchgear, transformers and pylons) and over the level crossing. About ¾ mile

181

L10

continued

after the level crossing turn right on Staythorpe Road, signed *Averham village*, and into **Averham**. At the T-junction turn right, signed *Kelham* and *Newark* to join the A617 at a second T-junction. Turn right on the A617, signed *Newark A617*, to pass through **Kelham** and over the western arm of the **River Trent**. This fairly busy main road is, unfortunately, really the most direct way into Newark, but it does have a parallel cycle track once you've crossed the river. After about 1½ miles there is a large roundabout at the junction with the A46 and A616. If you are not confident about negotiating this admittedly quite unpleasant junction, there are shared-use cycle and pedestrian paths which cross each arm of the roundabout in turn to join the B6326 and over the level crossing by Newark Castle station into **Newark**.

Start: Newark Castle (GR 796 540) or Fiskerton (GR 737 513)

Distance: 6 miles

Terrain: entirely on-road; flat.

Refreshment opportunities: Newark, pubs in the villages

Ordnance Survey maps: Landranger sheet 120 Mansfield and Worksop; Explorer sheet 271 Newark-on-Trent.

Public transport links: East Coast Main Line GNER from London Kings Cross and Doncaster to Newark Northgate, Central Trains services from Nottingham to Newark Castle, calling also at Fiskerton and Rolleston (not all services on this line call at these smaller stations, and these are in any case request stops: inform the conductor when you get on or give a hand signal to the driver of the approaching train).

Other routes: Route **26** explores some of the villages south-east and south-west of Newark. Route **40** is a linear route linking Newark with Nottingham, south of the River Trent. Link route **L11** joins Newark to routes **28** and **34** at Norwell.

Route

L11

start

7 miles • on-road • almost flat • Norwell or Newark

Link: Norwell and Newark (28, 36 and 26, 40, L10)

This link route joins routes **28** Southwell Trail and the Dumbles, and **36** North Trent Valley, to Newark and the Newark-based routes, and also provides a link in a possible linear route between Newark and the north of the county.

From Norwell to Newark: Leave the centre of **Norwell** southwards on a minor road opposite ***The Plough***, signed *Bathley*. A short distance after rounding a left-hand bend over a stream the road climbs through a wood and then goes gently downhill again. About 1½ miles from Norwell, opposite the entrance to ***Foxholes Farm***, turn right, signed *Bathley* and *Newark*. Go straight on at a minor crossroads after about 400yds where you have to give way, still signed *Bathley* and *Newark*. In **Bathley**, keep round to the right on what is marked on the ground as the through route, passing to the right of the Crown. Ignore the next left turn, continuing straight on to **Little Carlton**. At the T-junction with the A616 at the south end of the village, turn right signed *Sheffield A616*. After about 300yds at a small unsigned crossroads, shortly before the line of pylons crosses the main road, turn left into a narrow minor road. At an oblique T-junction about ½ mile further on, bear left, effectively straight on, into **Kelham**. Continue straight on to a T-junction with the A617; turn left, signed *Newark A617*. This is a fairly busy main road, but it does have a parallel cycle track once you've crossed the river. After about 1½ miles there is a large roundabout at the junction with the A46 and A616. If you are not confident about negotiating this admittedly quite unpleasant junction, there are shared-use cycle and pedestrian paths which cross each

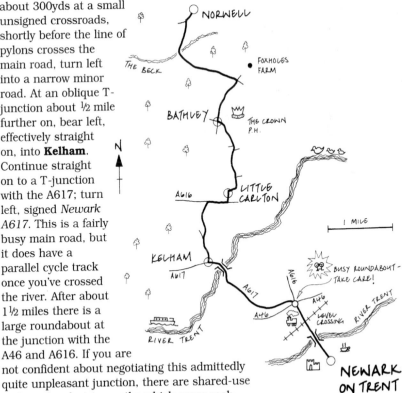

183

L11 *continued*

arm of the roundabout individually to join the B6326 and over the level crossing by Newark Castle station into **Newark**.

From Newark to Norwell: Leave **Newark** northwards on the B6326 over the level crossing by Newark Castle station. This road reaches a large and rather unpleasant roundabout junction with the A46, A616 and A617. Unfortunately there is no alternative, but there are shared-use cycle and pedestrian paths which cross each arm of the roundabout individually. Take the second exit from the roundabout, A617, signed *Kelham* and *Mansfield*. The A617 is quite a busy road but it does have a parallel cycle path between the roundabout and the river crossing. After about 1½ miles, just after crossing the western arm of the **River Trent**, in **Kelham**, turn right on a minor road, signed *South Muskham* and *Ollerton*, and then at the next junction continue straight on, signed *Ollerton*. Take the first fork on the right after Kelham, about 300yds after the speed derestriction sign. It is completely unsigned. At the T-junction with the A616 (unsigned at this point), with an unnamed entrance to a farm opposite, turn right past the village sign for **Little Carlton**, then after about 300yds, turn left, signed *Bathley*. At the north end of Little Carlton follow the road round to the left to Bathley. In **Bathley**, follow the road through the village, passing the Crown on the right. Soon after leaving the village go straight on at a minor crossroads where you have to give way, signed *Norwell*, then after about 400yds at a T-junction, opposite the entrance to **Foxholes Farm**, turn left, signed *Norwell* and *Ossington*. The road climbs steadily through a wood, then drops to an attractive bridge and old watermill, swinging right for Norwell. At the T-junction in the centre of **Norwell** village, turn left, signed *Norwell Woodhouse* and *Kneesall* to follow route **28** Southwell Trail and the Dumbles, or right, signed *Cromwell* and *Carlton on Trent* for route **36** North Trent Valley.

Start: either Newark on Trent (GR 797 541) or Norwell (GR 769 616)

Distance: 7 miles

Terrain: all on-road, almost flat with one hill.

Refreshment opportunities: Newark and pubs in one or two of the villages

Ordnance Survey maps: Landranger sheet 120 Mansfield and Worksop; Explorer sheet 271 Newark-on-Trent

Public transport links: East Coast Main Line from London Kings Cross and Doncaster to Newark Northgate, Central Trains services from Nottingham to Newark Castle.

Other routes: Route **28**, Southwell Trail and the Dumbles, and route **34**, Northern Trent Valley are linked to Newark by this route. Route **26** explores some of the villages south-east and south-west of Newark. Route **40** is a linear route linking Newark with Nottingham, south of the River Trent, while link route **L10** joins Newark to route 30 at Fiskerton.

Langwith-Whaley Thorns to Clumber Park
(RHL and 17, 27, 38, L8)

This link offers a very attractive and entirely rural public-transport-based route to and from Clumber Park (for more on Clumber Park see Route 27). It is described in both directions. It combines well with the homeward leg of Route 17 or the Clumber Park–Worksop section of the 'National Cycle Network' Route 6 to give a route between the two stations via Clumber.

Langwith-Whaley Thorns to Clumber Park: At **Langwith-Whaley Thorns** station go up the ramps from the platform and turn left on the path down to a mini-roundabout at the junction of Main Street and North Street. Turn left on North Street (chicanes and oncoming traffic priority) for about 300yds and then take the second right turn, where North Street becomes *The Woodlands*. This is Chapel Street, becoming Woodland View, then, at an unsigned T-junction by Whaley Thorns Primary School, turn left. The road climbs steadily and at the top of the hill follow the road markings round to the right (no sign) to reach the A616. Go straight over the main road for Holbeck, and bear right just after passing the **Holbeck** village sign, for *Norton*. Take care as you meet an unexpected oblique minor cross roads – no signs or indications of priority – continuing straight ahead until you reach the A60 after about 1 mile. Cross the main road into Infield Lane, signed *Norton* and *Carburton*, and after ¾ mile go left at the T-junction in **Norton** village for *Carburton*. This road skirts the southern edge of the **Great Lake of Welbeck Park**, and towards the eastern end of the lake look out for the heronry on the far shore. After about 2½ miles you reach the staggered crossroads with the B6034; the Carburton Old School tea shop is on the right.

L12

continued

Go right and left across the B-road to follow signs for *Clumber Park*, passing by the hamlet of **Carburton** before reaching the gateway at the entrance to the park. Bicycles are not charged to enter the park. About 200yds beyond this there is a bridge over the **River Poulter**; 100yds past the bridge fork right to pass round a low wooden barrier. Continue for about 400yds then, at a crossroads, go straight on (crossing 'NCN' Route 6) and bear left, following park signs for *Shop*, *Restaurant* and *Chapel*. These three features are about 600yds further on.

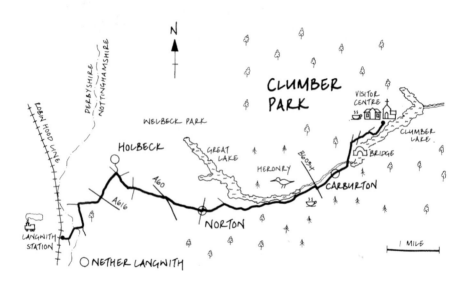

From Clumber Park to Langwith-Whaley Thorns: From the exit from the shop and restaurant in **Clumber Park**, turn left on the tarred road that runs parallel to the lake shore. After about 500yds there is a barrier (to keep car traffic out): go past this for about 200yds to a crossroads with open space to the right; turn left (no signpost), ignoring two cycle route symbols which point straight ahead. After about 300yds, at a triangle of roads, with Clumber Bridge in sight down to the left, fork right (no sign) and at the far side of the triangle go straight ahead, signposted *Carburton* and *B6034* ('NCN' Route 6 crosses here). Continue for about 400yds, passing round the barrier to join the Limetree Avenue road at an oblique junction. Bear left through the gatehouse at the exit to the park to a staggered crossroads with the B6034. Go right and left (signed *Norton, Cuckney*)

and follow this road past **Welbeck Park Great Lake** on the right for about 2½ miles to Norton. In **Norton** follow the road round to the left and almost immediately turn right (signed *Worksop*), and after about ¾ mile go straight across the A60, signposted *Holbeck*. Go straight on at an oblique crossroads of very minor roads and up to a T-junction. Turn left, signed *Langwith, Creswell*, to cross the A616 (signed *Langwith, Whaley Thorns*) and at the next T-junction, after about ½ mile, follow the road markings

L12

continued

round to the left (no sign). Go gently downhill to **Whaley Thorns** and on the outskirts of the village turn right at Whaley Thorns Primary School into Woodland View, which becomes Chapel Steet. At the end of the road, at a T-junction opposite a sign The Woodlands, turn left on traffic-calmed North Street to Langwith-Whaley Thorns station.

Start: Langwith-Whaley Thorns station (GR 529 708) or Clumber Park Restaurant and Shop (GR 625 746)

Distance: 9½ miles

Terrain: all on-road, gently rolling.

Refreshment opportunities: Old School, Carburton; Clumber Park Restaurant

Ordnance Survey maps: Landranger sheet 120 Mansfield and Worksop; Explorer sheet 28 (270) Sherwood Forest

Public transport links: Robin Hood Line to Langwith-Whaley Thorns (no Sunday service).

Other routes: Route **17** Worksop and Clumber Park, route **27** Clumber Park and Meden Vale. Routes **38** and **L8** start from Hardwick village in Clumber Park; route **17** describes the link from the shop and restaurant area in Clumber Park to Hardwick village. **'NCN' Route 6** crosses this route, L12, just north of Clumber Bridge in Clumber Park.

Going for a bike ride

You can ride any kind of bike for most of the routes in this book (though a specialised road-racing or time-trial one with flimsy tyres might not be so good off road) but some bikes are easier to ride than others. Provided your bike is in good mechanical condition – and we give you a checklist later – there are really only four fundamental factors which make a real difference between easy-going bikes and those that aren't. These are your **riding position** (which really means having a bike the right size correctly set up), the **gearing** and **your own fitness** (which determine how easily you'll go up hills), and finally the very simple matter of having your **tyres pumped up**. Everything else is secondary, even the weight of the bike within reason – and your fitness will develop fast once you start cycling.

Riding position and the right size of bike

Your body contacts the bike at five points – two hands, two feet and one seat. Comfort depends on getting the right balance of your weight between these, and making sure that your saddle is at the right height for effective pedalling.

For anything except a mountain-bike, the correct size of frame is about two-thirds your full inside leg measurement, from crutch to ground, measured without shoes. So, somebody with an inside leg measurement of 33 inches (84cm) would need a 22in (56cm) frame. This frame size is usually measured from the centre of the 'bottom bracket axle' (the axle the pedal cranks are fixed to) to the centre line of the 'top tube' ('crossbar'), following the line of the 'seat tube' (the bit of the frame that leads from the bottom bracket towards the saddle). This is really a maximum: what's essential is that you should be able to stand on the ground astride the bike's top tube in front of the saddle without difficulty or discomfort. If you can't, the bike really is too big for you. Sizes for mountain-bikes are usually specified at least a couple of inches shorter than this, and they usually allow a good deal of saddle height adjustment. If you're buying a new bike, a good specialist cycle dealer will make sure you buy the right size. We strongly advise going to a proper bike shop rather than going for the latest mail-order 'bargain'.

To obtain a riding position which lets you pedal comfortably and effectively, the saddle has to be adjusted by moving the 'seat pillar [or post]' (the tube the saddle is fixed to and which fits into the seat tube of the frame) up or down, by undoing the bolt or clamp at the top of the seat tube. The right height, whatever the type of bike, is where your leg is not uncomfortably stretched at the lowest point when pedalling, and not too bent at the highest. Start by raising the saddle until the top is about 90% of your inside leg measurement above the bottom bracket, still measured along the angle of the seat tube: for our 33in (84cm) inside leg example that would be about 29¾ in or 75.5cm. The top of the saddle should be horizontal. You can test the height by getting somebody to hold the bike up while you sit on the saddle and pedal slowly backwards with your heels on the pedals, using shoes with thin heels. Your leg should be just about straight at the longest reach but not so stretched that you can feel the tendons behind the knee pulling. If it isn't, move the saddle up or down by very small amounts, testing as you go, until it's right. When you're riding, too low a saddle can give you an ache in the muscles along the top of the thigh just above the knee; one that's too high makes you roll uncomfortably on the saddle as you pedal.

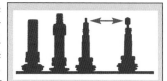

One of the simplest ways to make a bike run more easily is to pump the tyres up. Correct pressures are marked on the tyre wall (see p196).There are three types of tyre valve, shown left to right: car-type Schraeder, fitted to most mountain bikes; Woods, as found on many older bikes, especially roadsters; and Presta or 'High Pressure' (HP), fitted to most sporty road bikes. Each one needs a different pump fitting or connector (though a deep-drilled Presta HP one will usually fit a Woods). Before you can pump up a Presta valve, you have to undo the small knurled top nut (arrowed) and give it a quick dab with a finger to make sure it isn't sticking: this often catches people out as they try to pump through a valve which is still screwed down tight.

When you are sitting on the saddle in the normal riding position, with the ball of your foot, not the instep, on the pedal, your knee joint should be just over or a little behind the centre of the front pedal when the pedal cranks are horizontal – the quarter-to-three position. You may have to move the saddle forwards or backwards by loosening the clamp on the saddle frame wires underneath. If you're buying a new or secondhand bike from a good bike shop, the dealer should sort all this out for you.

For small children who may not yet be very skilled at controlling the bike you may have to set the saddle lower than this so that they can sit on it and still touch the ground with both feet. Once they're confident enough to be happy to start off with only one foot touching the ground you can move the saddle up a bit at a time until they are in the most efficient pedalling position.

Experienced cyclists find the most comfortable height for the handlebars (the whole handlebar for flat or mountain-bike bars, the straight top portion for dropped ones) is a little below level with the saddle. You may well find that you want them a bit higher than this, at least to begin with, although you will still be leaning forward. In any case, for leisure riding you are unlikely to be using the 'drop' part of dropped bars very much.

You may find that the forward reach is not comfortable, quite possibly too long; it depends partly on how the upper half of your body relates to your arm length, while women often prefer a fairly upright position because of the way the pelvic bone structure determines the comfortable leaning angle. To change handlebar reach you need a different length of handlebar stem, which is really a job for the bike shop unless you are sure you are competent to do it – for many types of handlebar stem it involves removing brake levers and any handlebar covering and replacing them afterwards. (Another problem is that diameters of handlebars where they fit into the stem are one of the few things on bikes not yet completely standardised, while mountain bikes can be different, too. Whenever you go to a bike shop for any new or replacement component it is always worth taking the original one with you if you're in the slightest way unsure about sizing.)

Gears

Most modern bikes have variable gears: you can change how far the bike travels for each turn of the pedals. A 'high' gear travels further for each pedal turn, but you have to put more force on the pedals, while a 'low gear' travels a shorter distance per turn but with less force. The object is to change the gears so that you can keep up a comfortable pedalling speed, and comfortable pressure on the pedals, no matter how fast or slow you're travelling. In general, comfortable pedalling rates are between 70 and 90 pedal revs per minute: you may find this seems quite fast to begin with but as you get more experienced you'll find that pedalling briskly seems more natural.

There are two types of gear change mechanism: **hub gears** (which have a miniature gearbox inside the rear wheel hub) and **derailleur gears** which shift the chain between a series of different-sized sprockets on the rear wheel hub and between two or three different-sized chainwheels at the front. Nowadays the number of rear sprockets can range from five to ten, with eight or nine the commonest on new bikes. Remember: bigger rear sprockets and smaller front chainwheels (both are the inside ones) give lower gears, while bigger front chainwheels and smaller rear sprockets (the outside ones) give higher gears. The advantage of hub gears has always been simplicity of use: there are separate click positions on the gear control for each gear. Their disadvantage was that the range of gears was restricted and often the jumps between gears were too big. The advantage of derailleur gears has always been the wide gear range available, while modern ones are now 'indexed' so that they, too, have definite click-positions on the gear lever for each gear. Hub gears are fighting back with new seven and even fourteen-speed versions.

The large number of rear sprockets, multiplied by the number of front chainrings means that modern bikes with derailleurs have enormous numbers of different gears: the three on the front and nine at the back on current mountain- and touring bikes gives a total of 27! This might make it sound very complicated but you do *not* go through the lot in sequence – and, definitely unlike a car, you certainly *don't* work your way up to top and stay there. We think the simplest way to use a bike equipped like this is to use the big, outer chainwheel for very easy conditions, the middle one for moderate conditions, and the tiny inside one for when it's hard – which usually means uphill, or perhaps off-road. Then you can then make your 'fine-tuning' changes to get a comfortable gear changing up or down with the rear gear alone. The aim, as we said, is to be able to turn the pedals at a comfortable rate ('cadence' is the fashionable word) in all conditions, though it feels natur-

Derailleur gearing

Top: big front chainring, smallest rear sprocket = highest gear

Bottom: smallest front chainring, biggest rear sprocket = lowest gear

al to pedal a bit slower uphill (say 50 to 60rpm) and faster when it's very easy. The chain has to be moving – that is, you have to be pedalling – to change a derailleur gear, and it's best to just ease off your foot pressure on the pedals for a moment as you change while still keep pedalling. It's better to change down earlier rather than later on a hill, while your feet are still turning at a reasonable speed. With a hub gear you freewheel briefly to take the load off the gear while you're changing.

If you really do find riding hard, or that you can't keep up a reasonably brisk pedalling rate, then your whole gear range could be too high – this is most likely on sports 'racer'-style bikes of a few years back which were often fitted with the same gear ratios as fit racers used. Discuss it with the bike shop.

Comfort on a bike

Saddles A comfortable saddle is a very personal choice. It has to be wide enough to support your ischial bones at the back (the small bony bumps you can feel by sitting on your hands), while not so wide that it chafes your legs further forward. The distance between the ischial bones varies enormously between individuals and is on average greater for women than for men. A saddle has to be firm enough to give good support while at the same time not being so hard that it bruises. A very wide soft saddle may seem the most comfortable when you sit on a bike in the shop but might well not be after a few miles on the road. The real answer is to try as many different saddles as you can – ones on your friends' bikes, ones on other bikes in the shop – until you find one that suits *you*. Then stick to it – even if you later trade in the bike for another one. Saddles often get blamed for causing soreness – because that's where you feel it – but the cause can be wrong clothing or a too stretched-out or forward-leaning riding position.

Once your riding position and saddle are right, what affects comfort most are riding within your natural personal limits and suitable clothing.

Taking it steady Many people seem to think that once you get on a bike you have to go as fast as you can. You don't: if you were out on a country ramble would you expect to break into a sprint? Everybody has their own natural cycling rhythm and comfortable effort of riding, which are likely to change with experience and fitness. Go at your own speed, especially uphill. If you're with other people who want to go faster or slower, arrange to meet up with them every so often. Don't struggle to keep up – and it's not all that easy to hang back to ride at a much slower speed.

In the same way, everyone has a natural time they can keep up their comfortable level of effort for. To begin with this may be, say, only an hour at a time, followed by a longish rest. At least to start with be prepared to underestimate your strength. You might surprise yourself – after all, four hours' riding at only 7 or 8mph, spread over the whole day with stops, will still take you around 30 miles.

Clothing For comfortable cycling you need clothing that allows free movement, protects from heat and cold and doesn't chafe where you sit on it. You can wear virtually what you like for the sort of routes in this book (OK then, perhaps not a trench coat and wellies!)

Helmets

Cycle helmets have received a lot of publicity – a great deal of it from non-cyclists – over recent years. A helmet can help to protect your head from certain types of impact but it doesn't make you invulnerable. The current tests for compliance with the published standard only require it to protect in an impact at about 12mph – comparable with falling off a bike – and not in more violent collisions with motor vehicles. The view of both Pedals and the CTC is that the choice of whether or not (and when) to wear a helmet must remain a personal decision by the user, or parent or guardian. If you do choose to wear one, then:

● Choose one that conforms at least to the current British Standard (BS6863), or to the more stringent requirements of the American Snell Institute.

● Make sure that it is the right size, properly secured and properly worn. This is just as important for children's helmets as for adults'.

● Be prepared for it to affect the way in which you move your head and hear other traffic at first and take extra care.

● Replace it if it suffers any hard blow or shows surface damage.

● Remember that it is not some sort of magic protection, making you immune from injury: you still need to be just as careful and wary of other traffic when riding.

but it should still follow the same principles as special cycle clothing. Clothes for the upper haf of the body need to be quite long at the back, otherwise the leaning-forward position can leave a chilly gap, and shorts or trousers must be flexible enough to allow full movement. Jeans usually don't, while tracksuit bottoms or loose casual trousers are often baggy enough to rub on the chain. 'Proper' nylon-Lycra cycling 'skin shorts' or tights may look strange or rather revealing but they really are comfortable to wear. Unlike conventional trousers and underwear, they have no hard seams across the saddle area and a special lining which is meant to be worn next to the skin. Wearing seamed underwear inside them completely defeats the object. Obviously, this means they have to be washed as often as you'd wash underwear. These skin shorts also make a good undergarment under trousers or tapered tracksuit bottoms designed for cycling in cooler weather.

The other thing which makes cycling different from walking, and has a big effect on clothing, is 'windchill' as a result of the higher speed of cycling. On a gentle open downhill – even on Nottinghamshire's modest slopes – you can easily freewheel at 25mph or more. If you've just ridden up the hill and are sweating a bit, you'll feel the windchill all the more. Going uphill, cycling clothes – tops, in particular – have to be porous enough for sweat to escape; going downhill, they have to be windproof enough to prevent chilling. The best compromise is to have several thin layers so that you can adjust what you are wearing as necessary. You will soon learn what your best combination is. This windchill from your own movement also means that bits of the body that aren't keeping warm by working, particularly hands and, in winter, feet – can get much cooler than you'd expect. Gloves can be a great comfort even on only moderately cool days.

Shoes for cycling need to have a fairly stiff sole to spread the pedalling load. Special cycling shoes have almost rigid soles but this makes them not so comfortable for walking in, some of the ones with a built-in cleat to fit the 'step-in' ski-binding style of pedal even more so. Mountain-bike pedals, except the 'step-in' versions, are designed to be used with anything up to walking boots.

Whatever anybody tells you, if it rains, there is no way of keeping completely dry on a bike. All that you can hope for is to keep out the worst and keep warm – but not so hot that you get even wetter by sweating. Some people find tops made out of one of the 'breathable' fabrics that are supposed to let moisture out effective (Gore-Tex is the best-known), others find them too clammy. It is cold from chilling that is the main discomfort of being damp. If you can stay warm until you can change into dry clothing you'll have won the battle.

Clothing, tools, food, and anything else you want to take with you, have to be carried. The best place for any load is generally on the bike, not on your back. Some mountain-bikers prefer a small securely-held backpack or water-carrier – partly because it's not always easy to fit bags to a full-suspension bike. On the road, though, bike-mounted loads, with bags on a proper carrier rack or even a front basket or bag, are more comfortable.

Servicing your bike

Bikes don't have a regular servicing schedule like cars. Perhaps they should – so we suggest the following (with any of these, if you don't feel competent to carry out the work yourself get a good bike shop to give the machine the once-over).

Before using a bike, particularly if it hasn't been used for some time, and also at intervals of a couple of months:

● Check that tyres, brake cables, transmission (front chain-wheel, chain, gears, rear sprockets) and wheels are in a good state of repair. Tyres should be checked for holes, bulges and twists; if in any doubt, buy new ones. Brake cables should operate smoothly with no stiffness or grating. Again, if in doubt lubricate or if necessary replace them. Brake blocks or pads (on brakes that act on the wheel rim) should have at least ¼ in (5–6mm) of thickness left. Wheels should be true (that is to say, the rim shouldn't wobble from side to side when you spin the wheel), with their full number of spokes evenly tensioned, and wheel hubs should run smoothly with no crackling or grating. The chain and gearing should not be so worn that you feel unevenness or grinding when you ride.

● Check that bolted-on components, such as brake mechanisms where they attach to the frame, brake levers where they are fitted onto the handlebars, mudguards, the saddle where it fits onto the seat pillar, the seat pillar where it fits into the frame, lights, carriers or baskets, are all tightly fixed. Check that wheel hubs are tightly bolted to the frame, or firmly clamped by 'quick-release' mechanisms. Check also that the handlebar stem cannot be easily twisted out of line with the front wheel: it should be exactly lined up with the front wheel and the saddle should be exactly lined up with the top tube of the frame.

● On a bike with a single gear or a hub gear, check that the back wheel is far enough back for the chain to be reasonably tight. You have to undo the wheelnuts with a spanner to do this. The correct adjustment is when you can move the chain up or down about half an inch midway between the front chainwheel and the rear hub. After this, you may have to readjust a hub gear: if you don't know how, ask your bike shop.

● Check that bearings – wheel hub, bottom bracket, pedals, steering head – are correctly adjusted. They should rotate freely and smoothly but at the same time not be loose. (Some of these bearings nowadays contain sealed ball-races that are effectively maintenance-free.)

● Check that brakes are correctly adjusted and working. The levers should pull the brakes firmly onto the rim within about the first half of their possible movement, long before they pull up against the handlebar. The law – as well as common sense – requires you to have an efficient brake operating on each wheel. (There are slightly different regulations for very small children's bikes, tricycles and 'fixed-wheel' bikes with no freewheel.)

Every few times you go out:

● Lubricate, with a medium oil, the chain and exposed bearings or sliding surfaces: where bare cable wires go through stops or guides or over pulleys, bearing pivots of derailleur gear mechanisms, front or rear. Don't overdo it: each, even a chain needs no more than a drop or two. Too much oil can run down spokes or spatter onto the tyres and rims. The need for lubrication varies with the weather, particularly rain.

Every time you go out:

● Check that tyres are pumped up correctly. The correct pressure is moulded on the side of the tyre, but you need a pump with a gauge, or a separate pressure gauge, to check these. If in doubt, get the shop to pump them up with a 'track pump' which has a gauge and then get used to how hard that feels between finger and thumb. (If you or your family have several bikes it could well be worth investing in your own track pump.)

● Quickly check the tyres for bulges or twisted sections, major cuts in the tread or sidewall, and for glass or thorns.

● Spin the wheels to make sure that they're not touching the brakes or mudguards.

● Check that there is no stiffness or jerkiness in the steering (lift the front wheel off the ground and try turning the handlebars).

● Check that the chain is lightly lubricated (but not too much).

● Check that the brakes work.

Where you can cycle

By right

● On any **public roads** that are not motorways (in Nottinghamshire, that's the M1, west and north-west of Nottingham, and the A1(M) Doncaster bypass north of Blyth), nor on which there is a valid no cycling order. These latter are marked by the standard 'no cycling' sign: a red circular sign with a black bicycle symbol on a white background. They are usually either short sections of heavily-trafficked road, such as the section of the A52 from the Dunkirk flyover to the Derby Road roundabout in Nottingham, or pedestrianised streets. For the major part of our routes we have chosen quiet minor roads.

● On **designated cycle tracks**. These are marked by a blue circular sign with a white bicycle symbol, if for cyclists only, and with pedestrian figures in addition if the path is for the use of both cyclists and pedestrians. Rectangular blue signs with a white cycle symbol are recommended cycle routes on roads used by other traffic, generally quiet residential roads. We have incorporated quite a number of both urban and rural cycle tracks into our routes where we can. One long-distance cycle route, Route 6 of the 'National Cycle Network' completed in millennium year runs from north to south through Nottinghamshire and is described in a special section of this guide.

● On **bridleways** – but you must be prepared to give way to walkers and horse-riders if necessary. Bridleways are usually marked at either end and at most road crossings by finger posts reading 'Public bridleway' or 'Bridleway'. In addition, they may be waymarked by small blue arrows. Sometimes a bridleway follows the line of a private road, and sometimes the 'Private Road' sign is a lot more prominent than the bridleway one – presumably deliberately; nevertheless you are entitled to ride a bicycle on the bridleway. Oddly, you are not in theory allowed to ride a tricycle or anything with even more wheels on a bridleway!

Legal entitlement to ride doesn't mean it's always physically possible, though: a bridleway's surface may be muddy, badly rutted or even rocky. Surfaces can vary with the weather and season: very muddy in winter and after wet weather, or with hoofmarks baked into ridges like concrete in a drought. Vegetation, such as nettles, can make them very narrow in summer. As far as possible, where we use bridleways as parts of our routes they are ridable using conventional bikes at most seasons, though you might have to walk short sandy stretches. If we think any on our routes are only really suitable for mountain-bikes, we say so.

There is another classification, 'road used as public path' (often shortened to RUPP). These are steadily being reclassified as footpaths, bridleways or 'byways open to all traffic' (which naturally get shortened to BOAT). (A byway is defined as a road which the highway authority is not obliged to keep surfaced.) You may take it that you can cycle on any remaining RUPPs, and of course on any which have been reclassified as bridleways or byways. Surface quality varies as much as any other path.

The position on cycling on country public footpaths is ill-defined. You certainly have no legal right, as with a bridleway, but nevertheless riding on one is not a criminal offence, though you leave yourself open in theory to proceedings for trespass. Probably more important is the damage you may cause to goodwill between cyclists as a whole and landowners and walkers. It's also worth noting that, while a bridleway must not legally have any obstructions that a horse can't negotiate, such as stiles, you are very likely to meet them on footpaths. You may *not* ride legally on a footway beside a road (the pavement) except to cross it or if it is signed for shared pedestrian and cycle use.

As a privilege

● On certain **designated canal towpaths**, with a permit from British Waterways. These permits are free and are obtainable

CYCLE CODES OF CONDUCT

Riding on the road

● Make sure that your bike is safe to ride – read the servicing advice on pp195-197.

● Ride on the left of the road – but don't cringe in the gutter. If you ride about 18 inches out from the kerb you won't have to swerve round drains or debris that accumulate there.

● Remember that you are part of the traffic. Ride in a straight line as far as possible, don't weave in and out of lanes or round parked cars. If there are many parked cars, follow the overtaking line unless traffic density makes it essential to pull in between them. When passing parked cars with people in them look out for the possibility of a door opening unexpectedly (it's an offence but it happens).

● Act predictably by obeying traffic lights, no entry signs etc, and being in the right part of the road for any manoeuvre you may want to make. Don't block a left-turn-only lane at traffic lights or other junctions if you're going straight ahead. Get into the proper right-turn lane for a right turn if you're confident enough; if you're not, it may be better to get off your bike and walk across to where you want to be.

● Signal if you're going to change direction – but look behind in good time first to make sure it's safe. If you can, look directly at, and catch the eye of, whoever you're signalling to.

● Be conspicuous in your positioning on the road. All vehicles have blind spots behind door and window pillars and so on. Don't creep into a place where a van, lorry or bus driver can't see you.

● Don't go to the left of a vehicle, moving or stopped, that's signalling a left turn. Don't go to the left of a bus near a bus stop and keep an eye out for people hailing taxis from the kerb.

● In slow-moving traffic don't ride into a gap between long vehicles which could close before you get to the front.

● Expect drivers to do daft things. They shouldn't, of course – but they do. Don't get angry!

● Use your ears as well as your eyes, and make use of every scrap of available evidence as to what's going on around you – reflections in shop windows, feet moving between parked cars and so on. Don't muffle your ears with a personal stereo.

● Use lights after sunset.

● Don't try to race other traffic – including other cyclists.

Riding off-road

Several bodies have issued codes of practice for cycling off-road in both town and country. The points below are condensed from these. The main point to remember is that you have to share with walkers on urban shared-use paths, and with walkers and horse-riders on bridleways and byways.

● Give way as appropriate and when necessary to pedestrians and horse-riders – be prepared to slow down when approaching them.

● Let pedestrians and riders know that you are there, say with the gentle verbal warning. Don't surprise them – many pedestrians may be hard of hearing, while horses often shy at the mere sight of a bicycle. If a rider is obviously having difficulty in controlling a horse or pony, stop and wait until they have passed or pulled off the path to let you by.

● When passing other path users give them as much room as possible.

● Be particularly cautious at blind spots such as junctions, bends, entrances and near obstructions, such as trees.

● On urban shared-use paths where the pedestrian and cycle sections are divided by a white line or kerb, keep to the cycle section, marked by the bike signs painted on the path.

● Ride carefully and under control downhill.

● Take particular care on unstable or wet surfaces.

Out in the country:

● Enjoy the countryside and respect its life and work

● Guard against all risk of fire

● Re-fasten all gates that you find closed

● Keep to rights of way across farmland

● Cross fences, hedges and walls only at gates or open gaps

● Leave livestock, crops and machinery alone

● Take your litter home

● Help to keep all water sources clean

● Protect wildlife, plants and trees

● Don't make unnecessary noise

In the forest:

● Except in designated areas, ride only on firm-based tracks and paths.

● Do not obstruct gates (for example, by leaving bikes locked to them) and keep clear of forestry operations.

● Don't pass any vehicle loading timber until you are told it is safe to do so.

Beside the canal:

● Ride with care on slippery or rough bits – by definition a canal towpath has a canal on one side of it! Ride at a moderate pace, and don't make slippery sections worse by deliberately – or accidentally – skidding.

● You may need to get off and walk when passing under a low bridge and you must when going by a lock.

● Don't bunch up along the towpath.

● Watch out for anglers (modern carbon-fibre rods are black and *very* long), and spikes and mooring ropes from moored boats.

from East Midlands Navigations, tel 01636 704 481; or can be downloaded from the www.britishwaterways.co.uk web site. The permit has a 'cycle code' of advice printed on the back. The whole 66km (42-mile) length of the Grantham Canal towpath is a permitted route, although the surface varies greatly from section to section; a considerable length of it, from Gamston eastwards, has now been made up with a firm crushed-stone surface. Also permitted is the 7.5km (5-mile) stretch of the Nottingham and Beeston Canal from Turnover Bridge to Meadow Lane lock, and on the Erewash Canal the 4.9km (3 miles) from Hallam Fields Lock to Dock Holme Lock. Most of this is in Derbyshire. Even where a section of canal towpath is incorporated into a designated cycle route, such as the Nutbrook Trail, you still need a permit.

● On *firm-surfaced tracks* (that is to say, not on soft-based horse tracks or routes marked for walkers only) in *Forestry Commission forests.* There may be restrictions when the tracks are being used for forestry operations such as tree-felling. Some of these firm tracks have been waymarked by Forest Enterprise (the FC's commercial arm) as cycle routes, notably in Sherwood Pines Forest Park in Clipstone Forest. There are shorter but still very enjoyable stretches in some of the other woods nearer to Nottingham, such as Sansom Wood, Blidworth Woods, Haywood Oaks and Fox Covert Plantation (near Calverton).

● On certain paths and roads in Country Parks and some National Trust properties, such as Clumber Park – where cars have to pay to enter but bikes go in free!

On payment
● On the road through the grounds of Newstead Abbey. A concessionary fee is payable by cyclists using the 'National Cycle Network' Route 6.

Maps for cycling

Although we mean you to be able to follow any of the routes in this book without one, a map can add to your enjoyment by showing you what features of interest lie just off the route and also by helping you to make up your own routes and links. The most useful map for general cycling is the Ordnance Survey Landranger series, in deep pink covers at a scale of 1:50 000 – 2cm on the map represent 1km on the ground; about 1¼ inches represent one mile. Each sheet covers an area 40km (about 25 miles) square. Unfortunately they're quite expensive (currently – 2004 – £5.99 a sheet), and to cover the whole of Nottinghamshire you'd need six sheets: 111 *Sheffield and Doncaster*; 112 *Scunthorpe*; 120 *Mansfield, Worksop*; 121 *Lincoln*; 129 *Nottingham and Loughborough*; and 130 *Grantham*. Most of our routes lie on the Mansfield/Worksop and Nottingham sheets, 120 and 129.

These maps are detailed enough to show all roads and most paths and tracks. They also show which of the latter are rights of way by marking them in red: public bridleways are shown by a line of long red dashes (– – – –), RUPPs as a succession of alternating short and long red dashes (– - - -), and BOATs as a succession of small red crosses and short dashes (+-+-+-+-).

For off-road riding, the Explorer series in orange covers at a scale of 1:25 000 can be useful. These are double the scale of the Landrangers at 4cm to the km or about 2½ inches to the mile; sheets vary in size and some are printed on both sides of the paper. The three Nottinghamshire sheets are 270 *Sherwood Forest* (covering the area from Hucknall as far north as Worksop, and from Sutton- and Kirkby-in-Ashfield in the west to Southwell and Ollerton in the east), 260 *Nottingham/Vale of Belvoir*, covering an area from Hucknall, Calverton and Bleasby in the north to Gotham and Kinoulton in the south and as far east as Bottesford, and 271 *Newark-on-Trent*, covering the area from North Wheatley in the north to Flintham in the south and from Southwell in the west to beyond the county boundary in the east. One or two of the northernmost routes stray for short distances onto sheet 269 *Chesterfield and Alfreton*, and one or two of the southerly ones similarly onto 246 *Loughborough*. These maps show more detail than the Landrangers, in particular field boundaries and on which side of them bridleways etc lie, which is helpful to off-road riders. Rights of way are marked in green, less heavily and obscuring less detail than in the earlier Pathfinder series. The surfaced road colouring, close to that used on the Landranger series, is also now much easier to follow.

Grid references Both types of Ordnance Survey map allow positions of features etc to be defined to the nearest 100 metres by means of a 'grid reference'. The maps are divided into 1km squares by a grid of blue lines which are numbered on the edges of the map, and every 10km on the actual map page.

The position of a point is defined by estimating the number of tenths of a square it is to the right (that is, *east*) of the nearest vertical line to its left: this forms the first part of the grid reference ('GR' in our route descriptions) made up of the number of the line, e.g. 58, and the number of estimated tenths of a square, say 3, to give 583. Then the second part of the reference is obtained in the same way by estimating the number of tenths of a square up (*north*) from the nearest horizontal line below it, e.g. 52 for the line, and 2 for the estimated tenths, to give 522. The complete six-figure grid reference, which only repeats every 100km and is accurate to about 100m, is 583 522. The two groups of numbers are always given in this order (mathematically, *x*

'National Cycle Network' Route 6

Northern Nottinghamshire Section: Shireoaks to Ravenshead

Shireoaks to Worksop: mostly Chesterfield Canal towpath. **Worksop to Sherwood Pines**: on-road to Worksop College, then mostly firm stone-surfaced path and forest track. **Sherwood Pines to Blidworth**: beautiful new tarred surface. **Blidworth to Ravenshead**: mix of stone-surfaced path and on-road sections.

White numbers in dark circles indicate places where *City County Forest* routes meet or run near 'NCN' Route 6 – see individual routes for links

203

'National Cycle Network' Route 6

*Southern Nottinghamshire
Section: Ravenshead to
Long Eaton*

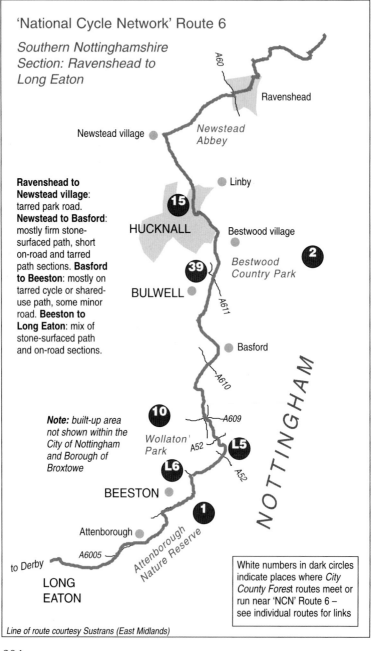

**Ravenshead to
Newstead village:** tarred park road.
Newstead to Basford: mostly firm stone-surfaced path, short on-road and tarred path sections. **Basford to Beeston:** mostly on tarred cycle or shared-use path, some minor road. **Beeston to Long Eaton:** mix of stone-surfaced path and on-road sections.

Note: built-up area not shown within the City of Nottingham and Borough of Broxtowe

Ravenshead

Newstead village

Newstead Abbey

Linby

15

HUCKNALL

Bestwood village

2

39

Bestwood Country Park

BULWELL

A611

Basford

A610

10

A609

Wollaton Park

A52

L5

L6

A52

BEESTON

1

Attenborough

Attenborough Nature Reserve

to Derby

A6005

LONG EATON

NOTTINGHAM

White numbers in dark circles indicate places where *City County Forest* routes meet or run near 'NCN' Route 6 – see individual routes for links

Line of route courtesy Sustrans (East Midlands)

and y coordinates, respectively). For ease of reading, we print the groups with a space between; not everybody does. If you check on sheet 120, *Mansfield and Worksop*, you will find that our example, 583 522, is the grid reference of Papplewick Pumping Station, a prominent local landmark on route 14.

The key panel printed down the side of the maps incorporates a section on 'How to give a grid reference'. Don't be put off: you don't have to be a whiz with grid references to follow our routes but if you *are* using an Ordnance Survey map it's a very useful system for defining and finding the positions of such places as starting points of routes – and, of course, teashops.

Other routes

There are several other sources of published routes in Nottinghamshire: the County Council, several of the district councils and Forest Enterprise have all devised cycle routes in various parts of the county. Contact addresses are given in the 'Useful addresses' section at the end of the book.

Cycle routes in the City of Nottingham are shown on two free maps, covering the north and south of the conurbation, produced by the City Council. The maps mark on- and off-road cycle routes, together with quiet 'cycle-friendly' roads in the city, as well as the location of cycle parking facilities in the city centre. The County Council's *Cycling in Nottinghamshire* shows where the National Cycle Network and the National Byway pass through the county, as well as other routes in the county towns.

Cycling in Greater Nottingham – from Bulwell in the north to Ruddington in the south, and west-to-east from Stapleford to Carlton – is dealt with in the Pedals' publication *The Pedal Pusher's Guide to Nottingham*, now in its third edition. The routes suggested are mainly on-road but include a few sections where you may have to walk, and (with a warning where needed) some off-road sections which may not always have the best of cycling surfaces.

The 'National Cycle Network'
Route 6 of the 'National Cycle Network', conceived by sustainable transport charity Sustrans, runs through the west of the county,

entering near Worksop in the north and leaving near Attenborough in the south. The sketch maps on pp203-204 show where it meets or runs near our routes; some suggested links are given with our route details. Route 6 is waymarked throughout with discreet blue signs with a white cycle symbol and a white-on-red '6'.

Organised rides

Nottinghamshire County Council promotes each year a pro-gramme of leisurely cycle rides in all parts of the county under the label 'Rural Rides'. Distances are generally modest and there is a mixture of on- and off-road rides. Leaders are council offi-cers, or volunteers, mainly from Pedals and the CTC. Rural Rides leaflets are available from: Environment Department, Nottinghamshire County Council, Trent Bridge House, Fox Road, West Bridgford, Nottingham NG2 6BJ; tel 0115 977 2166. They may also be found in local libraries, Tourist Information Centres, visitor centres and some bike shops.

The Nottinghamshire District Association of the CTC organis-es regular led cycle rides with a range of paces and distances. Pedals has some evening rides in the summer. There are more details and contact addresses on pp218-220.

Taking a bike with you

Bikes on trains

You can take bicycles free of charge and unbooked on the **Robin Hood Line** which runs from Nottingham to Worksop via Bulwell, Hucknall, Newstead, Kirkby-in-Ashfield, Sutton Parkway, Mansfield, Mansfield Woodhouse, Shirebrook, Langwith-Whaley Thorns, Creswell, and Whitwell. Several of our routes start from or finish at stations on this line, or have links to them. It offers one of the best ways of getting out into the quiet and sometimes unknown delights of the northern part of Nottinghamshire. Monday-to-Saturday services are basically half-hourly between, Nottingham and Mansfield Woodhouse, hourly further north.

Unfortunately, at present (2004) there is no service on Sundays but there are long-term hopes for one. The service is operated with two- or three-car diesel units, sometimes more at busier times. Train layouts vary: there may be a small separate luggage compartment (which *may* be marked with a cycle symbol), or there may be wheelchair/cycle space near the middle. You load and unload your bike yourself; it may not be possible to get a bike on board during rush hours. The service is operated by Central Trains and supported by the City of Nottingham Council and Nottinghamshire and Derbyshire County Councils.

You can also take bikes free and unbooked on other Central Trains services to stations on routes in this guide: from Nottingham to Newark Castle and beyond, from Nottingham to Grantham, from Nottingham to Beeston and Attenborough (and on to Derby, Leicester or beyond), and from Nottingham to Langley Mill, Alfreton and Chesterfield. A maximum of two cycles per train can be carried free of charge on a first-come, first-served basis. Tandems and tricycles are not carried but trailer-style bikes with a separate child-carrying 'half-bike' clamped behind an adult one can be carried if they can be taken apart: in this case they count as two bikes. Booking (fee £1 for up to two cycles) is necessary for Central Trains' long-distance services.

On High Speed diesel '125' Trains, Midland Main Line from Nottingham to Loughborough (not all trains stop here) and Leicester, and on GNER east coast main line services ('125s' or electric), from Newark Northgate to Retford and Doncaster, several bikes can be carried. You have to book (which is usually possible up to a few minutes before the train leaves), although bike reservations are free. There is a luggage van at one end of the train, the *opposite* end to the first-class coaches on 125s, the *same* end as first class on the electric trains on the East Coast line. Ask station staff where the van will be – these trains are *very* long if you find at the last moment you have to leg it from one end to the other!

Bicycles can be taken on off-peak Midland Main Line Turbo-star diesel unit trains, subject to space being available. You can't book a bike space in advance although, again, there is no charge if you can get your bike on. There is a shared wheelchair/cycle space near the middle of the train and though we've never been involved in – or witnessed – a clash we would expect that the conductor would give priority to wheelchairs.

On all services, a folding bike that folds away completely or is carried in a bag can be taken on any train (or tram or bus) as hand baggage free of charge. As far as we know, as yet no bus service in Nottinghamshire carries bikes. It is also not possible to take bikes with you on Nottingham's trams, although most tram stops have cycle parking facilities – lockers or 'Sheffield' stands.

Bikes on cars

Frankly, we'd rather you didn't use a car to get to the start of a ride – but as the last section showed, getting farther afield may not be easy by other means. We also appreciate that families with young children might like to start them off first on some of the traffic-free routes in country parks and forests. Please try to fill your car if you can: if two couples, say, are going to go on a ride together, use one car rather than two. If you're parking a car out in the country, make sure it is not obstructing the entrance to a field, track or path.

Apart from using a trailer, there are three ways to carry bikes on a car: inside, if there's room; on a roof rack; and on a rear-mounted rack.

The back of an estate car, MPV or hatchback, possibly with one or more of the seats folded down is the best – the bikes are out of the weather, not liable to come adrift and reasonably secure when the car is parked. When you're carrying more than one bike it is a good idea to put an old blanket or thick plastic sheet between the bikes so that pedals, chains and gear mechanisms don't get tangled or damaged. Some people take pedals off, though this is probably only worth it for longer journeys.

If you are carrying bikes on any kind of rack you must make sure that the rack is securely mounted on the car (read the instructions!) and that the bikes are securely fixed to the rack. Special bike roof racks have bolt-on or clamp fittings that hold the bikes secure. If you are carrying them on an ordinary rack – whether upright or lying down – make sure that they are tightly strapped on. Elastic 'bungee' straps alone are *not* enough. The type of leather or nylon strap sold by bike shops as 'toestraps' is very good for this since they can be adjusted more closely than straps with buckles.

When using a rear-mounted rack, remember that it is a legal requirement that the number plate, indicators and brake and tail lights should not be obscured. You may need an accessory lighting board and number-plate. Remove pumps, lights, cycle computers, bags and bike bottles – anything that can fall off or be stolen – before mounting bikes on any rack, and remember that the bikes may not be secure against theft if the car is parked.

Before loading any rack, check that you are not exceeding the rack's specified weight limit (to be on the safe side, consider each adult bike to weigh 30 lb or a child's one 20 lb). All racks, and in particularly roof ones, can affect the handling of the vehicle and its susceptibility to side-winds, as well as increasing fuel consumption. Drive a bit slower than usual if you are carrying bikes and remember the bikes when you're reversing if you're using a rear rack, and if you're going under a height-restricting barrier with a roof rack.

What to take on a bike ride

Always
- Pump – with a fitting to match the valve on your tyres
- Spare inner tube (or two) of the size to fit your bike
- Puncture repair outfit (in case you get two punctures!)
- Tyre levers (three is usual)
- Wheel spanners (usually 14mm for the front, 15mm for the back) if your bike hasn't got 'quick-release' hubs
- Lock and key if you're expecting to stop at a teashop or pub
- Money (and/or credit card, depending how far you expect to live it up)
- Some form of identification
- Spare fleece/long sleeved top (depending on weather of course)
- Waterproofs (depending on probability of rain)
- Water bottle

Could be useful
- Maps
- Picnic lunch (according to taste)
- Small first-aid kit
- Emergency nibble in case you get what cyclists call the 'bonk' (or used to before *The Sun* newspaper hijacked the term for something quite different; mountain-bike magazines are now reclaiming it) – a weak-kneed quivering from lack of food.
- Gloves/track mitts
- Lights if you expect to be out after dark, or near to lighting-up time (which is officially sunset)
- Vacuum flask in cooler weather
- And, of course, *City County Forest*!

TEA STOPS

While we have indicated as far as possible in the listing below opening days and hours, it is advisable to check ahead by phone if you are relying on a particular stop, especially outside the summer months and at weekends – in the case of tearooms attached to shops, bakeries etc. Map grid references are given only for tea stops outside towns or large villages, or if the address might otherwise be misleading. The listings for Nottingham and the larger towns are not claimed to be complete but give a selection of refreshment places on or near the routes.

Bawtry

The Town House Tea Rooms
21 Market Place
Tel 01302 719 397
Open daily, 9am to 5.30pm

Bawtry Garden Centre Coffee Shop
(near junction of A638 and A614)
Tel 01302 711 639
Open Mon, Tues, Thurs, Fri 9am to 5pm; Wed 10am to 5pm; Sat and Sun 10am to 5pm

(OS map 111; GR 649918)

Jayster's
20 Station Road
Tel 01302 714 338
Open Mon–Sat, 8am to 2.30pm

Bestwood Park

Bestwood Lodge
Bestwood Lodge Drive, Bestwood Country Park
Tel 0115 920 3011
Open daily
(OS map 129; GR 569 466)

Bingham

Dickie's on the Square
7 Market Place
Tel 01949 839 019
Open Mon–Fri 8am to 4pm; Sat 9.30am to 3.30pm

Bleasby

Manor Farm Tea Shoppe
Tel 01636 831 316
Open daily 10.30am to 5pm
(OS map 129; GR 707 499)

Blidworth

Blidworth Woods car park (off Longdale Lane)
Van, sit outside on benches
Open Fri–Wed
(OS map GR 120 592 525)

Bothamsall

Haughton Park Farm Tearooms
(near Bothamsall)

Tel 01623 860 320
Open April–end September, daily 10am to 6pm; October–March, Wed–Sun, 10am to 5.30pm
(OS map 120; GR 683 740)

Burton Joyce

Mulberries Coffee Shop
Tall Trees Garden Centre
Lowdham Road
Bulcote
Tel 0115 931 2356
Open Mon–Sat 9.30am to 6pm; Sun 10am to 5pm
(*Bulcote* – on A612 , 1 mile east of Burton Joyce: OS map 129; GR 661 452)

Calverton

Patchings Farm
Oxton Road
Tel 0115 965 3479
Open daily 9am to 10pm
(OS map 129; GR 597 499)

Carburton

Olde School Tearoom
Ollerton Road
Tel 01909 483 517
Open Tues–Sun 10am to 5pm
(OS map 120; GR 606 727)

Clipstone

Vicar Water Country ParkCafé
Tel 01623 466 340
Open Thurs–Sat, plus Tues, Wed in school holidays 10.30am to

210

3pm (4pm at weekends and in the summer season)

Clumber Park

Clumber Park
Restaurant Caféteria
Tel 01909 484 122
Open daily 10am to 6pm during British Summer Time; 10am to 4pm during Greenwich Mean Time (winter)
There is an admission charge to Clumber Park for cars, while cyclists and National Trust members get in free
(OS map 120; GR 626 746)

Creswell Crags

(Derbyshire – by about 100yds!)
Creswell Crags Visitor Centre, Creswell
Tel 01909 720 378
Open February–October, daily, 10.30am to 4.30pm;
November–January, Sundays only, same times. Drinks and snacks from machine only.
(Approximately 1 mile east of Creswell village, 4 miles south-west of Worksop. OS map 120; GR 537 744)

East Leake

Old Barn Café
Manor Farm Animal Centre and Donkey Sanctuary
Manor Farm, Castle Hill
Tel 01509 852 525
Open weekdays 10am to 3.45pm; weekends and bank holidays 10am to 4.45pm summertime,

10am to 3.45pm wintertime

Hampshire's
Gotham Lane
Tel 01509 852 811
Open Mon–Fri 7am to 3.30pm; Sat 7am to 2.30pm

Eastwood

The White Peacock Teashop
Scargill Walk
Tel 01773 765 237
Open Mon, Tues, Thurs Fri, Sat, 9am to 4pm; Wed, 9am to 1pm

Edwinstowe

The Coffee House
High Street
Tel 07960 431 611
Open Mon–Sat 10am to 5pm; Sun (summer only) 11am to 4pm

Edwinstowe Bistro
High Street
Tel 01623 824 880
Open Mon, Tues, Thurs Fri, Sat, 10.30am to 4pm; Sun 12 noon to 4pm

Robin's Rest Tearoom
41 High Street
Tel 01623 822 115
Open Tues–Sat 9.30am to 6pm; Sun 11am to 6pm

See also **Sherwood Pines Forest Park**, and **Sherwood Forest Art and Craft Centre**

Gamston

(near Nottingham)
Safeway Store
Tel 0115 981 1787

Open Mon–Fri 8am to 6pm; Sat 8am to 7pm; Sun 10am to 4pm

Greasley

Minton's Tea Room
100 Church Road
Tel 0701 0704 701
Open Wed–Sat, 10am to 4pm; Sun, 12.30pm to 5pm

Gunthorpe

Gunthorpe Lock Tearoom
Riverside
Tel 0115 966 4833
Open Mon–Fri 9.30am to 5pm; Sat and Sun 9.30am to 6pm

Hardstoft

(Derbyshire)
The Herb Garden
Hall View Cottage, Hardstoft, Pilsley
Tel 01246 854 268
Open Wed–Sun and Bank Holidays,
March–September 10am to 6pm
(OS map 120; GR 436 633)

Hardwick Hall

(Derbyshire)
National Trust Shop and Restaurant
Tel 01246 850 430
Open April–October, Wed, Thur, Sat, Sun and Bank Holiday Mondays, 11am to 5pm
There is an admission charge to the grounds in which the restaurant is situated, although National Trust members can get in free
(OS map 120; GR 463 637)

211

Tel 01623 550 172
Open daily April –
September 11am to 4pm;
October to March 11am
to 3pm
*(OS map 120; GR 472
595)*

Keyworth
The White House Coffee
Shop
Main Street
Tel 0115 937 2895
Open Mon, Tues, Thurs,
Fri 8.30am to 3.30pm;
Thurs 8.30am to 3pm;
Wed and Sat 8.30am to
1.30pm

Harworth
Lazy Days Diner
113 Scrooby Road
Tel 01302 759 282
Open Mon–Fri 8am to
3pm; Sat 8am to 2pm

Tasty Dish Café
75 Scrooby Road
Tel 01302 746 691
Open Mon–Sat 7.30am
to 10pm; Sun 10am to
10pm

Hoveringham
Ferry Farm Country Park
and Restaurant
Parlour Tea Room
Boat Lane
Tel 0115 966 5037 or
0115 966 4512
Open March–September,
Tues–Sun 10am to
5.30pm; plus Bank
Holiday Mondays
There is an admission
charge to the park in
which the tea room is sit-
uated
*(OS map 129; GR 703
463)*

Hucknall
Butlers Hill Café
174 Portland Road
Tel 0115 956 6121
Open Mon–Fri 7am to
2.45pm; Sat 7am to 2pm

The Coffee Pot
10a South Street
Tel 0115 963 2757
Open Mon–Sat 9am to
2.30pm

Tesco
Ashgate Road (near the
railway/tram station)
Tel 0845 677 9797
Open Mon 8am to 8pm;
Tues–Sat 7am to 8pm;
Sun 10am to 4pm

Collins and Thorntons
68 High Street (opposite
main Post Office)
Tel 0115 963 0213
Open Mon–Sat 9am to
4.30pm

Huthwaite
Brierley Forest Park
Visitor Centre, entrance
off Skegby Road

Kirkby-in-Ashfield
Portland Park Visitor
Centre
Lindleys Lane, off Station
Street
Tel 01623 721 617
Open Tues–Fri 10am to
2pm; Sun 9am to 3pm

Langar
Langar Parachute
Clubhouse
Langar Airfield
Opening times vary, nor-
mally Sat and Sun to
about 4pm and all week
during the summer, sub-
ject to weather and
demand.

Naturescape Wild Flower
Farm Tearooms
Coach Gap Lane
(off Langar Airfield
Industrial Estate)
*(OS map 129: GR 733
342)*

Mansfield
Harold's Coffee Shop
39a West Gate
Tel 01623 427 030

212

Open Mon–Sat, 9.30am to 3pm
(OS map 120; GR 627 588)

Mapperley
Brookfields Garden Centre
Mapperley Plains,
Tel 0115 926 8200
(OS map 129; GR 604 454)

Misson
Misson Mill Café
Bawtry Road
Open Mon–Fri 9am to 3pm

Misterton
The Dovecote Café
Grove Wood Road
Tel 07759 585 969
Open Mon, Tues, Wed, Fri 8.30am to 6pm; Thurs, Sat and Sun 8.30am to 4.30pm

Newark on Trent
Baker's Oven
Stodman Street
(just off Market Square)
Tel 01636 701 937
Open Mon–Sat 8am to 4.45pm
(Plaque over shop reads: 'Prince Rupert stayed here after his quarrel with the King, 19 October 1645')

Feeling Peckish
33 Castlegate
Tel 01636 673 333
Open Daily 9am to 3pm

Gannets Café
35 Castlegate
Tel 01636 702 066
Open Mon–Fri 9am to 4pm; Sat 9am to 5pm;

Sun 9.30am to 4pm

Lord Byron's Coffee Lounge
27/28 Market Place
Tel 01636 613 390
Open Mon–Sat 9am to 2.30pm

Newstead Abbey
Newstead Abbey Tea Rooms
Mansfield Road, Ravenshead
Tel 01623 455 900
Open daily 11am to 5.30pm
There is an admission charge to Newstead Abbey grounds
(OS map 120; GR 542 538)

Nottingham
(We've only included those on our routes!)

The Castle Cafe
Castle Road
Tel 0115 915 3650
Open Daily 10am to 4.30pm
There is an admission charge on Saturdays, Sundays and Bank Holidays to the Castle grounds, where the cafe is situated. Cycling is not permitted in the grounds, and you may have to leave your bike outside.

Café L
The Djanogly Art Gallery, University Boulevard
Tel 0115 951 3192
Open Mon–Fri 9am to 4.30pm; Sat 9am to 4pm; Sun and Bank Holidays 2pm to 5pm

Cosy Teapot Café
Carrington Street
(about 50yds north of Nottingham Midland Station)
Tel 0115 950 1194
Open Mon–Sat 8am to 2pm

Sue's Cob Shop
147 Trent Boulevard
Tel 0115 914 2019
(on routes 35 and 40)
Open Mon–Sat, 7am to 5pm

Wollaton Park
Courtyard Coffee Shop
Tel 0115 915 3900
Open daily 10.30am to 4.30pm

Ollerton
Ollerton Water Mill Tea Shop, Market Place
Tel 01623 824 094 or 01623 822 469
Open April to October, Wed–Sun, 10.30am to 5pm; March and November, Sat and Sun only, 10.30pm to 4.30pm; Bank Holiday Mondays, 10.30am to 5pm
(OS map 120; GR 653 674)

Ravenshead
Longdale Craft Centre
Longdale Lane
Tel 01623 796 952
Open daily 10am to 6pm
(OS map 120; GR 575 528)

Portland College
Nottingham Road
Tel 01623 499 111
Open Mon–Fri 8.30am to 4.30pm; Sat, Sun and Hank Holidays 9.30am to

4.30pm
(OS map 120; GR 552 568)

Retford

Baker's Oven
40 Carolgate
Tel 01777 708 280
Open Mon–Sat 8am to 4.30pm

Britalia Coffee Shop
Grove Street
Tel 01777 705 643
Open Mon–Sat 10am to 2pm

Ruddington

The Village Coffee Shop
14 High Street
Tel 0115 940 5736
Open Mon–Sat 7.30am to 2pm
(OS map 129: GR 573 331)

Rufford

The Coach House
Rufford Country Park,
Old Rufford Road
(A614), near Ollerton
Tel 01623 822 056
Open January and February 11am to 4pm; March–December 10.30am to 5pm
(OS map 120; GR 645 647)

Sherwood Forest

Art and Craft Centre
Tearoom
Edwinstowe
(next to Youth Hostel, off Church Street)
Tel 01623 824 033
Open April–September Mon–Sat 10am to 5.30pm, Sun 10.30 to 4.30; October–March Wed–Sat 10am to 4pm,

Sun 10.30 to 4.30

Sherwood Pines Forest Park

Visitor Centre
Tel 01623 822 500
Open Tues–Fri (and Mon in school holidays) 10am to 3.30pm; Sat and Sun 10 am to 4pm
(OS map 120; GR 612 637)

Six Hills

Six Hills Leisure Park and Golf Course
Tel 01664 434 080 (Jet Ski Centre Café)
Open Sat and Sun 10am to 5pm
(OS map 129; GR 653 214)

Southwell

Gossips Coffee House
24/26 King Street
Tel 01636 815 816
Open Mon–Sat 8.45am to 5pm; Sun 11am to 5pm

The Minster Centre
Southwell Minster
Church Street
Tel 01636 815 691
Open Mon–Sat 9.30am to 4.15pm; Sun 12noon to 5pm

Muscroft's Café and Restaurant
12 King Street
Tel 01636 816 0573
Open Tues–Sat 11am to 3pm

Reg Taylor's Garden Centre
Hill Farm Nurseries,
Normanton
Tel 01636 813 184
Open Mon–Fri 10am to

4.30pm; Sat 10.30am to 5pm; Sun 10.30 to 4pm
(OS map 120; GR 710 548)

Southwell Garden Centre
Fiskerton Road
Tel 01636 812 886
Open Mon–Fri 9.30am to 4.15pm; weekends 9am to 4.30pm
(OS map 120; GR 710 535)

Sutton-cum-Lound

Wetlands Waterfowl
Reserve
Tel 01777 818 099
Open daily 10am to 5pm
There is an admission charge to the Reserve but you do not have to pay to get to the teashop
(OS maps 111,120: GR 693 851)

Teversal

Teversal Trail Visitor
Centre
Carnarvon Street, off
Fackley Road
Tel 01623 442 021
Open April–September Tues 11am to 3pm; other days 11am to 4pm; October–March 11am to 3pm
(About 3/4 mile south-south-west of village centre. OS map 120; GR 480 613)

Thoresby

The Gallery Tea Rooms
Thoresby Park, near
Ollerton
Tel 01623 822 365
Open April–October Fri–Mon 2pm to 5pm
(OS map 120; GR 639 712)

214

Walesby
Walesby Garden Centre
Tearooms (Sandhurst
Nurseries), Brake Road
Tel 01623 860 382
Open daily 10am to
4.30pm
*(OS map 120; GR 677
704)*

Welbeck
Dukeries Garden Centre,
Welbeck
Tel 01909 476 506
Open Mon–Fri, 9.30am
to 4.45pm; weekends
9.30am to 5.30pm
*(OS map 120; GR 552
742)*

West Bridgford
ASDA Nottingham
Loughborough Road
Tel 0115 969 4200
Open Mon–Sat 8am to
9pm; Sun 10am to 3pm

Birds the Confectioners
Tea Room
Central Avenue
Tel 0115 981 0678
Open Mon–Fri 8am to
5.30pm; Sat 8am to
4.30pm

The Coffee Shop at
Corsons
Central Avenue
Tel 0115 981 4080
Open Mon–Sat 10am to
3pm

Worksop
Aphrodite Coffee Bar
9 Central Avenue
Tel 01909 474 040
Open Mon, Wed, Thurs,
Fri 9am to 4pm; Tues
9am to 3.30pm; Sat
8.30am to 4.30pm

Café Delight
79 Bridge Street
Tel 01909 476 509
Open Mon–Sat 8am to
5pm; Sun 10am to 4pm

The Coffee Pot
85 Bridge Street
Tel 01909 472 525
Open Mon, Tues, Thurs
9am to 4pm; Wed and
Sat 9am to 4.30pm

Copper Kettle
10 Newcastle Avenue
Tel 01909 530 500
Open Mon–Sat 8.30am
to 4.30pm

The Crusty Cob Café
23 Central Avenue
Tel 01909 530 270
Open Mon–Fri 7am to
4.30pm; Sat 7am to
3pm; Sun 8am to 2pm

Cypriana Coffee House
and Grill
Bridge Street
Tel 01909 473 666
Open Mon–Sat 8am to
5pm

GB Café
106 Bridge Street
Tel 01909 485 588
Open Mon–Sat 8am to
3.30pm

May's Café
Gateford Road
Tel 01909 475 639
Open Mon–Sat, 9am to
3.30pm; Sun 10am to
3pm

Mr Straw's Café Louge
130 Bridge Street
Open Mon–Sat

The Railway Café
Platform 2
Worksop Station
Tel 07788 447 717
Open Mon–Fri 6 am to
2.30pm; Sat 7am to 12
noon

The Speedy Pepper
Coffee Shop
9 Victoria Square
Tel 01909 477 110
Open Mon–Sat 10am to
4pm

BIKE
SHOPS

Beeston
Beeston Wheelies
123 High Road
Tel 0115 917 0028

Cycle Inn
35–37 Chilwell Road
Tel 0115 925 6647

Eastwood
Mick Brown/The Bike
Centre
233 Nottingham Road
Tel 01773 719 790

Hucknall
Pro-bike
171 Annesley Road
Tel/fax 0115 956 1955

Long Eaton
(Derbyshire)
The Bike Shop
68 Tamworth Road
Tel 0115 973 2862

Long Eaton Cycle Centre
49 Tamworth Road
Tel 0115 972 6335

Tracey Maid
Regent Mills, Regent
Street
Tel 0115 973 0719

**Mansfield
Woodhouse**
A & C Sports
1 Morven Avenue
Tel 01623 623 389

On Yer Bike
181Yorke Street
Tel 01623 421 033

Newark on Trent
A1 Cycle Repairers
57–59 Castle Gate
Tel 01636 707 277

Hawk Factory Cycle
Store
50a Lombard Street
Tel 01636 611642

Marriott's
16a Appleton Gate
Tel 01636 704 842

Nottingham

Arnold
The Bike Shop
15 High Street
Tel 0115 926 4733

Bulwell
Charlie's Cycles
200 Highbury Road
Tel 0115 976 3118

Carlton
Rex Robinson Cycles
27 Burton Road
Tel 0115 961 9069

Chilwell
Halfords Superstore
Chilwell Retail Park
Tel 0115 946 2820

City centre
Bunney's Bikes
97 Carrington Street
Tel 0115 947 2713

Freewheel
34–36 Goose Gate,
Hockley
Tel 0115 952 0200

Super Cycles
45–47 Carlton Road
Tel 0115 941 1133

Mapperley
Langdale Lightweights
455–457 Westdale Lane
Tel 0115 956 5505

Netherfield
Hawk Factory Cycle
Store
105 Victoria Road
Tel 0115 961 4555

Halfords Superstore
Victoria Retail Park
Tel 0115 940 0811

Sherwood
Olympic Cycles
213 Valley Road
Tel 0115 985 8001
Fax 0115 985 8002

West Bridgford
Radcliffe Road Cycles
152b Radcliffe Road
Tel 0115 982 2459

Retford
Discount Cycles
Carolgate
Tel 01777 703 128

Ruddington
Ruddington Cycles
10 High Street
Tel 0115 921 1393
sShokwave Mountain

Bikes
13 Church Street
Tel 0115 921 5030

Sutton-in-Ashfield
Halfords
Unit 2 Forest Street
Forest Retail Park
Tel 01623 510 590

Worksop
Halfords
Unit 3 Carlton Road
Tel 01909 530 521

TICs

Tourist Information
Centres can supply full
information on places to
visit and where to stay
(including campsites and
self-catering) in their
area. Most will book
accommodation for you
for a small charge under
the 'Book a Bed Ahead'
(BABA) scheme.

Newark on Trent
The Gilstrap Centre,
Castlegate
Tel 01636 789 62

Nottingham
1-4 Smithy Row
Tel 0115 947 0661

Ollerton
Sherwood Heath,
Ollerton Roundabout
Tel 01623 824 545

Retford
Arncott House Annexe
40 Grove Street
Tel 01777 860 780

Sherwood Forest Visitor Centre
Edwinstowe
Tel 01623 824 490

West Bridgford
County Hall,
Loughborough Road
Tel 0115 977 3558

Worksop
Worksop Library,
Memorial Avenue
Tel 01909 501 148

USEFUL BOOKS & GUIDES

Cycles and cycling
(in public libraries most are under the classification 976.6)

The Bicycle Repair Step-by Step; Rob van der Plas (Van der Plas Publications, 2002); ISBN 1 83506 732 6

The Bike Book; John Stevenson (Haynes, 2003); ISBN 1 89249 539 2

Cyclecraft; John Franklin (The Stationary Office Books, 1997); ISBN 0 11702 051 6

Jordan's Family Cycling; (Emap Active, 2002); ISBN 0 95330 876 6

Richard's 21st Century Bicycle Book; Richard Ballantine (Pan, 2000); ISBN 0 33037 717 5

Cycling in Nottinghamshire

Cycling in Nottinghamshire; Penny and Bill Howe (Sigma Leisure, 1995); ISBN 1 85058 443 5

On Your Bike: Derbyshire and Nottinghamshire; Tim Hughes and Jo Cleary (Countryside Books, 2002); ISBN 1 83506 732 6

Pedal Pusher's Guide to Nottingham; compiled by Lawrence Geary (Pedals, 1999); ISBN 0 9536412 0 1

Guides to designated cycle routes in Nottinghamshire
(Generally available free from the local authority).

Cycling in Nottinghamshire: Your complete guide (Nottinghamshire County Council, 2004)

Cyclists and Tram Tracks (NET, 2004)

Cycling in Rushcliffe (Rushcliffe Borough Council, 2003)

Nottingham Cycle Map North and Nottingham Cycle Map South (Nottingham City Council, 2004)

Nottingham's Canal Towpath (Nottingham City Council, 2003)

Nottinghamshire and country matters

A Dictionary of English Place-Names; A D Mills (Oxford Paperbacks, 1998); ISBN 0 19280 074 4

Nottinghamshire; Jeff and Margaret Hopewell (Shire Publications, 1999); ISBN 0 7478 0194 0

Nottinghamshire Curiosities; Geoffrey Oldfield (Dovecote Press, 1992); ISBN 0 946159 98 X

The Nottinghamshire Village Book; (Countryside Books, 1994); ISBN 1 85306 057 7

Tales of Old Nottinghamshire; Polly Howatt (Countryside Books, 1991); ISBN 1 85306 160 3

Nottinghamshire; Authur Mee (The Kings England Press, 1989); ISBN 1 872243 800 8

Nottinghamshire: Buildings of England; Niklaus Pevsner (Yale University Press, 2002); ISBN 0 30009 636 4

What is Pedals?

Pedals was founded in 1979 to encourage more people to use bikes and to campaign for safer and more attractive conditions for cyclists in the Nottingham area.

The Power Behind Nottingham's Cyclists

Pedals has helped to get Nottingham one of England's largest networks of urban cycle routes and is pressing for many more facilities, especially in the City Centre and the north side of Nottingham,together with better links to surrounding countryside. Pedals also campaigns for much more attention to be given to cyclists' needs in all highway planning and traffic management, including making traffic-calming more cycle-friendly.

Pedals has helped to get hundreds of cycle stands installed locally and is campaigning for further secure cycle parking, including cycle lockers. Pedals campaigns for better surfaces on roads and cycle paths and for prompter attention to defects including vandalised signs and broken glass.

Pedals started the Great Nottinghamshire Bike Ride in 1982, now run by Nottinghamshire County Council. The GNBR is the largest mass cycle ride in the country, outside the south-east. Pedals in 1983 started the Summer Guided Cycle Rides Programme, and continues to play a major part in these events, now run by the County Council.

Pedals supports the Ridewise project, launched in 2004 to provide training for adult cyclists and help them cope with busy modern traffic conditions.

Pedals has produced three editions of the Pedal Pushers' Guide to Nottingham, the first handbook of maps and practical advice for local cyclists. The latest edition is available for £4.95 (including postage and packing) from Pedals Publications, 96 Pierrepont Road, West Bridgford, Nottingham NG2 5DW.

Pedals produces a newsletter three times a year to keep you informed of developments and issues for cyclists, as well as to tell members about our monthly meetings and other forthcoming events.

Pedals members get a 10% discount on cash sales with selected local dealers (see Pedals Pushers' Guide for details).

Pedals was fully involved in helping to organisation of the Velo City '93 Conference, a major international cycling conference, in Nottingham from 6-9 September 1993.

● For more information write to Pedals, 162 Musters Road, West Bridgford, Nottingham NG2 7AA; telephone 0115 981 6206; or or visit the web site at www.pedals.org.uk where you can download a membership form.

What is the CTC?

The Cyclists' Touring Club (known everywhere as the CTC) was founded as long ago as 1878 by a group of cyclists to exchange information and to press for the legal right to use the highways – this being well before the first motorcar. The horse was the prime user of the roads and no doubt cyclists were disliked, just as inconsiderate cyclists nowadays upset equestrians.

By the 1890's the ordinary bicycle (penny farthing) had evolved into the safety bicycle, which was basically the same as the modern machine. This made cycling accessible to all who could afford a machine, which in those days was the upper and middle classes, and for a period before the introduction of the motorcar, was the in-thing.

In Nottinghamshire a group of cyclists, led by the Rev. W. H. Kynaston, held a meeting at the Saracen's Head in Southwell on 15 May 1897 to form Nottinghamshire District Association of the CTC. This is still going strong, organising day rides from Nottingham, Newark and Mansfield as well asocial activities and cycling tours. The DA publishes a bi-monthly magazine 'Cyclonda' and has it's own web site: www.ctcnottsda.blogspot.com. For information about CTC activities in Nottinghamshire phone 0115 986 3214 or 0115 929 7706 or Email terrydpscott@hotmail.com.

The CTC works for all cyclists looking after their interests in such topics as protecting cyclists' right to use the roads, working for improved off-road access and for better public transport access. Membership of the CTC has a number benefits: free third party insurance; a fee bi-monthly magazine; legal aid from the CTC's legal experts; cycle and travel insurance especially designed for the cyclist; touring information about Britain, Europe and worldwide; advise from the club's technical department about cycle equipment and, of course, free membership of your local CTC group. The CTC also organises a comprehensive programme of cycling holidays for members. Annual get-togethers enjoyed by members are the York Cycle Rally held in June and the Birthday Rides – a weeklong series of rides and social events held at a different location in Britain each August.

● For more information about CTC nationally, write to CTC, 69 Meadrow, Godalming, Surrey GU7 3HS; telephone 0870 873 0060; fax 0870 873 0064, email cycling@ctc.org.uk or visit the web site at www.ctc.org.uk

What is RideWise?

Ridewise is an independent company with active support from Nottingham City Council and Nottinghamshire County Council, Nottinghamshire's Primary Care Trusts, Groundwork, Transport 2000, consultants Cleary Hughes Associates, PEDALS and members of the public.

The aim of RideWise is simple yet quite ambitious – to encourage more people to cycle by giving them the confidence to ride a bike on our roads in modern traffic conditions. It hopes to achieve this by providing a comprehensive training and support service for cyclists in Nottinghamshire, and by making cycling as normal a form of transport as walking, catching a bus or driving a car.

RideWise intends to get anyone who is interested back on their bikes. The team of fully trained instructors are able to teach any adult, teenager or child to be able to ride safely and confidently both on- and off-road. The trainers tailor the location and nature of instruction to what is appropriate for the individual.

RideWise also plans to deliver a series of cycle maintenance classes; develop courses to improve driver awareness; and provide cycle consultancy and advice to anyone who needs it, such as employers, developers, schools, retailers and the general public.

● For further information about Ridewise, contact the RideWise co-ordinator, telephone 0781 826 3738, email info@ridewise.org.uk, or visit the web site at www.ridewise.org.uk

the big wheel

turning transport around

www.thebigwheel.org.uk

The Big Wheel promotes integrated transport in Nottingham: bus, train, tram, car, walking and, of course, cycling. The organisation is backed by the Greater Nottingham Transport Partnership representing the City and County councils, plus large and small companies across the conurbation.

The Big Wheel is responsible for a number of initiatives to promote cycling. These include poster campaigns, as well as organising the Greater Nottingham Cycle Forum, where cyclists get together with transport planners to ensure their views are heard.

● To find out more about The Big Wheel visit www.thebig-wheel.org.uk

The Nottingham Green Partnership was established back in 1991 and has brought together the public sector, higher education, environmental groups and private businesses to make Nottingham a more sustainable city.

The Partnership is pleased to continue to support this guide as a valuable source of information for new and potential cyclists, promoting cycling in the city and beyond.

● For further information about the Nottingham Green Partnership, please contact Mike Peverill, Nottingham City Council, The Guildhall, Burton Street, Nottingham; telephone 0115 948 3500.

Nottingham NHS
Health Authority

'City County Forest' is a Pedals' initiative supported by Nottingham Health Authority as part of the Nottingham Health Action Zone.

Nottingham Health Authority serves 640,000 people registered with GPs in the districts of Broxtowe, Gedling, City of Nottingham, Rushcliffe and the Hucknall area of Ashfield. The Authority is responsible for the health of the population and for the strategic development of health and health services in the area. The Health Authority is also responsible for the NHS care provided by GPs, dentists, opticians and pharmacists. The Nottingham Health Authority area is one of 26 NHS Health Action Zones – areas of high deprivation selected to fast track health improvement and reduce health inequalities by working in partnership with other public, private and voluntary sector organisations.

Place-name index